SHAW

An Autobiography
1898–1950
The Playwright Years

Selected from his writings by
STANLEY WEINTRAUB

MAX REINHARDT
LONDON SYDNEY
TORONTO

UNIFORM WITH THIS VOLUME

Shaw: An Autobiography 1856-1898

00024430

Text © The Trustees of the British Museum, The Governors and Guardians of the National Gallery of Ireland, and The Royal Academy of Dramatic Art 1970
Introduction and editorial matter © Stanley Weintraub 1970
ISBN 0 370 01362 X
Printed in Great Britain for
Max Reinhardt Ltd
9 Bow Street, London WC2
by Lowe & Brydone (Printers) Ltd, London
First published in Great Britain 1971

23424

428 SHA

Contents

A Patchwork Self-Portrait, 1898–1950

Were I to tell the truth about myself I must needs seem vainglorious: were I to tell less than the truth I should do myself an injustice and deceive my readers.

—G.B.S.

WITHDRAWN

BERNARD SHAW observed in his nineties that there was no reason for him to write, add to, or collect autobiographical writings of the period following his marriage in 1898. His "life in the twentieth century," he felt, was "so public that any biographer can ascertain more of it than I can myself remember." Still, a subject's ability to write from the inside provides a perspective no biographer can match with all his facts and insights, and Shaw furnished sufficient materials with which to construct a patchwork self-portrait of his life in the twentieth century. While his many private letters provide yet another perspective, they do not comprise a self-portrait in the spirit of autobiography, which represents, rather, those facets of a life which a writer wants the world to see, and remember. In his autobiographical writings up until his death in 1950, at ninety-four, Shaw wrote voluminously on his plays and playwriting, and on people in his crowded orbit, yet the amount of verbiage on a particular subject is not a clear index to the relative importance of an event to Shaw, for he was often publicly silent on personal matters he preferred to keep private while he sometimes wrote a great deal on subjects whose significance he wished to inflate. Such disproportion is the autobiographer's privilege, and when reflected here it indicates Shaw's own emphases.

Since some parts of the memoir were written as late as Shaw's last years, the general perspective must be that of G.B.S. looking at his life from his nineties—an angle of vision maintained in places with some strain since his references to contemporaries long passed from the scene by the fifth decade of the twentieth century were in some cases written as early as 1898. Nevertheless the judgments rendered on personalities—H. G. Wells is the best example—were unaltered by time.

There are also blind spots. For example, Shaw wrote almost nothing for public print about his marriage.* His changing politics were another kind of blind spot, as his increasing disenchantment with democratic institutions led him into love affairs with dictators of every ideological hue, not all of which he had recanted by the end of his life. In Russia in the early thirties, for example, he was not only carefully shepherded by the Communists, but came so prepared to praise that halter and blinders were hardly necessary. About his other travels, which took him around the world, he had little to say for print, although scenes and incidents from his experience turned up in such late plays as *The Simpleton of the Unexpected Isles* (1935) and *Buoyant Billions* (1946).

As would be expected, he maintained the G.B.S. mask for his public appearances, revealing little of the warm, compassionate Shaw underneath except on the rare occasions when the mask slips—as it does, for example, in his moving reference to the last visit he had from Cecil Chesterton in 1916, and his feelings, in his nineties, on the death in 1946 of a long-estranged surrogate son, Harley Granville-Barker.

As is appropriate in the autobiography of a man of ideas, his autobiographical writings, especially those concerned with the work of his mature and later years, emphasize the progress of the mind as much as the progress of the man. For Shaw, who lived the public life of the celebrity throughout the period encompassed by this concluding segment of his autobiography, the private life of the inner man was something especially to be savored, but it was also the stuff from which his plays were made, and it inevitably emerges in his first-person writings as well. This is the most paradoxical side of the man, as we see him alternately cranky and compassionate, democratic-minded and dictator-loving, iconoclastic and deeply religious, arrogant and humble, narrow and visionary, humane and heartless, pragmatic and philosophical. With Walt Whitman he might have claimed, "I resist anything better than my own diversity."

The material comprising the *Autobiography 1898–1950* was composed at different times and under vastly varying conditions and levels

* See *Shaw: An Autobiography 1856–1898*, pp. 170–71.

of inspiration—prefaces and program notes to his plays, book reviews, economic and social treatises, lectures and speeches, drafts of articles, interviews based on carefully prepared texts, letters Shaw caused to be published himself, journalism of all kinds including reports as a war correspondent, a variety of autobiographical afterthoughts, and even deliberate, formal autobiography.* The strategy of weaving such first-person material, with varying tones and intentions, into an autobiographical narrative offers perplexing challenges, although all of Shaw's words in the narrative are words which were originally intended to represent him in public print or actually published. Although it is not the autobiography of Shaw's public years that Shaw himself could have written, it is what he did write. Not a formal memoir, but a patchwork self-portrait, it nevertheless reveals much of the man who was G.B.S.

Stanley Weintraub

* There is also an unassimilable—but revealing—autobiographical essay in the third person, a clever parody of Frank Harris's biographical style written for Harris, and included in this volume as an appendix.

Shaw

PREFACE

Who I Am

THE CELEBRATED G.B.S. is about as real as a pantomime ostrich. But . . . I have played my game with a conscience. I have never pretended that G.B.S. was real: I have over and over again taken him to pieces before the audience to shew the trick of him. And even those who in spite of that cannot escape from the illusion, regard G.B.S. as a freak. The whole point of the creature is that he is unique, fantastic, unrepresentative, inimitable, impossible, undesirable on any large scale, utterly unlike anybody that ever existed before, hopelessly unnatural, and void of real passion. Clearly such a monster could do no harm, even were his example evil (which it never is). . . .

I have been asked whether the portrait resembles me. The question interests me no more than whether Velasquez's Philip was like Philip or Titian's Charles like Charles. No doubt some mean person will presently write a disparaging volume called The Real Shaw, which will be . . . true in its way. . . . Perhaps some total stranger to the Irish-British environment may produce a study as unexpected, and as unflattering, as the very interesting picture of Nelson by a Turkish miniaturist which hangs in the National Portrait Gallery. Like all men, I play many parts; and none of them is more or less real than another. To one audience I am the occupier of a house in Adelphi Terrace; [1] to another I am "one of those damned Socialists." A discussion in a club of very young ladies as to whether I could be more appropriately described as an old josser or an old geezer ended in the carrying of an amendment in favor of an old bromide. I am also a soul of infinite worth. I am, in short, not only what I can make of myself, which varies greatly from hour to hour and emergency to no-emergency, but what you can see in me. And the whole difference between an observer of genius and a common man is not a difference in the number of objects they perceive, but in their estimate of the importance of the objects. Put one man into Fleet Street and ask him what he sees there; and he may give you an accurate description of the color of the buses, the sex of the horses, the numbers of the motor-cars, the signs of the public-houses, and the complexions and probable ages of the people. Another man, who could not answer a single question on these points, may tell you that what he sees is a Jacob's ladder with angels moving up and down between heaven and earth.

It happens that I resemble my sainted namesake in refusing to eat flesh, fish, or fowl, to smoke tobacco (or anything else), or to stimulate myself with drugs or spirits. I do not go about in a monk's frock and rope-girdle; but I spend no more on clothes than men with a twenty-fifth of my income, if so much. For nearly fifty years past I have had at my disposal an unearned income sufficient to enable me to live comfortably without doing a stroke of work; but I work daily like any proletarian. If saintliness consists in these abstinences and exertions I may claim a place in the Communion of Saints beside St Bernard or any other hero of the hagiographers.

On this a ridiculous legend has grown to the effect that a stern Puritan bringing-up imposed Law's Serious Call on me from my childhood. No fable could be farther from the truth. The only belief impressed on me in my Irish Protestant childhood was that all Roman Catholics go to hell as such when they die, and all Protestants to heaven if they are good children. I grew out of this when I was promoted from petticoats to knickerbockers; and the rest of my development was in a family atmosphere so sceptical, Bohemian, anarchic, and on its educational side aesthetic, that in my teens I was a professed atheist, with no reverence whatever for the Trinity, but a profound and lasting respect for Michael Angelo and Raphael, for Handel, Mozart, and Beethoven. To literature I took without enthusiasm or ambition because it was in my lifeblood. At all events, I am the last man in the world to be cited as ascetic either in theory or practice.

Far from being an abstinent man, I am the worst drunkard of a rather exceptionally drunken family; for they were content with alcohol, whereas I want something so much stronger that I would as soon drink paraffin oil as brandy. Cowards drink alcohol to quiet their craving for real stimulants: I avoid it to keep my palate keen for them. And I am a pitiable example of something much worse than the drink craze: to wit, the work craze. Do not forget Herbert Spencer's autobiography, with its cry of warning against work. I get miserably unhappy if my work is cut off. I get hideous headaches after each month's bout: I make resolutions to break myself of it, never to work after lunch, to do only two hours a day; but in vain: every day brings its opportunity and its temptation: the craving masters me every time; and I dread a holiday as I dread nothing else on earth.

Authors are not free from pecuniary cares, very far from it; but nobody who had any regard for his pecuniary interests would adopt literature as a profession. There are religious orders in which the rule is so completely monastic that every penny the members would own as laymen belongs to the order. They may not even choose the fashion of the clothes they wear. But their daily bread is secure; and wherever they go they are entitled to at least three days hospitality from the order. I asked a friend of mine who belonged to such an order what bad effects, if any, it had on its votaries. He thought a moment, and said, "Well, it develops one's individuality so frightfully that at forty years of age every member is a confirmed crank." . . . The explanation seems to be that freedom from economic pressure makes room for an excessive development of individuality in people who have any individuality to develop and are not, like soldiers, specially trained not to think for themselves.

My craft of playwright can be exercised singlehanded on a desert island; and the effect is that authors are harder to organize even for their own protection than hogs. On paper they are models of every virtue: in business they are inveterate anarchists, quarrelsome, sentimental, unable to debate without losing their tempers, and treating differences from their opinion as personal insults. Journalism, being a social activity, civilizes them; but the romancers who sit alone and arrange the world out of their own heads, uncontradicted and unedited, never, unless they have a strong sense of humor, learn how to live in political society, and have to be indulged by statesmen as visitors from another world. . . .

When I was first in company with Anatole France he asked who I was. Answering for myself I said, "I am, like you, a man of genius." This was, according to his French code, so immodest that it startled him into riposting with, "Ah well: a whore (*courtisane*) has the right to call herself a pleasure merchant."[2] I was not offended; for it is true that all artists make their livings as pleasure merchants and not as seers and philosophers; and the similarity of the case of the *courtisane* was not new to the author of Mrs Warren's Profession. But why did he not say "a confectioner has the right to call himself a pleasure merchant," which would have been equally true? Or a jeweller? Or a trader in any of the hundreds of articles in our shops that are not necessities of life and have an aesthetic value only? . . . I myself cannot bear to admit that I am a mere pleasure merchant. I use the pleasure given by my art as a playwright to induce people to read my plays or see them performed, and thereby enable me to live by them; but I am uncomfortably aware of the fact that needy and shallow playwrights have to exploit the viler pleasures given by indecency, scurrility, profanity, immorality, and falsehood solely for the sake of the money they draw. Even the best play must be enough of a potboiler to attract an audience, however small and select. Our greatest dramatic poet, Shakespear, had to practise his art "as you like it" to enable himself to retire as a country gentleman with a coat of arms.

No doubt every man has a shy child in him, artist or no artist. But every man whose business it is to work directly upon other men, whether as artist, politician, advocate, propagandist, organizer, teacher, or what not, must dramatize himself and play his part. To the laborer who merely digs and vegetates, to the squire who merely hunts and eats, to the mathematician and physicist, the men of the orchestra and the tribune may seem affected and theatrical; but when they themselves desire to impress their needs or views on their fellows they find that they, too, must find a pose or else remain paralyzed and dumb. In short, what is called a pose is simply a technical condition of certain activities. It is offensive only when out of place: he who brings his public pose to the dinner table is like the general who brings his sword there, or the dentist who puts his forceps beside his plate, just to shew that he has one. He cannot, however, always leave it behind him.

Granted that St Bernard and St Thomas were as resolute egoists as I, having equally disregarded the interests and wishes of our families in our determination to go our ways, and choosing always the course of life most congenial to us at all costs to ourselves and others, why did they go so far as to kill themselves at half my age by overwork and privation? It was not because they believed themselves to be the servants and instruments of God; for I believe myself to be the servant and instrument of creative evolution, which comes to the same thing, and entitles me to rank equally with them as a religious person: that is to say, a person to whom eating, drinking and reproduction are irksome necessities in comparison with the urge to wider and deeper knowledge, better understanding, and greater power over ourselves and our circumstances. So far, there is no reason why I, too, should not be canonized some day. Perhaps I shall.

I am myself a literary artist, and have made larger claims for literature—or, at any rate, put them forward more explicitly—than any writer of my generation as far as I know, claiming a continuous inspiration for modern literature of precisely the same character as that conceded to the ancient Hebrew Scriptures, and maintaining that the man of letters, when he is more than a mere confectioner, is a prophet or nothing. But to listen for a writer's message, even when the fellow is a fool, is one thing: to worship his tools and his tricks, his pose and his style, is an abomination. Admire them by all means, just as you admire the craft of the masons and the carpenters and sculptors who built your cathedral; but dont go inside and sing Te Deums to them.

G.B.S.

1

Plays for Puritans

SINCE I gave my Plays, Pleasant and Unpleasant, to the world . . . years ago, many things have happened to me. I had then just entered on the fourth year of my activity as a critic of the London theatres. They very nearly killed me. I had survived seven years of London's music, four or five years of London's pictures, and about as much of its current literature, wrestling critically with them with all my force and skill. After that, the criticism of the theatre came to me as a huge relief in point of bodily exertion. The difference between the leisure of a Persian cat and the labor of a cockney cab horse is not greater than the difference between the official weekly or fortnightly playgoings of the theatre critic and the restless daily rushing to and fro of the music critic, from the stroke of three in the afternoon, when the concerts begin, to the stroke of twelve at night, when the opera ends. The pictures were nearly as bad. An alpinist once, noticing the massive soles of my boots, asked me whether I climbed mountains. "No," I replied. "These boots are for the hard floors of the London galleries." Yet I once dealt with music and pictures together in the spare time of an active young revolutionist, and wrote plays and books and other toilsome things into the bargain. But the theatre struck me down like the veriest weakling. I sank under it like a baby fed on starch. My very bones began to perish, so that I had to get them planed and gouged by accomplished surgeons. I fell from heights and broke my limbs in pieces. The doctors said: "This man has not eaten meat for twenty years: he must eat it or die." I said: "This man has been going to the London theatres for three years; and the soul of him has become insane and is feeding unnaturally on his body." And I was right. I did not change my diet; but I had myself carried up into a mountain where there was no theatre; and there I began to revive. Too weak to work,[1] I wrote books and plays. . . .

. . . When I began I could not get my plays acted in this country at all. I therefore proposed to publish them as books. Heinemann, whom I consulted, told me that plays were not read in this country; those which were published sold in batches according to the number of characters in the play, one copy per character and one for the prompter, shewing that they were purchased for the rehearsing of amateur performances and for no other purposes. He allowed me to see an actual ledger account to satisfy me on the point.

I contended that the business was in a vicious circle: the plays were issued in unreadable acting versions, with revolting stage directions like telegrams with all the definite articles left out, and peppered with technical prompters' terms that insulted the human imagination. . . . I made a resolution . . . that no play of mine, however full its stage directions, should ever mention the stage or use any technical term that could remind the reader of the theatre or destroy the imaginative illusion. Grant Richards, who was then starting in business, published two volumes of plays written in this manner; and their success practically re-established the public habit of reading plays, though I am sorry to say that my system of stage direction is so little understood that even burlesques of it often include references to "the centre of the stage," and such specifications as "to the right of the stage, a small table," &c., &c. Naturally, what my parodists overlooked is not noticed by authors generally; and though I am followed purely as a fashion, the point of my fashion is missed, and telegram English and references to the theatrical mechanism still survive, and still make people prefer novels to plays as instruments to produce illusion. . . . Whereas my earlier plays were printed first and acted afterwards, my later ones were "produced" by me, and acted, years before they were collected in volumes, to be finally revised for press in the light of my practical stage experience with them, and prefaced by essays to which they had no more relation (if so much) than a text has to a sermon. . . .

They tell me that So-and-So, who does not write prefaces, is no charlatan. Well, I am. I first caught the ear of the British public on a cart in Hyde Park, to the blaring of brass bands, and this not at all as a reluctant sacrifice of my instinct of privacy to political necessity, but because, like all dramatists and mimes of genuine vocation, I am a natural-born mountebank. I am well aware that the ordinary British citizen requires a profession of shame from all mountebanks by way of homage to the sanctity of the ignoble private life to which he is condemned by his incapacity for public life. Thus Shakespear, after proclaiming that Not marble nor the gilded monuments of Princes should outlive his powerful rhyme, would apologize, in the approved taste, for making himself a motley to the view; and the British citizen has ever since quoted the apology and ignored the fanfare. When an actress writes her memoirs, she impresses on you in every chapter how cruelly it tried her feelings to exhibit her person to the public gaze; but she does not forget to decorate the book with a dozen portraits of herself. I really cannot respond to this demand for mock-modesty. I am ashamed neither of my work nor of the way it is done. I like explaining its merits to the huge majority who dont know good from bad. It does them good; and it does me good, curing me of nervousness, laziness, and snobbishness. I write prefaces as Dryden did, and treatises as Wagner, because I *can;* and I would give half a dozen of Shakespear's plays for one of the prefaces he ought to have written. I leave the delicacies of retirement to those who are gentlemen first and literary workmen afterwards. The cart and trumpet for me.

This is all very well; but the trumpet is an instrument that grows on one; and sometimes my blasts have been so strident that even those who are most annoyed by them have mistaken the novelty of my shamelessness for novelty in my plays and opinions. Take, for instance, . . . The Devil's Disciple. It does not contain a single even passably novel incident. Every old patron of the Adelphi pit would, were he not beglamored in a way presently to be explained, recognize the reading of the will, the oppressed orphan finding a protector, the arrest, the heroic sacrifice, the court martial, the scaffold, the reprieve at the last moment, as he recognizes beefsteak pudding on the bill of fare at his restaurant. Yet when the play was produced in 1897 in New York by Mr Richard Mansfield, with a success that proves either that the melodrama was built on very safe old lines, or that the American public is composed exclusively of men of genius, the critics, though one said one thing and another another as to the play's merits, yet all agreed that it was novel—*original,* as they put it—to the verge of audacious eccentricity.

Now this, if it applies to the incidents, plot, construction, and general professional and technical qualities of the play, is nonsense; for the truth is, I am in these matters a very old fashioned playwright. . . . One day [William] Terriss sent for me, and informed me that since witnessing the production of Arms and the Man he regarded me as one of the "greatest intellectual forces of the present day." He proposed to combine my intellect with his knowledge of the stage in the construction of a play. . . . He wasted very little time indeed in flattering me: instead, he shewed me a bank-book containing a record of the author's fees on a very popular melodrama then running at the Adelphi. I believe he had no idea that he was an unrivalled executive instrument for my purposes as a dramatist, and that I accordingly had a strong artistic incentive to write for him; on the contrary, he had a confused idea that I was an extremely learned man, and that the only chance of inducing me to condescend to the Adelphi was by an appeal to my pocket, which he rightly regarded as a vital organ even in the most superior constitutions. He at first proposed a collaboration and produced . . . one of the most astounding scenarios I ever encountered. . . . When I endeavoured with all my reasoning powers to convince this terrible Terriss that such a scenario contained far too much action and far too little delineation of character, he declared firmly: "Mister Shaw, you have convinced me." With these words, and without the slightest hesitation, he threw the whole scenario into the fire with the attitude and decision of a man who well knows that he has another draft lying in his desk. Nevertheless, the fact that he greeted me as a great intellectual force and yet had implied that I was incapable of writing a popular melodrama delighted me beyond words, and I resolved to get together all the trite episodes, all the stale situations, which had done such good service in the last ten years in trashy plays, and combine them in a new melodrama, which should have the appearance of a deeply thought-out, original modern play. The result of it all was The Devil's Disciple. . . . When it was finished, there was no immediate occasion for it; and since plays did not interest him as works of art, I found it absolutely impossible to induce him to apply his mind seriously to it, in spite of a quite pathetic effort on his part to pay me that compliment. He was like a child in church longing to be at anything else.[2]

Robert Buchanan, a dramatist who knows what I know and remembers what I remember of the history of the stage, pointed out that the stage tricks by which I gave the younger generation of playgoers an exquisite sense of quaint unexpectedness, had done duty years ago in Cool as a Cucumber, Used Up, and many forgotten farces and comedies of the Byron-Robertson school, in which the imperturbably impudent comedian, afterwards shelved by the reaction to brainless sentimentality, was a stock figure. It is always so more or less: the novelties of one generation are only the resuscitated fashions of the generation before last.

But the stage tricks of The Devil's Disciple are not, like some of those of Arms and the Man, the forgotten ones . . . , but the hackneyed ones of our own time. Why, then, were they not recognized? Partly, no doubt, because of my trumpet and cartwheel declamation. The critics were the victims of the long course of hypnotic suggestion by which G.B.S. the journalist manufactured an unconventional reputation for Bernard Shaw the author. In England as elsewhere the spontaneous recognition of really original work begins with a mere handful of people, and propagates itself so slowly that it has become a commonplace to say that genius, demanding bread, is given a stone after its possessor's death. The remedy for this is sedulous advertisement. Accordingly, I have advertized myself so well that I find myself . . . almost as legendary a person as the Flying Dutchman. Critics, like other people, see what they look for, not what is actually before them. In my plays they look for my legendary qualities, and find originality and brilliancy in my most hackneyed claptraps. Were I to republish Buckstone's Wreck Ashore[3] as my latest comedy, it would be hailed as a masterpiece of perverse paradox and scintillating satire. Not, of course, by the really able critics—for example, you, my friend, now reading this sentence. The illusion that makes *you* think me so original is far subtler than that. The Devil's Disciple has, in truth, a genuine novelty in it. Only, that novelty is not any invention of my own, but simply the novelty of the advanced thought of my day. As such, it will assuredly lose its gloss with the lapse of time, and leave The Devil's Disciple exposed as the threadbare popular melodrama it technically is.

. . . Dick Dudgeon, the devil's disciple, is a Puritan of the Puritans. He is brought up in a household where the Puritan religion has died, and become, in its corruption, an excuse for his mother's master passion of hatred in all its phases of cruelty and envy. This corruption has already been dramatized for us by Charles Dickens in his picture of the Clennam household in Little Dorrit: Mrs. Dudgeon being a replica of Mrs. Clennam with certain circumstantial variations, and perhaps a touch of the same author's Mrs. Gargery in Great Expectations. In such a home the young Puritan finds himself starved of religion, which is the most clamorous need of his nature. With all his mother's indomitable selffulness, but with Pity instead of Hatred as his master passion, he pities the devil; takes his side; and champions him, like a true Covenanter, against the world. He thus becomes, like all genuinely religious men, a reprobate and an outcast. Once this is understood, the play becomes straightforwardly simple.

. . . Centuries ago our greatest English dramatizer of life, John Bunyan, ended one of his stories with the remark that there is a way to hell even from the gates of heaven, and so led us to the equally true proposition that there is a way to heaven even from the gates of hell. A century ago William Blake was, like Dick Dudgeon, an avowed Diabolonian: he called his angels devils and his devils angels. His devil is a Redeemer. Let those who have praised my originality in conceiving Dick Dudgeon's strange religion read Blake's Marriage of Heaven and Hell, and I shall be fortunate if they do not rail at me for a plagiarist. But they need not go back to Blake and Bunyan. Have they not heard . . . about Nietzsche and his Good and Evil Turned Inside Out? . . . There never was a play more certain to be written than The Devil's Disciple at the end of the nineteenth century. The age was visibly pregnant with it.

I grieve to have to add that my old friends and colleagues the London critics for the most part shewed no sort of connoisseurship either in Puritanism or in Diabolonianism when the play was performed for a few weeks at a suburban theatre (Kennington) in October, 1899, by Mr Murray Carson.[4] They took Mrs Dudgeon at her own valuation as a religious woman because she was detestably disagreeable. And they took Dick as a blackguard on her authority, because he was neither detestable nor disagreeable. But they presently found themselves in a dilemma. Why should a blackguard save another man's life, and that man no friend of his, at the risk of his own? Clearly, said the critics, because he is redeemed by love. All wicked heroes are, on the stage: that is the romantic metaphysic. Unfortunately for this explanation (which I do not profess to understand) it turned out in the third act that Dick was a Puritan in this respect also: a man impassioned only for saving grace, and not to be led or turned by wife or mother, Church or State, pride of life or lust of the flesh. In the lovely home of the courageous, affectionate, practical minister who marries a pretty wife twenty years younger than himself, and turns soldier in an instant to save the man who has saved him, Dick looks round and understands the charm and the peace and the sanctity, but knows that such material comforts are not for him. When the woman nursed in that atmosphere falls in love with him and concludes (like the critics, who somehow always agree with my sentimental heroines) that he risked his life for her sake, he tells her the obvious truth that he would have done as much for any stranger—that the law of his own nature, and no interest nor lust whatsoever, forbade him to cry out that the hangman's noose should be taken off his neck only to be put on another man's.

But then, said the critics, where is the motive? *Why* did Dick save Anderson? On the stage, it appears, people do things for reasons. Off the stage they dont: that is why your penny-in-the-slot heroes, who only work when you drop a motive into them, are so oppressively automatic and uninteresting. . . . The theatre critic's professional routine so discourages any association between real life and the stage, that he soon loses the natural habit of referring to the one to explain the other. The critic who discovered a romantic motive for Dick's sacrifice was no mere literary dreamer, but a clever barrister. He pointed out that Dick Dudgeon clearly did adore Mrs Anderson; that it was for her sake that he offered his life to save her beloved husband; and that his explicit denial of his passion was the splendid mendacity of a gentleman whose respect for a married woman, and duty to her absent husband, sealed his passion-palpitating lips. From the moment that this fatally plausible explanation was launched, my play became my critic's play, not mine. Thenceforth Dick Dudgeon every night confirmed the critic by stealing behind Judith, and mutely attesting his passion by surreptitiously imprinting a heartbroken kiss on a stray lock of her hair whilst he uttered the barren denial. As for me, I was just then wandering about the streets of Constantinople, unaware of all these doings. When I returned all was over. . . .

I claim as a notable merit in the authorship of . . . Captain Brassbound's Conversion . . . that I have been intelligent enough to steal its scenery, its surroundings, its atmosphere, its geography, its knowledge of the east, its fascinating Cadis and Krooboys and Sheikhs and mud castles from an excellent book of philosophic travel and vivid adventure entitled Mogreb-el-Acksa (Morocco the Most Holy) by Cunninghame Graham. My own first hand knowledge of Morocco is based on a morning's walk through Tangier, and a cursory observation of the coast through a binocular from the deck of an Orient steamer, both later in date than the writing of the play.

Cunninghame Graham is the hero of his own book; but I have not made him the hero of my play, because so incredible a personage must have destroyed its likelihood—such as it is. There are moments when I do not myself believe in his existence. And yet he must be real; for I have seen him with these eyes; and I am one of the few men living who can decipher the curious alphabet in which he writes his private letters. The man is on public record too. The battle of Trafalgar Square,[5] in which he personally and bodily assailed civilization as represented by the concentrated military and constabular forces of the capital of the world, can scarcely be forgotten by the more discreet spectators, of whom I was one. On that occasion civilization, qualitatively his inferior, was quantitatively so hugely in excess of him that it put him in prison, but had not sense enough to keep him there. Yet his getting out of prison was as nothing compared to his getting into the House of Commons. How he did it I know not; but the thing certainly happened, somehow. That he made pregnant utterances as a legislator may be taken as proved by the keen philosophy of the travels and tales he . . . tossed to us; but the House, strong in stupidity, did not understand him until in an inspired moment he voiced a universal impulse by bluntly damning its hypocrisy. Of all the eloquence of that silly parliament, there remains only one single damn. It has survived the front bench speeches of the eighties as the word of Cervantes survives the oraculations of the Dons and Deys who put him, too, in prison. The shocked house demanded that he should withdraw his cruel word. "I never withdraw," said he; and I promptly stole the potent phrase for the sake of its perfect style, and used it as a cockade for the Bulgarian hero of Arms and the Man. The theft prospered; and I naturally take the first opportunity of repeating it.

In what other Lepantos besides Trafalgar Square Cunninghame Graham has fought, I cannot tell. He is a fascinating mystery to a sedentary person like myself. . . . He handles . . . lethal weapons as familiarly as the pen: mediaeval sword and modern Mauser are to him as umbrellas and kodaks are to me. His tales of adventure have the true Cervantes touch of the man who has been there—so refreshingly different from the scenes imagined by bloody-minded clerks who escape from their servitude into literature to tell us how men and cities are conceived in the counting house of the volunteer corps. He is, I understand, a Spanish hidalgo: hence the superbity of his portrait by Lavery (Velasquez being no longer available). He is, I know, a Scotch laird. How he contrives to be authentically the two things at the same time is no more intelligible to me than the fact that everything that has ever happened to him seems to have happened in Paraguay or Texas instead of in Spain or Scotland. He is, I regret to add, an impenitent and unashamed dandy: such boots, such a hat, would have dazzled D'Orsay himself. With that hat he once saluted me in Regent Street when I was walking with my mother. Her interest was instantly kindled; and the following conversation ensued.

"Who is that?"

"Cunninghame Graham."

"Nonsense! Cunninghame Graham is one of your Socialists: that man is a gentleman."

This is the punishment of vanity, a fault I have myself always avoided, as I find conceit less troublesome and much less expensive. Later on somebody told him of Tarudant, a city in Morocco in which no Christian had ever set foot. Concluding at once that it must be an exceptionally desirable place to live in, he took ship and horse; changed the hat for a turban; and made straight for the sacred city, via Mogador. How he fared, and how he fell into the hands of the Cadi of Kintafi, who rightly held that there was more danger to Islam in one Cunninghame Graham than in a thousand Christians, may be learnt from his account of it in Mogreb-el-Acksa, without which Captain Brassbound's Conversion would never have been written.

Written in 1899, . . . Captain Brassbound's Conversion . . . had its copyright secured in the same year through a performance by Sir Henry Irving's company at the Court Theatre, Liverpool, when the title part was played by Mr Laurence Irving, and that of Lady Cicely Waynflete by Miss Ellen Terry.[6] . . . It did not come into the normal traffic of the English stage until 1906, when it was produced by Messrs Vedrenne & Barker at the Court Theatre, with Miss Ellen Terry as Lady Cicely. Miss Terry then made her jubilee tour of America, and subsequently of the British Provinces, with the play . . . which I had written for her. . . . In writing the play I did the sort of usual thing that an author does. The author, in writing for a particular genius, a particular personality, instead of thinking of gratifying that personality and enabling her or him to escape for a moment from himself or herself, seizes on the personality and dramatizes it. I did this with Ellen Terry. . . . But she said to me on one occasion: "I wish somebody would write a part for me to act. In this play of yours I have nothing to do but go on the stage and be myself, and the thing is done."

Even Miss Terry had to struggle in 1906 against adverse opinions of the play owing to the rather violent transition through which the art of the theatre was then passing. When any art drifts into that phase of extreme artificiality in which its touch with contemporary life is lost, the ensuing reaction to natural subjects and straightforward lifelike methods—the Return to Nature, as we say—may be welcome enough to the world at large; but it invariably and inevitably produces on the case-hardened professional critic an impression of perverse and outrageous violation of custom, undertaken wantonly in a spirit of mischief or as a bid for notoriety. In 1906 the Return to Nature was operating very grotesquely in this way in the London theatres; and Captain Brassbound's Conversion suffered. . . . Indeed it suffered specially because its thesis was trite, its story obviously taken from contemporary life, and its technical method ancient and simple. To begin with the method, it was far older than the platform-stage method of Shakespear or even the ritual method of ancient Athens, being frankly the time-honored trick of those dramatic interludes between the clown and the ringmaster which have enlivened circuses since men learnt the art of horsemanship. This method was stamped on the consciousness of literate Europe 250 years ago through its deliberate adoption by Molière.

The material of the play had been spread before the public for some years by the sharply contrasted travels of explorers like [Henry Morton] Stanley[7] and Mary Kingsley,[8] which shewed us, first, little troops of physically strong, violent, dangerous, domineering armed men shooting and bullying their way through risks and savage enmities partly conjured up by their fear-saturated imaginations, and partly promoted by their own terrified aggressions, and then, before we had recovered the breath their escapes had made us hold, a jolly, fearless, good tempered, sympathetic woman walking safely through all these terrors without a weapon or a threat, and finding more safety and civility than among the Apaches of Paris or the Hooligans of London. Mr Cunninghame Graham's attempt to penetrate the inviolate recesses of Morocco had shewn that the right sort of man could get on as well with the natives as the right sort of woman; and the incident of his being set back by the Cadi of Kintafi was made familiar by his book describing that adventure before it was lifted into the second act of Captain Brassbound's Conversion. The lesson of these popular and widely discussed adventures is the thesis of the play, as it has been the main thesis of Christendom for the last two thousand years. Yet this most old-fashioned, orthodox, and easily understood melodramatic comedy, which might justly have been slighted by an audience of Schopenhauers or Nietzsches as only fit for Sunday School children, was mistrusted and disparaged as paradoxical, unnatural, morbid, perverse, incomprehensible, and Heaven knows what not, by the critics of that remote day (1906), who lived so exclusively in the theatre that they had never heard of Stanley or Mary Kingsley, had forgotten the Gospels, and lost all sense of any connection between the life of the world and the life represented on the stage.

I wrote Caesar and Cleopatra for Forbes Robertson,[9] because he . . . had a right to require such a service from me. He stands completely aloof in . . . the Olympian region where the classic actor is at home. Forbes Robertson is the only actor I know who can find out the feeling of a speech from its cadence. His art meets the dramatist's art directly, picking it up for completion and expression without explanations or imitations, even when he follows up the feat by turning to ask what the prosaic meaning of the sentence is, only to find the author as much in doubt as himself on that point. Without him Caesar and Cleopatra would not have been written; for no man writes a play without any reference to the possibility of a performance: you may scorn the limitations of the theatre as much as you please; but for all that you do not write parts for six-legged actors or two-headed heroines, though there is great scope for drama in such conceptions. . . . Technically, I do not find myself able to proceed otherwise than as former playwrights have done. True, my plays have the latest mechanical improvements: the action is not carried on by impossible soliloquies and asides; and my people get on and off the stage without requiring four doors to a room which in real life would have only one. But my stories are the old stories; my characters are the familiar harlequin and columbine, clown and pantaloon (note the harlequin's leap in the third act of Caesar and Cleopatra); my stage tricks and suspenses and thrills and jests are the ones in vogue when I was a boy, by which time my grandfather was tired of them. . . . The very name of Cleopatra suggests at once a tragedy of Circe, with the horrible difference that whereas the ancient myth rightly represents Circe as turning heroes into hogs, the modern romantic convention would represent her as turning hogs into heroes. Shakespear's Antony and Cleopatra must needs be as intolerable to the true Puritan as it is vaguely distressing to the ordinary healthy citizen, because, after giving a faithful picture of the soldier broken down by debauchery, and the typical wanton in whose arms such men perish, Shakespear finally strains all his huge command of rhetoric and stage pathos to give a theatrical sublimity to the wretched end of the business, and to persuade foolish spectators that the world was well lost by the twain. Such falsehood is not to be borne except by the real Cleopatras and Antonys (they are to be found in every public house) who would no doubt be glad to be transfigured by some poet as immortal lovers. Woe to the poet who stoops to such folly! The lot of the man who sees life truly and thinks about it romantically is Despair. . . .

Surely the time is past for patience with writers who, having to choose between giving up life in despair and discarding the trumpery moral kitchen scales in which they try to weigh the universe, superstitiously stick to the scales and spend the rest of the lives they pretend to despise in breaking men's spirits. But even in pessimism there is a choice between intellectual honesty and dishonesty. . . . When your Shakespears and Thackerays huddle up the matter at the end by killing somebody and covering your eyes with the undertaker's handkerchief, duly onioned with some pathetic phrase, as The flight of angels sing thee to thy rest, or Adsum, or the like, I have no respect for them at all: such maudlin tricks may impose on tea-drunkards, not on me.

Besides, I have a technical objection to making sexual infatuation a tragic theme. Experience proves that it is only effective in the comic spirit. We can bear to see Mrs. Quickly pawning her plate for love of Falstaff, but not Antony running away from the battle of Actium for love of Cleopatra. Let realism have its demonstration, comedy its criticism, or even bawdry its horse-laugh at the expense of sexual infatuation, if it must; but to ask us to subject our souls to its ruinous glamor, to worship it, deify it, and imply that it alone makes our life worth living, is nothing but folly gone mad erotically—a thing compared to which Falstaff's unbeglamored drinking and drabbing is respectable and rightminded. Whoever, then, expects to find Cleopatra a Circe and Caesar a hog . . . had better lay down my book and be spared a disappointment.

As to Caesar himself, I have purposely avoided the usual anachronism of going to Caesar's books, and concluding that the style is the man. That is only true of authors who have the specific literary genius, and have practised long enough to attain complete self-expression in letters. It is not true even of these conditions in an age when literature is conceived as a game of style, and not as a vehicle of self-expression by the author. Now Caesar was an amateur stylist writing books of travel and campaign histories in a style so impersonal that the authenticity of the later volumes is disputed. They reveal some of his qualities just as the Voyage of a Naturalist Round the World reveals some of Darwin's, without expressing his private personality. An Englishman reading them would say that Caesar was a man of great common sense and good taste, meaning thereby a man without originality or moral courage.

In exhibiting Caesar as a much more various person than the historian of the Gallic wars, I hope I have not been too much imposed on by the dramatic illusion to which all great men owe part of their reputation and some the whole of it. I admit that reputations gained in war are specially questionable. Able civilians taking up the profession of arms, like Caesar and Cromwell, in middle age, have snatched all its laurels from opponent commanders bred to it, apparently because capable persons engaged in military pursuits are so scarce that the existence of two of them at the same time in the same hemisphere is extremely rare. The capacity of any conqueror is therefore more likely than not to be an illusion produced by the incapacity of his adversary. At all events, Caesar might have won his battles without being wiser than Charles XII or Nelson or Joan of Arc, who were, like most modern "self-made" millionaires, half-witted geniuses, enjoying the worship accorded by all races to certain forms of insanity. But Caesar's victories were only advertisements for an eminence that would never have become popular without them. Caesar is greater off the battle field than on it. Nelson off his quarterdeck was so quaintly out of the question that when his head was injured at the battle of the Nile, and his conduct became for some years openly scandalous, the difference was not important enough to be noticed. It may, however, be said that peace hath her illusory reputations no less than war. And it is certainly true that in civil life mere capacity for work—the power of killing a dozen secretaries under you, so to speak, as a life-or-death courier kills horses—enables men with common ideas and superstitions to distance all competitors in the strife of political ambition. It was this power of work that astonished Cicero as the most prodigious of Caesar's gifts, as it astonished observers in Napoleon before it wore him out. How if Caesar were nothing but a Nelson and a Gladstone combined! a prodigy of vitality without any special quality of mind! nay, with ideas that were worn out before he was born, as Nelson's and Gladstone's were! I have considered that possibility too, and rejected it. I cannot cite all the stories about Caesar which seem to me to shew that he was genuinely original; but let me at least point out that I have been careful to attribute nothing but originality to him. Originality gives a man an air of frankness, generosity, and magnanimity by enabling him to estimate the value of truth, money, or success in any particular instance quite independently of convention and moral generalization. He therefore will not, in the ordinary Treasury bench fashion, tell a lie which everybody knows to be a lie (and consequently expects him as a matter of good taste to tell). His lies are not found out: they pass for candors. He understands the paradox of money, and gives it away when he can get most for it: in other words, when its value is least, which is just when a common man tries hardest to get it. He knows that the real moment of success is not the moment apparent to the crowd. Hence, in order to produce an impression of complete disinterestedness and magnanimity, he has only to act with entire selfishness; and this is perhaps the only sense in which a man can be said to be *naturally* great. It is in this sense that I have represented Caesar as great. Having virtue, he had no need of goodness. He is neither forgiving, frank, nor generous, because a man who is too great to resent has nothing to forgive; a man who says things that other people are afraid to say need be no more frank than Bismarck was; and there is no generosity in giving things you do not want to people of whom you intend to make use. This distinction between virtue and goodness is not understood in England: hence the poverty of our

WITHDRAWN

drama in heroes. Our stage attempts at them are mere goody-goodies. Goodness, in its popular British sense of self-denial, implies that man is vicious by nature, and that supreme goodness is supreme martyrdom. Not sharing this pious opinion, I have not given countenance to it in any of my plays. In this I follow the precedent of the ancient myths, which represent the hero as vanquishing his enemies, not in fair fight, but with enchanted sword, superequine horse, and magical invulnerability, the possession of which, from the vulgar moralistic point of view, robs his exploits of any merit whatever.

The American notices of the play showed, in spite of all my warnings to the critics, a widespread and dense ignorance of the nature of great men in general and the career of Julius Caesar in particular. Just as all the military realism and elaborately accurate Balkan color of Arms and the Man was received in 1894 with incredulous ridicule as mere *opéra bouffe;* so everything in Caesar and Cleopatra, which is simply dramatised Mommsen or transcribed Plutarch, has been pooh-poohed as fantastic modern stuff of my own, whilst the few modern topical allusions I have indulged in, including the quotation from Beaconsfield on Cyprus,[10] have passed unchallenged as grave Roman history. As to Caesar, even Shakespear's Caesar, who is nothing but the conventional tyrant of the Elizabethan stage adapted to Plutarch's Roundhead account of him, would be too modern, too realistic, for some of the New York papers. The fact that Caesar was a real flesh and blood man, and not a statue with a phonograph in its mouth repeating "I came: I saw: I conquered" and "Et tu, Brute!" appears to strike . . . journalists as a whimsical paradox. Caesar was a very modern man indeed: first a young man about town dressed in the height of fashion; then a demagogue like Wilkes or Bradlaugh, with mobs in his pay; then at forty, discovering that handling a provincial army was child's play to a man accustomed to manipulate Roman mobs; then conqueror and explorer; then by force of circumstance and gameness for any destiny, political adventurer gambling with Pompey for the empire of the civilised world and winning; finally dead and turned to clay, assassinated by the Nonconformist Conscience. The reason Shakespear belittled him, and that no later English dramatist touched this greatest of all protagonists until I saw my chance and took it, was simply that Shakespear's sympathies were with Plutarch and the Nonconformist Conscience, which he personified as Brutus. From the date of Shakespear's play onward

England believed in Brutus with growing hope and earnestness, until the assassination in the Capital was repeated in Whitehall, and Brutus got his chance from Cromwell, who found him hopelessly incapable, and ruled in Caesar's fashion until he died, when the nation sent for Charles II, because it was determined to have anybody rather than Brutus. Yet as late as Macaulay and John Morley you find Brutus still the hero and Caesar still the doubtful character. It was Ibsen who killed him at last with the self-same steel that slew the Tennysonian King Arthur. That left the dramatic field free at last for Caesar and for Forbes Robertson.

Caesar and Cleopatra was written and published before it was acted. It was, except for the old copyrighting farce[11] which has no importance and is now abolished by the last Copyright Act, first produced in Berlin. During the rehearsals it was discovered that I had failed to remove one of the characters, Apollodorus the Sicilian (the hero of the carpet incident), from the stage in the third act. I had accordingly to write in a speech or two to dismiss him; and this speech of course appears in the later editions and is not in the earlier ones. Later on, when Forbes Robertson, for whom the part of Caesar was written, was at last able to take it up, he said one day at rehearsal that the scene with Septimius in the second act, which is one of the great acting points in the play, required a little more explanation and additional preparatory ferment to enable him to make the most of it, and I immediately wrote in about a dozen speeches to make it right for him. An edition printed from Forbes Robertson's prompt copy would contain those speeches, which I regret to say I have been too lazy to have inserted in my own editions.

But there is a further complication. The great length of Caesar and Cleopatra when performed in the old-fashioned way in acts separated by long intervals to allow the carpenters to put up and remove heavy scenic sets, led to several expedients to shorten it. I first cut out the third act; but the fascination of this episode of fun for the actors, and its success in Berlin, produced a rebellion against the author, and it had to be restored. To make room for it I struck out the first scenes of the first and fourth acts, and replaced them by a sort of grand overture in the form of a prologue to be spoken by the god Ra. . . .[12] But the difficulty was this tremendous exordium required another Forbes Robertson to deliver it; and the English stage produces only one at a time. But several ambitious actors tackled it, and established this version for a time on the stage. Now suppose some twentieth century Heminge and Condell print in folio a version of the play from the authentic prompt copies used by our Burbage, the original Caesar; and take my editions as the equivalent of the Shakespearean quartos. The quartos will have scenes omitted in the folio; and the folio will have an entirely different opening and several passages omitted from the quartos. The Literary Supplement of that day will be able to keep a correspondence going for months about the discrepancies.

2

Cerebral Capers

ONE DAY early in the eighteen hundred and sixties, I, being then a small boy, was with my nurse, buying something in the shop of a petty newsagent, bookseller, and stationer in Camden Street, Dublin, when there entered an elderly man, weighty and solemn, who advanced to the counter, and said pompously, "Have you the works of the celebrated Buffoon?"

My own works were at that time unwritten, or it is possible that the shop assistant might have misunderstood me so far as to produce a copy of Man and Superman. As it was, she knew quite well what he wanted; for this was before the Education Act of 1870 had produced shop assistants who know how to read and know nothing else. The celebrated Buffoon was not a humorist, but the famous naturalist Buffon. Every literate child at that time knew Buffon's Natural History[1] as well as Esop's Fables. And no living child had heard the name that has since obliterated Buffon's in the popular consciousness: the name of Darwin.

Ten years elapsed. The celebrated Buffoon was forgotten; I had doubled my years and my length; and I had discarded the religion of my forefathers. One day the richest and consequently most dogmatic of my uncles came into a restaurant where I was dining, and found himself, much against his will, in conversation with the most questionable of his nephews. By way of making myself agreeable, I spoke of modern thought and Darwin. He said, "Oh, thats the fellow who wants to make out that we all have tails like monkeys." I tried to explain that what Darwin had insisted on in this connection was that some monkeys have no tails. But my uncle was as impervious to what Darwin really said as any neo-Darwinian nowadays. He died impenitent, and did not mention me in his will.

Twenty years elapsed. If my uncle had been alive, he would have known all about Darwin, and known it all wrong.

In spite of the efforts of Grant Allen[2] to set him right, he would have accepted Darwin as the discoverer of Evolution, of Heredity, and of modification of species by Selection. For the pre-Darwinian age had come to be regarded as a Dark Age in which men still believed that the book of Genesis was a standard scientific treatise, and that the only additions to it were Galileo's demonstration of Leonardo da Vinci's simple remark that the earth is a moon of the sun, Newton's theory of gravitation, Sir Humphry Davy's invention of the safety lamp, the discovery of electricity, the application of steam to industrial purposes, and the penny post. It was just the same in other subjects. Thus Nietzsche, by the two or three who had come across his writings, was supposed to have been the first man to whom it occurred that mere morality and legality and urbanity lead nowhere, as if Bunyan had never written Badman. Schopenhauer was credited with inventing the distinction between the Covenant of Grace and the Covenant of Works which troubled Cromwell on his deathbed. People talked as if there had been no dramatic or descriptive music before Wagner; no impressionist painting before Whistler; whilst as to myself, I was finding that the surest way to produce an effect of daring innovation and originality was to revive the ancient attraction of long rhetorical speeches; to stick closely to the methods of Molière; and to life characters bodily out of the pages of Charles Dickens.

This particular sort of ignorance does not always or often matter. But in Darwin's case it did matter. . . . The discovery and vogue of evolution, from 1790 to 1830, made an end, for the pioneers of thought, of eighteenth century rationalist atheism and deism on the one hand, and, on the other, of what may be called Garden-of Edenism. In the middle of the nineteenth century the discovery by Darwin and Wallace of Natural Selection, which might have had as its subtitle "The revelation of a method by which all the appearances of intelligent design in the universe may have been produced by pure accident," practically destroyed religion in cultured Europe for a whole generation, in spite of Darwin's and Wallace's own reservations and the urgent warnings and fierce criticisms of Samuel Butler. With the beginning of the present century the return swing of the pendulum has inaugurated a counterfashion of saying that Natural Selection, instead of accounting for everything, accounts for nothing. That it accounts for nothing in any religious sense is of course true; for it leaves untouched the whole sphere of will, purpose, design, intention, even consciousness; and a religion is nothing but a common view of the nature of will, the purpose of life, the design of organism, and the intention of evolution. Such a common view has been gradually detaching itself from the welter of negation provoked by the extremely debased forms of religion which have masqueraded as Christianity in England during the period of petty commercialism from which we are emerging. . . .

Shelley and Wagner made attempts to . . . formulate this common view as a modern religion, and to provide it with a body of doctrine, a poesy, . . . to provide it with materials for a Bible: and I, with later lights of science to guide me than either of these prophets had, . . . made a further attempt in this Man and Superman. As I have not been sparing of such lighter qualities as I could endow the book with for the sake of those who ask nothing from a play but an agreeable pastime, I think it well to affirm plainly that the third act, however fantastic its legendary framework may appear, is a careful attempt to write a new Book of Genesis for the Bible of the Evolutionists. . . .

. . . Ibsen was Darwinized to the extent of exploiting heredity on the stage much as the ancient Athenian playwrights exploited the Eumenides; but there is no trace in his plays of any faith in or knowledge of Creative Evolution as a modern scientific fact. True, the poetic aspiration is plain enough in his Emperor or Galilean; but it is one of Ibsen's distinctions that nothing was valid for him but science; and he left that vision of the future which his Roman seer calls "the third Empire" behind him as a Utopian dream when he settled down to his serious grapple with realities in those plays of modern life with which he overcame Europe, and broke the dusty windows of every dry-rotten theatre in it from Moscow to Manchester.

In my own activities as a playwright I found this state of things intolerable. The fashionable theatre prescribed one serious subject: clandestine adultery: the dullest of all subjects for a serious author, whatever it may be for audiences who read the police intelligence and skip the reviews and leading articles. I tried slum-landlordism, doctrinaire Free Love (pseudo-Ibsenism), prostitution, militarism, marriage, history, current politics, natural Christianity, national and individual character, paradoxes of conventional society, husband-hunting, questions of conscience, professional delusions and impostures, all worked into a series of comedies of manners[3] in the classic fashion, which was then very much out of fashion, the mechanical tricks of Parisian "construction" being *de rigueur* in the theater. But this, though it occupied me and established me professionally, did not constitute me an iconographer of the religion of my time, and thus fulfil my natural function as an artist. I was quite conscious of this; for I had always known that civilization needs a religion as a matter of life or death; and as the conception of Creative Evolution developed I saw that we were at last within reach of a faith which complied with the first condition of all the religions that have ever taken hold of humanity: namely, that it must be, first and fundamentally, a science of metabiology. This was a crucial point with me; for I had seen Bible fetichism, after standing up to all the rationalistic batteries of Hume, Voltaire, and the rest, collapse before the onslaught of much less gifted Evolutionists, solely because they discredited it as a biological document; so that from that moment it lost its hold, and left literate Christendom faithless. My own Irish eighteenth-centuryism made it impossible for me to believe anything until I could conceive it as a scientific hypothesis, even though the abominations, quackeries, impostures, venalites, credulities, and delusions of the camp followers of science, and the brazen lies and priestly pretensions of the pseudoscientific cure-mongers, all sedulously inculcated by modern "secondary education," were so monstrous that I was sometimes forced to make a verbal distinction between science and knowledge lest I should mislead my readers. But I never forgot that without knowledge even wisdom is more dangerous than mere opportunist ignorance, and that somebody must take the Garden of Eden in hand and weed it properly.

Accordingly, in 1901, I took the legend of Don Juan in its Mozartian form and made it a dramatic parable of Creative Evolution. But being then at the height of my invention and comedic talent, I decorated it too brilliantly and lavishly. I surrounded it with a comedy of which it formed only one act, and that act was so completely episodical (it was a dream which did not affect the action of the piece) that the comedy could be detached and played by itself:-indeed it could hardly be played at full length owing to the enormous length of the entire work, though that feat has been performed a few times. . . .

But I hear you asking me in alarm whether I have actually put all this tub thumping into a Don Juan comedy. I have not. I have only made my Don Juan a political pamphleteer, and given . . . his pamphlet in full by way of appendix. . . . I supplied the published work with an imposing framework consisting of a preface, an appendix called The Revolutionist's Handbook, and a final display of aphoristic fireworks. . . . It is a common practice with romancers to announce their hero as a man of extraordinary genius, and then leave his works entirely to the reader's imagination; so that at the end of the book you whisper to yourself ruefully that but for the author's solemn preliminary assurance you should hardly have given the gentleman credit for ordinary good sense. You cannot accuse me of this pitiable barrenness, this feeble evasion. I not only tell you that my hero wrote a revolutionists' handbook: I give you the handbook at full length for your edification if you care to read it. And in that handbook you will find the politics of the sex question as I conceive Don Juan's descendant to understand them. Not that I disclaim the fullest responsibility for his opinions and for those of all my characters, pleasant and unpleasant. They are all right from their several points of view; and their points of view are, for the dramatic moment, mine also. This may puzzle the people who believe that there is such a thing as an absolutely right point of view, usually their own. It may seem to them that nobody who doubts this can be in a state of grace. However that may be, it is certainly true that nobody who agrees with them can possibly be a dramatist, or indeed anything else that turns upon a knowledge of mankind. Hence it has been pointed out that Shakespear had no conscience. Neither have I, in that sense.

. . . The effect was so vertiginous, apparently, that nobody noticed the new religion in the centre of the intellectual whirlpool. Now I protest I did not cut these cerebral capers in mere inconsiderate exuberance. I did it because the worst convention of the criticism of the theatre current at that time was that intellectual seriousness is out of place on the stage; that the theatre is a place of shallow amusement; that people go there to be soothed after the enormous intellectual strain of a day in the city: in short, that a playwright is a person whose business it is to make unwholesome confectionery out of cheap emotions. My answer to this was to put all my intellectual goods in the shop window under the sign of Man and Superman. That part of my design succeeded. By good luck and acting, the comedy triumphed on the stage; and the book was a good deal discussed. Since then the sweet-shop view of the theatre has been out of countenance; and its critical exponents have been driven to take an intellectual pose which, though often more trying than their old intellectually nihilistic vulgarity, at least concedes the dignity of the theatre, not to mention the usefulness of those who live by criticizing it. And the younger playwrights are not only taking their art seriously, but being taken seriously themselves.

I should make formal acknowledgment to the authors whom I have pillaged in . . . Man and Superman . . . if I could recollect them all. The theft of the brigand-poetaster from Sir Arthur Conan Doyle is deliberate; and the metamorphosis of Leporello into Enry Straker, motor engineer and New Man, is an intentional dramatic sketch of the contemporary embryo of Mr H. G. Wells's anticipation of the efficient engineering class which will, he hopes, finally sweep the jabberers out of the way of civilization.

. . . The conception of Mendoza Limited I trace back to a certain West Indian colonial secretary,[4] who, at a period when he and I and Mr Sidney Webb were sowing our political wild oats as a sort of Fabian Three Musketeers, without any prevision of the surprising respectability of the crop that followed, recommended Webb, the encyclopedic and inexhaustible, to form himself into a company for the benefit of the shareholders. Octavius I take over unaltered from Mozart; and I hereby authorize any actor who impersonates him, to sing "Dalla sua pace" (if he can) at any convenient moment during the representation. Ann was suggested to me by the fifteenth century Dutch morality called Everyman, which Mr William Poel . . .[5] resuscitated so triumphantly.

. . . As I sat watching Everyman at the Charterhouse, I said to myself, Why not Everywoman? Ann was the result: every woman is not Ann; but Ann is Everywoman.

That the author of Everyman was no mere artist, but an artist-philosopher, and that the artist-philosophers are the only sort of artists I take quite seriously, will be no news to you. Even Plato and Boswell, as the dramatists who invented Socrates and Dr Johnson, impress me more deeply than the romantic playwrights. Ever since, as a boy,

I first breathed the air of the transcendental regions at a performance of Mozart's Zauberflöte, I have been proof against the garish splendors and alcoholic excitements of the ordinary stage combinations of Tappertitian romance with the police intelligence. Bunyan, Blake, Hogarth, and Turner (these four apart and above all the English classics), Goethe, Shelley, Schopenhauer, Wagner, Ibsen, Morris, Tolstoy, and Nietzsche are among the writers whose peculiar sense of the world I recognize as more or less akin to my own.

. . . I cannot be a bellettrist. No doubt I must recognize, as even the Ancient Mariner did, that I must tell my story entertainingly if I am to hold the wedding guest spellbound in spite of the siren sounds of the loud bassoon. But "for art's sake" alone I would not face the toil of writing a single sentence. I know that there are men who, having nothing to say and nothing to write, are nevertheless so in love with oratory and with literature that they delight in repeating as much as they can understand of what others have said or written aforetime. I know that the leisurely tricks which their want of conviction leaves them free to play with the diluted and misapprehended message supply them with a pleasant parlor game which they call style. I can pity their dotage and even sympathize with their fancy. But a true original style is never achieved for its own sake: a man may pay from a shilling to a guinea, according to his means, to see, hear, or read another man's act of genius; but he will not pay with his whole life and soul to become a mere virtuoso in literature, exhibiting an accomplishment which will not even make money for him, like fiddle playing. Effectiveness of assertion is the Alpha and Omega of style. He who has nothing to assert has no style and can have none: he who has something to assert will go as far in power of style as its momentousness and his conviction will carry him. Disprove his assertion after it is made, yet its style remains. Darwin has no more destroyed the style of Job nor of Handel than Martin Luther destroyed the style of Giotto. All the assertions get disproved sooner or later; and so we find the world full of a magnificent débris of artistic fossils, with the matter-of-fact credibility gone clean out of them, but the form still splendid. . . .

3

The Court Experiment

THE FIRST PERFORMANCE of a play of mine was a desperate adventure, in which . . . Jack Grein spent all his savings. My first regular West End production was financed by . . . Annie Elizabeth Fredericka Horniman, a lady of property, who produced my Arms and the Man at the old Avenue Theatre in 1894, and put me on the map as a playwright by drastically emptying her own pocket. . . . Now what had made serious drama possible to a limited extent . . . was that a play could pay its way even if the theatre were only half full until Saturday and three-quarters full then. A manager who was an enthusiast and a desperately hard worker, with an occasional grant-in-aid from an artistically disposed millionaire, and a due proportion of those rare and happy accidents by which plays of the higher sort turn out to be potboilers as well, could hold out for some years, by which time a relay might arrive in the person of another enthusiast. Thus and not otherwise occurred that remarkable revival of the British drama at the beginning of the century which made my own career as a playwright possible in England.

. . . Yet for ten years all the money that came to me from the theatre came from Germany and America. . . . In Germany and Austria I had no difficulty: the system of publicly aided theatres there, Court and Municipal, kept drama of the kind I dealt in alive; so that I was indebted to the Emperor of Austria for magnificent productions of my works at a time when the sole attention paid to me by the British Court was the announcement to the English-speaking world that certain plays of mine were unfit for public performance, a substantial set-off against this being that the British Court, in the course of its private playgoing, paid no regard to the bad character given me by the chief officer of its household. . . .[1]

In the year 1904, when I was forty-eight years old, I was an unacted playwright in London, though certain big box office successes abroad, notably those of Agnes Sorma as Candida in Germany and Richard Mansfield in New York as the Devil's Disciple, had proved that my plays were both actable, and possibly highly lucrative. But . . . there were no murders, no adulteries, no sexual intrigues in them. The heroines were not like heroines: they were like women. Although the rule of the stage was that any speech longer than twenty words was too long, and that politics and religion must never be mentioned and their places taken by romance and fictitious police and divorce cases, my characters had to declaim long speeches on religion and politics in the Shakespearean or "ham" technique. . . . When little private clubs of connoisseurs like the Independent Theatre and the Stage Society ventured on single performances of them, the Strand (as theatre-land was then called) could not accept them as plays at all, and repudiated them as pamphlets in dialogue form by a person ignorant of the theatre and hopelessly destitute of dramatic faculty.

. . . In looking about for an actor suitable for the part of the poet in Candida at a Stage Society performance, I had found my man in a very remarkable person named Harley Granville-Barker. He was at that time twenty-three years of age, and had been on the stage since he was fourteen. He had a strong strain of Italian blood in him, and looked as if he had stepped out of a picture by Benozzo Gozzoli.[2] He had a wide literary culture and a fastidiously delicate taste in every branch of art. He could write in a difficult and too precious but exquisitely fine style. He was self-willed, restlessly industrious, sober, and quite sane. He had Shakespear and Dickens at his finger ends. Altogether the most distinguished and incomparably the most cultivated person whom circumstances had driven into the theatre at that time.

I saw him play in Hauptmann's Friedensfest and immediately jumped at him for the poet in Candida. His performance of this part—a very difficult one to cast—was, humanly speaking, perfect.

Presently a gentleman[3] with a fancy for playing Shakespearean parts, and money enough to gratify it without much regard to public support, took the Court Theatre in Sloane Square, made famous by the acting of John Hare, . . . Ellen Terry, and by the early comedy-farces of Pinero. He installed therein as his business manager . . . J. E. Vedrenne, who, when his principal was not indulging in Shakespearean matinées, kept the theatre going by letting it by night to amateurs. Granville-Barker was engaged for one of these revivals in the ordinary course of his professional routine.

. . . The Court Theatre presently became virtually his theatre, with Vedrenne in the manager's office. They began with matinées of Candida, the expenses of which were guaranteed by a few friends; but the guarantee was not needed: the matinées paid their way. More matinées of my plays followed with Barker as the leading actor; and before long Vedrenne and Barker were in a position to take the theatre over from the Shakespearean enthusiast as a full-blown management; and I ceased to write plays for anybody who asked me, and became playwright in ordinary to this new enterprise.

But it is not enough to have a fascinating actor for your heroes: you must also have an interesting actress for your heroine. . . . This difficulty was acute when I had to find a heroine for Man and Superman. Everybody said that she must be ultra-modern. I said that I wanted a young Mrs Siddons or Ristori, and that an ultra-modern actress would be no use to me whatever in the part. I was in despair of finding what I wanted when one day there walked into my rooms in the Adelphi a gorgeously good-looking young lady in a green dress and huge picture hat in which any ordinary woman would have looked ridiculous, and in which she looked splendid, with the figure and gait of a Diana. She said: "Ten years ago, when I was a little girl trying to play Lady Macbeth, you told me to go and spend ten years learning my business. I have learnt it: now give me a part." I handed her the book of Man and Superman without a moment's hesitation, and said simply, "Here you are." And with that young lady I achieved performances of my plays which will probably never be surpassed. For Lillah McCarthy was saturated with declamatory poetry and rhetoric from her cradle, and learnt her business out of London by doing work in which you were either heroic or nothing . . . in the course of a tour round the world as the beautiful Mercia in The Sign of the Cross after playing Lady Macbeth at the age of sixteen like an immature Mrs Siddons. . . .

It is an actress's profession to be extraordinary; but Lillah was extraordinary even among actresses. The first natural qualification of an actress who is not a mere puppet, impotent without a producer, is imagination. Lillah had a great deal too much of it: she was of imagination all compact. It was difficult to get her feet down to the ground, and almost impossible to keep them there. . . . She was beautiful, plastic, statuesque, most handsomely made, and seemed to have come straight from the Italian or eighteenth century stage without a trace of the stuffiness of the London cup-and-saucer theatres.[4]

. . . Her technique fell in with mine as if they had been made for one another, as indeed they had. She created the first generation of Shavian heroines with dazzling success. Not merely playgoing London came to see her: indeed I doubt if playgoing London ever did to any great extent. Political London, artistic London, religious London, and even sporting London made the long series of performances in which she figured a centre of almost every vein of fashion except the hopeless old theatrical fashion. And she did this by playing my heroines exactly as she would have played Belvidera in Venice Preserved if anyone had thought of reviving that or any other of Mrs Siddons's great parts for her.

During the career of Mrs Siddons a play was regarded as an exhibition of the art of acting. Playwrights wrote declamatory parts for actors as composers did for singers or violinists, to display their technical virtuosity. This became an abuse: Wagner was quite justified in his complaint that singers thought only of how they sang, and never of what they were singing. Actors who had learnt how "to bring down the house" with a tirade were quite as pleased when the tirade was trash as when it was one of Shakespear's best. The cup-and-saucer drama, and the actor who, having no force to reserve, made a virtue of reserved force, were inevitable reactions against the resultant staginess, staginess being definable as much ado about nothing. The art of acting rhetorical and poetical drama, vulgarized and ridiculous, very soon became a lost art in the fashionable London theatres. Rhetoric and poetry vanished with it. But when I dragged rhetoric and poetry back its executive technique became again indispensable. . . . Lillah McCarthy's secret was that she combined the . . . art of the grand school with a natural impulse to murder the Victorian womanly woman; . . . this being just what I needed. . . .

We were now complete. The Court experiment . . . from April 1904 to June 1907 . . . went through with flying colors. Barker, aiming at a National Repertory Theatre, with a change of program every night, was determined to test our enterprise to destruction as motor tyres are tested, to find out its utmost possibilities. I was equally reckless. Vedrenne, made prudent by a wife and family, was like a man trying to ride two runaway horses simultaneously. Barker worked furiously: he had not only to act, but to produce all the plays except mine, and to find and inspire all the artists who he drew into the theatre to carry out his ideas. . . .

There is no reasonable probability of any private enterprise of the kind being more ably or public-spiritedly managed or more fortunate in obtaining a large stock of suitable plays. Its artistic success, and its beneficial reaction on the theatre generally, have been admitted on all hands. It was even commercially successful in the sense that the managers, though they did not get the commercial value of their time, skill, and labor, at least scraped a living and made a considerable reputation. . . .

. . . You may say that genius does not wait for its opportunity: it creates it. But that is not true of any particular opportunity when there are alternatives open. Men of genius will not become the slaves of the ordinary fashionable theatres when they have the alternative of writing novels. The genius of Dickens, who at first wanted to write for the theatre, was lost to it because there was no theatre available in which his art could have breathed. I . . . myself tried hard to tempt Mr Wells, Mr Kipling, Mr Conrad, and Mr Maurice Hewlett to leave their safe and dignified position as masters of the art of fiction, and struggle with new difficulties and a new *technique*—though the technical difficulties are absurdly exaggerated—for the sake of redeeming the British drama from banality. But it was too much to ask. They all knew the story of the manager who, after receiving favorably a suggestion of a play by Stevenson, drew back in disgust on learning that the author in question was not what he called "*the* Stephenson," meaning the librettist of a well-known light opera,[5] but one Robert Louis Stevenson, of whom he had never heard. . . . But I kept pressing for the enlistment of other authors, and urging Barker to write, which he did slowly, repeatedly protesting that as it was not his profession, and was mine, it was easy for me and very hard for him. Galsworthy, Masefield, Laurence Housman, and St John Hankin (for the moment forgotten or neglected, but a master of serious comedy) came into our repertory, financed at first by revivals of my potboiler, You Never Can Tell.

Barker's production of his own plays and Galsworthy's were exquisite: their styles were perfectly sympathetic, whereas his style and taste were as different from mine as Debussy's from Verdi's. With Shakespear and with me he was not always at his happiest best; but he was absolutely faithful to the play and would not cut a line to please himself; and the plays pulled him through with the bits that suited him enchanting and the scenery and dressing perfect.

Producing kills acting: an actor's part dies if he is watching the others critically. You cannot conduct an orchestra and play the drums at the same concert. As long as I was producing and Barker acting all was well: he acted beautifully; and I took care to make the most of him.

He adopted my technique of production, but was utterly inconsiderate in its practice. I warned him again and again that the end of it would be a drastic Factory Act regulating the hours of rehearsals as strictly as the hours of weaving in a cotton mill. But he would not leave off until the unfortunate company had lost their last trains and buses and he had tried himself beyond human powers of maintaining the intense vigilance and freshness which first-rate production, or indeed any production, demands. I myself put a limit to such attention at three hours or less between breakfast and lunch, [and] absolutely refused to spend more time than that in the theatre.

. . . As we rehearsed our scenes and rejoiced in the growing interest and expectancy of our actors as they took the play in, we knew that no matter how enthusiastic our audience on the first night would be, no matter how triumphant the success of our actors, the next day—always a day of reaction at the best of times—would bring down on them all a damp cloud of grudging, petulant, ill-conditioned disparagement, suggesting to them that what they had been working so hard at was not a play at all, but a rather ridiculous experiment which was no credit to anybody connected with it. . . . If you turn . . . to the first-night notices of the productions you will see what I mean. There you will find a chronicle of failure, a sulky protest against this new and troublesome sort of entertainment that calls for knowledge and thought instead of for the usual *clichés*. . . . The mischief done was very considerable in the cases of new authors; and the discouragement to our actors must have had its effect, bravely as they concealed it. . . .

Now, we were all—we authors—very much indebted to our actors, and felt proportionately disgusted at the way in which they were assured that they were wasting their time on us. . . . I will only give, as an instance, the fact that my own play John Bull's Other Island failed as completely in America without Mr Louis Calvert as Broadbent as it succeeded here, where it was carried on his massive shoulders. The success was his, not mine: I only provided the accessories. Well, you will say, but did not the press acknowledge this? is not the play always spoken of as a masterpiece? is not Mr Calvert's Broadbent as famous as Quin's Falstaff? Yes, it is—*now*. But turn back to the first-night notices, and you will learn that the masterpiece is not a play at all, and that Mr Calvert only did the best he could with an impossible part. It was not until Man and Superman followed that the wonderful qualities of John Bull were contrasted with the emptiness and dullness of its successor. It was not until Major Barbara came that the extinction of all the brilliancy that blazed through Man and Superman was announced. And not until The Doctor's Dilemma had been declared my Waterloo was it mentioned that Major Barbara had been my Austerlitz. . . . Praise comes too late to help plays that have already helped themselves.

John Bull's Other Island was written in 1904 at the request of Mr. William Butler Yeats, as a patriotic contribution to the repertory of the Irish Literary Theatre. Like most people who have asked me to write plays, Mr Yeats got rather more than he bargained for. The play was at that time beyond the resources of the . . . Abbey Theatre. . . .

There was another reason for changing the destination of John Bull's Other Island. It was uncongenial to the whole spirit of the new-Gaelic movement, . . . bent on creating a new Ireland after its own ideal, whereas my play is a very uncompromising presentment of the real old Ireland. The next thing that happened was the production of the play in London at the Court Theatre by Messrs Vedrenne and Barker, and its immediate and enormous popularity with delighted and flattered English audiences. This constituted it a successful commercial play, and made it unnecessary to resort to the special machinery or tax the special resources of the Irish Literary Theatre for its production.

. . . Writing the play for an Irish audience, I thought it would be good for them to be shewn very clearly that the loudest laugh they could raise at the expense of the absurdest Englishman was not really a laugh on their side; that he would succeed where they would fail; that he could inspire strong affection and loyalty in an Irishman who knew the world and was moved only to dislike, mistrust, impatience, and even exasperation by his own countrymen; that his power of taking himself seriously, and his insensibility to anything funny in danger and destruction, was the first condition of economy and concentration of force, sustained purpose, and rational conduct. But the need for this lesson in Ireland is the measure of its demoralizing superfluousness in England. English audiences very naturally swallowed it eagerly and smacked their lips over it, laughing all the more heartily because they felt that they were taking a caricature of themselves with the most tolerant and large-minded good humor. They were perfectly willing to allow me to represent Tom Broadbent as infatuated in politics, hypnotized by his newspaper leader-writers and parliamentary orators into an utter paralysis of his common sense, without moral delicacy or social tact, provided I made him cheerful, robust, goodnatured, free from envy, and, above all, a successful muddler-through in business and love. Not only did no English critic allow that the success in business of Messrs English Broadbent and Irish Doyle might possibly have been due to some extent to Doyle, but one writer actually dwelt with much feeling on the pathos of Doyle's failure as an engineer (a circumstance not mentioned nor suggested in my play) in contrast with Broadbent's solid success. . . .

I am persuaded . . .—without pretending to know more about it than anyone else—that Broadbent's special contribution was simply the strength, self-satisfaction, social confidence, and cheerful bumptiousness that money, comfort, and good feeding bring to all healthy people; and that Doyle's special contribution was the freedom from illusion, the power of facing facts, the nervous industry, the sharpened wits, the sensitive pride of the imaginative man who has fought his way up through social persecution and poverty. I do not say that the confidence of the Englishman in Broadbent is not for the moment justified. The virtues of the English soil are not less real because they consist of coal and iron, not of metaphysical sources of character. The virtues of Broadbent are not less real because they are the virtues of the money that coal and iron have produced. But as the mineral virtues are being discovered and developed in other soils, their derivative virtues are appearing so rapidly in other nations that Broadbent's relative advantage is vanishing. In truth I am afraid (the misgiving is natural to a by-this-time slightly elderly playwright) that Broadbent is out of date. The successful Englishman of today, when he is not a

D

transplanted Scotchman or Irishman, often turns out on investigation to be, if not an American, an Italian, or a Jew, at least to be depending on the brains, the nervous energy, and the freedom from romantic illusions (often called cynicism) of such foreigners for the management of his sources of income. At all events I am persuaded that a modern nation that is satisfied with Broadbent is in a dream. . . .

Years ago I wrote a play called Major Barbara, and one of the things I am proudest of in connection with that play is that I induced certain prominent members of the Salvation Army to come to the theatre, for the first time in their lives, to see that play; and they liked it. At that time I tried to persuade the Salvation Army to make use of the very remarkable quantity of artistic talent that they have in their ranks, and which they use in the way of singing certain kinds of songs which are dramatically effective at their meetings. I tried to induce them deliberately to go in for theatrical entertainments, and I offered them the second act of my play—the conversion by a member of the Salvation Army of a sinner—as a sample of what might be done. I was met very sympathetically by the more genuine and religious people in the Army, but I suspect they were hampered by some people whose support they could not afford to dispense with, and who had rather curious ideas on the subject of art, and did not like the idea of anything being enacted by the Salvation Army unless it was literally true. They seemed to have the idea that to invent a story or write a drama was to tell a lie—it was to pretend that something had happened that had never taken place. . . .

We must not forget that though the old fables are dead for some of us they are not yet dead for everybody. I recall something that happened to me one night when I attended a great meeting of the Salvation Army in the Albert Hall to commemorate Mrs Booth, the wife of the Army's founder. I had been invited because I had written a play with a Salvation lass as the heroine, and, in a letter to the Press, corrected an ignorant ribald who had libelled the excellent Salvation bands. I was placed in the very centre and focus of the great amphitheatre. I could sing not altogether discordantly and unskilfully; and as there is no better fun than community singing, and the Army hymn tunes were delightfully exciting and quite free from the dullness that has given "sacred music" a bad name, I led the singing in my crowded box with tremendous gusto. A tribute to my performance came from a young Salvation lass, who, her eyes streaming with tears, grasped both my hands and cried "Ah! *we* know, dont we?"

. . . In Major Barbara . . . during its run the spectacle was seen for the first time of a box filled with Salvation Army officials in uniform, sitting in a theatre and witnessing a play. Their testimony was useful. Some of the critics, in an inept attempt to be piously shocked, tried to present the play as a gibe at the Army, on the ground that the Salvationists were represented as being full of fun, and that they took money from the distiller. The Army received this with the scorn it deserved, declaring that Barbara's fun was perfectly correct and characteristic, and that the only incident that seemed incredible to them was her refusal to accept that money. Any good Salvationist, they said, would, like the commissioner in the play, take money from the devil himself, and make so good use of it that he would perhaps be converted, as there is hope for everybody

When Major Barbara was produced in London, the second act was reported in an important northern newspaper as a withering attack on the Salvation Army, and the despairing ejaculation of Barbara deplored by a London daily as a tasteless blasphemy. And they were set right, not by the professed critics of the theatre, but by religious and philosophical publicists like Sir Oliver Lodge[6] and Dr Stanton Coit,[7] and strenuous Nonconformist journalists like William Stead,[8] who not only understood the act as well as the Salvationists themselves, but also saw it in its relation to the religious life of the nation, a life which seems to lie not only outside the sympathy of many of our theatre critics, but actually outside their knowledge of society. Indeed nothing could be more ironically curious than the confrontation Major Barbara effected of the theatre enthusiasts with the religious enthusiasts. On the one hand was the playgoer, always seeking pleasure, paying exorbitantly for it, suffering unbearable discomforts for it, and hardly ever getting it. On the other hand was the Salvationist, repudiating gaiety and courting effort and sacrifice, yet always in the wildest spirits, laughing, joking, singing, rejoicing, drumming, and tambourining: his life flying by in a flash of excitement, and his death arriving as a climax of triumph. And, if you please, the playgoer despising the Salvationist as a joyless person, shut out from the heaven of the theatre, self-condemned to a life of hideous gloom; and the Salvationist mourning over the playgoer as over a prodigal with vine leaves in his hair, careering outrageously to hell amid the popping of champagne corks and the ribald laughter of sirens! Could misunderstanding be more complete, or sympathy worse misplaced?

. . . Surely the truth is that the Salvationists are unusually happy people. And is it not the very diagnostic of true salvation that it shall overcome the fear of death? Now the man who has come to believe that there is no such thing as death, the change so called being merely the transition to an exquisitely happy and utterly careless life, has not overcome the fear of death at all: on the contrary, it has overcome him so completely that he refuses to die on any terms whatever. I do not call a Salvationist really saved until he is ready to lie down cheerfully on the scrap heap, having paid scot and lot and something over, and let his eternal life pass on to renew its youth in the battalions of the future.

Then there is the nasty lying habit called confession, which the Army encourages because it lends itself to dramatic oratory, with plenty of thrilling incident. For my part, when I hear a convert relating the violences and oaths and blasphemies he was guilty of before he was saved, making out that he was a very terrible fellow then and is the most contrite and chastened of Christians now, I believe him no more than I believe the millionaire who says he came up to London or Chicago as a boy with only three halfpence in his pocket. Salvationists have said to me that Barbara in my play would never have been taken in by so transparent a humbug as Snobby Price; and certainly I do not think Snobby could have taken in any experienced Salvationist on a point on which the Salvationist did not wish to be taken in. But on the point of conversion all Salvationists wish to be taken in; for the more obvious the sinner the more obvious the miracle of his conversion. When you advertize a converted burglar or reclaimed drunkard as one of the attractions at an experience meeting, your burglar can hardly have been too burglarious or your drunkard too drunken. As long as such attractions are relied on, you will have your Snobbies claiming to have beaten their mothers when they were as a matter of prosaic fact habitually beaten by them, and your Rummies of the tamest respectability pretending to a past of reckless and dazzling vice . . .

The Salvation Army still spends in a struggle with poverty the zeal that was meant for a struggle with sin and the money that Undershaft and Bodger subscribe for the reasons set forth in the play. And the author is still of the opinion that the best comedies for British audiences are those which they themselves provide by trying to run an international civilization on the precepts of our village Sunday Schools and the outlook of our suburban nurseries.

The play develops itself. I only hold the pen. But sometimes the first thing in my head is some situation like the arrest in The Devil's Disciple, which may or may not prove a central one in the finished play. Sometimes it is a remark made in my hearing which is pregnant with a whole play: for instance, The Doctor's Dilemma grew from a remark made by Sir Almroth Wright to an assistant in his laboratory at St Mary's Hospital when he was demonstrating his technical methods for me.[9]

Some time back Sir Almroth . . . delivered a scientific address in London containing a great deal of valuable matter. The Press took no notice of that valuable matter; but Sir Almroth having casually let fall a remark that he was rather skeptical of the value of washing, we read everywhere, "Distinguished physician says we should not wash ourselves." I sympathize with Sir Almroth Wright, because we are fellow countrymen. One has to be an Irishman to understand the antipathy and instinctive dislike that every Irishman has to washing. Anyone going to Ireland will understand the feeling.

I must not expose any professional man to ruin by connecting his name with the entire freedom of criticism which I, as a layman, enjoy; but it will be evident to all experts that my play could not have been written but for the work done by Sir Almroth Wright in the theory and practice of securing immunization from bacterial diseases by the inoculation of "vaccines" made of their own bacteria: a practice incorrectly called vaccinetherapy (there is nothing vaccine about it) apparently because it is what vaccination ought to be and is not.[10] Until Sir Almroth . . . , following up one of Metchnikoff's[11] most suggestive biological romances, discovered that the white corpuscles of phagocytes which attack and devour disease germs for us do their work only when we butter the disease germs appetizingly for them with a natural sauce which Sir Almroth named opsonin, and that our production of this condiment continually rises and falls rhythmically from negligibility to the highest efficiency, nobody has been able even to conjecture why the various serums that were from time to time introduced as having effected marvellous cures, presently made such direful havoc of some unfortunate patient that they had to be dropped hastily. The quantity of sturdy lying that was necessary to save the credit of inoculation in those days was prodigious; and had it not been for the devotion shewn by the military authorities throughout Europe, who would order the entire disappearance of some disease from their armies, and bring it about by the simple plan of changing the name under which the cases were reported, or for our own Metropolitan Asylums Board, which carefully suppressed all the medical reports that revealed the sometimes quite appalling effects of epidemics of revaccination, there is no saying what popular reaction might not have taken place against the whole immunization movement in therapeutics.

The situation was saved when Sir Almroth . . . pointed out that if you inoculated a patient with pathogenic germs at a moment when his powers of cooking them for consumption by the phagocytes was receding to its lowest point, you would certainly make him a good deal worse and perhaps kill him, whereas if you made precisely the same inoculation when the cooking power was rising to one of its periodical climaxes, you would stimulate it to still further exertions and produce just the opposite result. And he invented a technique for ascertaining in which phase the patient happened to be at any given moment. The dramatic possibilities of this discovery and invention will be found in my play. But it is one thing to invent a technique: it is quite another to persuade the medical profession to acquire it. Our general practitioners, I gather, simply declined to acquire it, being mostly unable to afford either the acquisition or the practice of it when acquired. Something simple, cheap, and ready at all times for all comers, is, as I have shewn, the only thing that is economically possible in general practice, whatever may be the case in Sir Almroth's famous laboratory in St Mary's Hospital. It would have become necessary to denounce opsonin in the trade papers as a fad and Sir Almroth as a dangerous man if his practice in the laboratory had not led him to the conclusion that the customary inoculations were very much too powerful, and that a comparatively infinitesimal dose would not precipitate a negative phase of cooking activity, and might induce a positive one. And thus it happens that the refusal of our general practitioners to acquire the new technique is no longer quite so dangerous in practice as it was when The Doctor's Dilemma was written: nay, that Sir Ralph Bloomfield Bonington's way of administering inoculations as if they were spoonfuls of squills may sometimes work fairly well.

In my play called The Doctor's Dilemma . . . the character of

Dubedat illustrates one of my pet theses, which is that no man is scrupulous all round. . . . He has, according to his faculties and interests, certain points of honor, whilst in matters that do not interest him he is careless and unscrupulous. One of the several models[12] who sat unconsciously for Dubedat was morbidly scrupulous as to his religious and political convictions, and would have gone to the gallows sooner than recant a syllable of them. But he had absolutely no conscience about money and women: he was a shameless seducer and borrower, not to say a thief. In contrast with men who were scrupulously correct in their family and business life he seemed a blackguard, and was a blackguard; but there were occasions on which they cut a very poor figure beside him: occasions when loyalty to their convictions called for some risk and sacrifice. When Dubedat says on his deathbed that he has fought the good fight, he is quite serious. He means that he has not painted little girls playing with fox terriers to be exhibited and sold at the Royal Academy, instead of doing the best he could in his art. Much as I have written against anarchic Bohemianism as the curse of artists, and declared that there is no lack of clever people but a great lack of sober, honest, and industrious ones, always declining to offer a high order of talent as an excuse for a low order of conduct, none the less I am aware that bourgeois morality is largely a system of making cheap virtues a cloak for expensive vices. . . .

I have recognized this by dramatizing a rascally genius, with the disquieting result that several highly intelligent and sensitive persons have passionately defended him, on the ground, apparently, that high artistic faculty and an ardent artistic imagination entitle a man to be recklessly dishonest about money and recklessly selfish about women, just as kingship in an African tribe entitles a man to kill whom he pleases on the most trifling provocation. I know no harder practical question than how much selfishness one ought to stand from a gifted person for the sake of his gifts or on the chance of his being right in the long run. The Superman will certainly come like a thief in the night, and be shot at accordingly; but we cannot leave our property wholly undefended on that account. On the other hand, we cannot ask the Superman simply to add a higher set of virtues to current respectable morals; for he is undoubtedly going to empty a good deal of respectable morality out like so much dirty water, and replace it by new and strange customs, shedding old obligations and accepting new and heavier ones. Every step of his progress must horrify conventional people; and if it were possible for even the most superior man to march ahead all the time, every pioneer of the march towards the Superman would be crucified. Fortunately what actually happens is that your geniuses are for the most part keeping step and marking time with the rest, an occasional stumble forward being the utmost they can accomplish, often visibly against their own notions of propriety. . . . Dubedat . . . had his faith, and upheld it.

Even the very remarkable measure of pecuniary success which the Vedrenne-Barker experiment achieved at the Court Theatre will not bear close examination from the public point of view. The vogue of my own plays, helped at a critical moment by the patronage of the King,[13] made the Court Theatre and its principal author fashionable; and as in addition to the four plays which I wrote expressly for the enterprise, I was able to place at its disposal no less than eight others[14] which were virtually new to the public, it was really trading on a windfall unprecedented in the commercial history of the stage. Thus although at the Court Theatre thirty-two plays by seventeen authors were produced in the course of 946 performances, no less than 701 of these performances were of plays by me. Only two other living authors paid their way, although four of the seventeen were dramatists of European celebrity, six were highly distinguished English writers, and the remaining three, who were comparative novices, quite justified the opportunity afforded them. Yet it was impossible to give these authors their fair share of the performances. Incomparably the noblest play produced at the Court Theatre was The Trojan Women of Euripides in the beautiful translation of Professor Gilbert Murray.* When I say that it was performed only eight times, whilst my amusing but hackneyed comedy You Never Can Tell was performed 149 times (not counting the later performances at the Savoy), it will be seen how utterly unable the Court managers were to pursue an impartial

* The Euripidean verses in the second act of Major Barbara are not by me, nor even directly by Euripides. They are by Professor Gilbert Murray, whose English version of The Bacchae came into our dramatic literature with all the impulsive power of an original work shortly before Major Barbara was begun. The play, indeed, stands indebted to him in more ways than one. . . . The part of Adolphus Cusins, the very unusual *jeune premier* of the play, owes its originality to the fact that . . . Murray, the Regius professor of Greek at Oxford University, served the author as a . . . model. He quotes his own famous translations of Euripides.

artistic and educational policy. Having no regular endowment, they were compelled to use the popularity of my plays as a financial [prop]. It was by a quite uncommercial accident that I shared their aims and, having an independent income, could afford to let them make extraordinary sacrifices of their commercial opportunities by repeatedly withdrawing my plays at the height of their success to produce equally deserving ones with the certainty of changing a handsome nightly profit into a serious loss. But they could not, as honest men, carry these sacrifices to the point of making themselves insolvent; and so they had to exploit my plays far more than would have become a National Theatre. Howbeit, . . . my plays effected a lodgment on the London stage, and were presently followed by the plays of Granville-Barker, Gilbert Murray, John Masefield, St John Hankin, Laurence Housman, Arnold Bennett, John Galsworthy, John Drinkwater, and others which would in the nineteenth century have stood rather less chance of production at a London theatre than the Dialogues of Plato, not to mention revivals of the ancient Athenian drama. . . .

In the end [Barker] had to give up acting and devote himself entirely to producing, or, under all the pressure I could put on him, to writing plays. The Court was abandoned for larger and more central theatres, not always one at a time. The pace grew hotter and hotter; the prestige was immense; but the receipts barely kept us going and left no reserves with which to nurse new authors into new reputations.

At last we were in debt and had to put up the shutters. . . . The deficit was . . . £6000. . . . Having ruined Vedrenne in spite of his remonstrances, we could not ask him to pay the debts; and we were bound to clear him without a stain on his character. Barker paid all he possessed; I paid the rest; and so the firm went down with its colors flying, leaving us with a proved certainty that no National Theatre in London devoted to the art of the theatre at its best can bear the burden of London rents and London rates. . . .

The combination, Lillah-Barker-Shaw, still remained, and was reinforced by Shakespear. Barker reached the summit of his fame as a producer by restoring Shakespear to the London stage,[15] where he lingered only in the infamous mutilations of his works by the actor-managers and refreshment bar renters.

But this was done at the cost of an extravagance which could not be sustained. Without Vedrenne to plead for economy Barker was reckless.

Lord Howard de Walden[16] came nobly to the rescue financially; and Barker gave him full value artistically, but made ducks and drakes of his heavily taxed spare money.

Quite early in this history, . . . Lillah and Barker got married. I knew that this was all wrong; that there were no two people on earth less suited to one another; that in the long run their escapade could not stay put. But there was nothing to be done but make the best of it. Certainly, for the moment, it worked very well, and had every air of being a brilliant success. She was an admirable hostess; and her enjoyment of the open air and of travelling made her a most healthy companion for him. He, in spite of the vagabondage of his profession, was not in the least a Bohemian; and the dignity of marriage was quite right for him and good for him. The admirations and adorations the pair excited in the cultured sections of London society could be indulged and gratified in country houses where interesting and brilliant young married couples were welcome. And professionally they were necessary to one another, just as I was necessary to them. It actually made for the stability of the combination that they were never really in love with one another, though they had a very good time together. The appalling levity with which actors and actresses marry is a phenomenon much older than Hollywood; and I had no excuse for being surprised and every reason for finding the arrangement a convenient one. Still, I was instinctively dismayed.

My misgivings were finally justified by a domestic catastrophe. When we had tested the possibility of a highbrow repertory theatre in London to the insolvency and winding-up of the Vedrenne-Barker management, Barker, cleaned out financially, went to New York to consider an offer of the directorship of the new Millionaires Theatre there. Finding the building unsuitable, he turned down the offer, and was presently overtaken by the 1914–18 Armageddon and came back to present himself to me in the guise of a cadet gunner, and later on (he being obviously wasted as a gunner), as an intelligence officer in a Sam Browne belt. He looked the part to perfection.

In New York, however, the Italian volcano in him had erupted unexpectedly and amazingly. He fell madly in love—really madly in the Italian manner—and my first effective intimation was a demand that I should, before the end of the week, procure him a divorce, or a promise of one, from Lillah.

Not yet realizing that I was dealing with a lunatic, I naturally thought that Lillah was prepared for this, and that they had talked it out and agreed to it before she left America. As I had never believed in the permanence of their marriage, and thought that a divorce would restore the order of nature in their case and be a very good thing for both of them, I approached Lillah to arrange the divorce. I was at once violently undeceived. Lillah was as proud as ten thousand empresses. The unprepared proposal for a divorce struck her simply as an insult: something that might happen to common women but could never happen to her. I had a difficult time of it; for I at once lost the confidence of both parties: of Lillah because instead of indignantly repudiating the proposed outrage and renouncing Barker as the infamous author of an unheard-of act of *lèse majesté*, I was acting as his go-between and treating the divorce as inevitable and desirable: of Barker, because my failure to obtain a decree nisi within twenty-four hours shewed that I was Lillah's accomplice in the worst of crimes, that of delaying his instant remarriage. There were no broken hearts in the business; for this wonderful pair, who had careered together so picturesquely, and made such excellent and quite kindly use of the coincidence of their ages and gifts, had never really cared a rap for one another in the way of what Shakespear called the marriage of true minds; so that now, in the storm raised by the insensate impatience of the one and the outraged pride of the other, there was no element of remorse or tenderness, and no point of contact at which they could be brought to reason. They had literally nothing to say to each other; but they had a good deal to say to me, mostly to the effect that I was betraying them both.

And now it may be asked what business all this was of mine. Well, I had thrown them literally into one another's arms as John Tanner and Ann Whitefield; and I suppose it followed that I must extricate them. I succeeded at last; but I could have done it easily six months sooner if they had been able to escape for a moment from their condition of passionate unreasonableness; and I came out of the conflict much battered from both sides, Barker blaming me for the unnecessary delay; and Lillah for having extorted her consent by arguments that almost amounted to blackmail.

Happily the very unreality in their marriage that made the tempest over its dissolution so merciless also cleared the sky very suddenly and completely when it was over. The ending was quite happy. In a prophetic moment in the struggle I had told Lillah that I foresaw her, not as Barker's leading lady to all eternity, but as a handsome chatelaine with a title[17] and a distinguished "honest to God" husband, welcoming a crowd of the best people on the terrace of a beautiful country house. She took this as being in the worst possible taste, her imagination being just then full of a tragic and slaughterous Götterdämmerung of some kind as the end of Lillah. But it is exactly what . . . happened to her. When these twain who worked with me in the glory of their youth settled down handsomely in the dignity of their maturity, I rejoiced in their happiness and leisure.

My part in the divorce had been complicated by the attitude of the lady who had enchanted Barker. This lady was not a private nobody. She was a personage of distinguished talent as a novelist and poetess.[18] Unfortunately for me, she was an American, which meant that the latest great authors for her were Henry James and Meredith: the final politicians Jefferson and Washington. Socialism was to her simple sedition, and Shaw a most undesirable acquaintance for her beloved. Nothing I could do could conciliate her or maintain our alliance. After their retirement to Devon and then to Paris he became a highly respectable professor. Besides his Prefaces to Shakespear, he wrote two more plays, and collaborated with his wife in translations from the Spanish. Virtually we never met again. Our old sympathy remained unaltered and unalterable; but he never dared to shew it; and I could not intrude where I was not welcome.[19] He had well earned a prosperous and happy retirement after his long service and leadership in the vanguard. . . . The wild oats he sowed with me have produced a better harvest than she foresaw. . . .

We [had] clicked so well together that I regarded him as my contemporary until one day at rehearsal, when someone remarked that I was fifty, he said, "You are the same age as my father." After that it seemed impossible that he should die before me. The shock the news gave me made me realise how I had cherished a hope that our old intimate relation might revive. But

Marriage and death and division
Make barren our lives

and the elderly professor could have had little use for a nonagenarian ex-playwright.

4

The Practical Impossibilities of Censorship

AS A PLAYWRIGHT I was held up as an irreligious pornographer, and as such a public enemy, not to say a thorough-paced cad, for many years by an irresponsible censorship which could not be challenged in parliament or elsewhere. I am by profession a playwright. I have been in practice since 1892. I am a member of the Managing Committee of the Society of Authors and of the Dramatic Sub-Committee of that body. I have written . . . plays . . . which have been translated and performed in all European countries. . . . They have been performed extensively in America. Three of them have been refused licenses by the Lord Chamberlain.[1] . . . I have suffered both in pocket and reputation by the action of the Lord Chamberlain. In other countries I have not come into conflict with the censorship except in Austria, where the production of a comedy of mine was postponed for a year because it alluded to the part taken by Austria in the Servo-Bulgarian war.[2] This comedy was not one of the plays suppressed in England by the Lord Chamberlain. . . .

I am not an ordinary playwright in general practice. I am a specialist in immoral and heretical plays. My reputation has been gained by my persistent struggle to force the public to reconsider its morals. In particular, I regard much current morality as to economic and sexual relations as disastrously wrong; and I regard certain doctrines of the Christian religion as understood in England today with abhorrence. I write plays with the deliberate object of converting the nation to my opinions in these matters. I have no other effectual incentive to write plays, as I am not dependent on the theatre for my livelihood. If I were prevented from producing immoral and heretical plays, I should cease to write for the theatre, and propagate my views from the platform and through books. I mention these facts to shew that I have a special interest in the achievement by my profession of those rights of liberty of speech and conscience which are matters of course in other professions. I object to censorship not merely because the existing form of it grievously injures and hinders me individually, but on public grounds.

In 1902 the Stage Society, technically a club giving private performances for the entertainment of its own members, and therefore exempt from the Lord Chamberlain's jurisdiction, resolved to perform . . . Mrs Warren's Profession . . . at last, after a delay of only eight years; and I . . . shared with Ibsen the triumphant amusement of startling all but the strongest-headed of the London theatre critics clean out of the practice of their profession. . . . None of the public theatres dared brave his displeasure . . . by harboring the performance; but another club which had a little stage, and which rather courted a pleasantly scandalous reputation, opened its doors for one night and one afternoon. . . .

In consequence of the Lord Chamberlain having refused to licence it . . . , an impression was created in America, naturally, that it was a hideously indecent and horrible play, because, as the American public were aware that many plays which are licensed here are exceedingly indecent, they naturally concluded that anything that the Censor refused to licence must be of almost incredible indecency *a fortiori*. As a consequence of that, all the worst elements in the New York population came in enormous crowds. There were almost riots outside the theatre, and fabulous prices were paid for seats. The police then went in and arrested the entire company, and marched them off to the police court—actors, actresses, manager, and everybody else. The magistrate had to adjourn the case, because, he said, that he would have to read the play and he publicly expressed his extreme loathing of the unpleasant task before him. . . . He adjourned the case, intending to read the play in the meantime. At the next hearing he exhibited a certain amount of temper, which one would almost think suggested disappointment. He said that he had read the play and that there was not in it what he had expected it to contain from the accounts given of it.

. . . The result was "that the defendants stand acquitted by the decision of the Court, in which it is stated that there is nothing in the words themselves or in any particular phrase or expression which can be said to be indecent, and that the Court is compelled to resort to the theme and motive of the play to find the indecency complained of. It must be said for the playwright," proceeds the decision, "that he has in this instance made vice less attractive than any other dramatists whose plays have escaped the censorious attention of the police. His attack on social evils is one which may result in effecting some reforms." They acquitted the defendants.[3] . . . Nevertheless, . . . the impression produced that I am an indecent and unconscientious author is one which will follow me to the very end of my career.

Few books of the year 1909 can have been cheaper and more entertaining than the report of . . . the Select Committee of both Houses of Parliament which sat . . . to inquire into the working of the censorship, against which it was alleged by myself and others that as its imbecility and mischievousness could not be fully illustrated within the limits of decorum imposed on the press, it could only be dealt with by a parliamentary body subject to no such limits. . . . Its full title is REPORT FROM THE JOINT SELECT COMMITTEE OF THE HOUSE OF LORDS AND THE HOUSE OF COMMONS ON THE STAGE PLAYS (CENSORSHIP) TOGETHER WITH THE PROCEEDINGS OF THE COMMITTEE, MINUTES OF EVIDENCE, AND APPENDICES. What the phrase 'the Stage Plays' means in this title I do not know; nor does anyone else. The number of the Bluebook is 214. How interesting it is may be judged from the fact that it contains verbatim reports of long and animated interviews between the Committee and such witnesses as Mr William Archer, Mr Granville-Barker, Mr J. M. Barrie, Mr Forbes Robertson, Mr Cecil Raleigh, Mr John Galsworthy, Mr Laurence Housman, Sir Herbert Beerbohm Tree, Mr W. L. Courtney, Sir William Gilbert, Mr A. B. Walkley, Miss Lena Ashwell, Professor Gilbert Murray, Mr George Alexander, Mr George Edwardes, Mr Comyns Carr, the Speaker of the House of Commons, the Bishop of Southwark, Mr Hall Caine, Mr Israel Zangwill, Sir Squire Bancroft, Sir Arthur Pinero, and Mr Gilbert Chesterton, not to mention myself and a number of gentlemen less well known to the general public, but important in the world of the theatre. The publication of a book by so many famous contributors would be beyond the means of any commercial publishing firm. His Majesty's Stationery Office sells it to all comers by weight at the very reasonable price of three-and-threepence a copy. . . .

Let me now tell the story of the Committee in greater detail, partly as a contribution to history; partly because, like most true stories, it is more amusing than the official story.

All commissions of public enquiry are more or less intimidated both by the interests on which they have to sit in judgment and, when their members are party politicians, by the votes at the back of those interests; but this unfortunate Committee sat under a quite exceptional cross fire. . . .

It may . . . be asked how a Liberal government had been persuaded to meddle at all with a question in which so many conflicting interests were involved, and which had probably no electoral value whatever. Many simple souls believed that it was because certain severely virtuous plays by Ibsen, by M. Brieux, by Mr Granville-Barker, and by me, were suppressed by the censorship, whilst plays of a scandalous character were licensed without demur. No doubt this influenced public opinion; but those who imagine that it could influence British governments little know how remote from public opinion and how full of their own little family and party affairs British governments, both Liberal and Unionist, still are. The censorship scandal had existed for years without any parliamentary action being taken in the matter, and might have existed for as many more had it not happened in 1906 that Mr Robert Vernon Harcourt entered parliament as a member of the Liberal Party, of which his father had been one of the leaders during the Gladstone era. Mr Harcourt was thus a young man marked out for office both by his parentage and his unquestionable social position as one of the governing class. Also, and this was much less usual, he was brilliantly clever, and was the author of a couple of plays of remarkable promise.[4] Mr Harcourt informed his leaders that he was going to take up the subject of the censorship. The leaders, recognizing his hereditary right to a parliamentary canter of some sort as a prelude to his public career, and finding that all the clever people seemed to be agreed that the censorship was an anti-Liberal institution and an abominable nuisance to boot, indulged him by appointing a Select Committee of both Houses to investigate the subject. The then Chancellor of the Duchy of Lancaster, Mr Herbert Samuel[5] . . . who had made his way into the Cabinet twenty years ahead of the usual age, was made Chairman. Mr Robert Harcourt himself was of course a member. With him, representing the Commons, was Mr Alfred Mason, a man of letters who had won a seat in parliament as offhandedly as he . . . discarded it, or as he once appeared on the stage to help me out of a difficulty in casting Arms and the Man when that piece was the newest thing in the advanced drama. There was Mr Hugh Law, an Irish member, son of an Irish Chancellor, presenting a keen and joyous front to English intellectual sloth. Above all, there was Colonel Lockwood[6] to represent at one stroke the Opposition and the average popular man. This he did by standing up gallantly for the Censor, to whose support the Opposition was in no way committed, and by visibly defying the most cherished conventions of the average man with a bunch of carnations in his buttonhole as large as a dinner-plate, which would have made a Bunthorne[7] blench, and which very nearly did make Mr Granville-Barker (who has an antipathy to the scent of carnations) faint.

The House of Lords then proceeded to its selection. As fashionable drama in Paris and London concerns itself almost exclusively with adultery, the first choice fell on Lord Gorell, who had for many years presided over the Divorce Court. Lord Plymouth, who had been Chairman to the Shakespear Memorial project . . . was obviously marked out for selection; and it was generally expected that the Lords Lytton and Esher, who had taken a prominent part in the same movement, would have been added. This expectation was not fulfilled. Instead, Lord Willoughby de Broke, who had distinguished himself as an amateur actor, was selected along with Lord Newton, whose special qualifications for the Committee, if he had any, were unknown to the public. Finally Lord Ribbesdale, the argute son of a Scotch mother, was thrown in to make up for any shortcoming in intellectual subtlety that might arise in the case of his younger colleagues; and this completed the two teams.

In England, . . . the theatre is not respected. It is indulged and despised as a department of what is politely called gaiety. It is therefore not surprising that the majority of the Committee began by taking its work uppishly and carelessly. When it discovered that the contemporary drama, licensed by the Lord Chamberlain, included plays which could be described only behind closed doors, and in the discomfort which attends discussions of very nasty subjects between men of widely different ages, it calmly put its own convenience before its public duty by ruling that there should be no discussion of particular plays, much as if a committee on temperance were to rule that drunkenness was not a proper subject of conversation among gentlemen.

This was a bad beginning. Everybody knew that in England the censorship would not be crushed by the weight of the constitutional argument against it, heavy as that was, unless it were also brought home to the Committee and to the public that it had sanctioned and protected the very worst practicable examples of the kind of play it professed to extirpate. For it must be remembered that the other half of the practical side of the case, dealing with the merits of the plays it had suppressed, could never secure a unanimous assent. If the Censor had suppressed Hamlet, as he most certainly would have done had it been submitted to him as a new play, he would have been supported by a large body of people to whom incest is a tabooed subject which must not be mentioned on the stage or anywhere else outside a criminal court. Hamlet, Oedipus, and The Cenci, Mrs Warren's Profession, Brieux's Maternité, and Les Avariés, Maeterlinck's Monna Vanna and Mr. Granville-Barker's Waste may or may not be great poems, or edifying sermons, or important documents, or charming romances: our tribal citizens know nothing about that and do not want to know anything: all that they do know is that incest, prostitution, abortion, contagious diseases, and nudity are improper, and that all conversations, or books, or plays in which they are discussed are improper conversations, improper books, improper plays, and should not be allowed. . . .

It was part of this nervous dislike of the unpleasant part of its business that led to the comic incident of the Committee's sudden discovery that I had insulted it, and its suspension of its investigation for the purpose of elaborately insulting me back again. Comic to the lookers-on, that is; for the majority of the Committee made no attempt to conceal the fact that they were wildly angry with me; and I, though my public experience and skill in acting enabled me to maintain my appearance of imperturbable good-humor, was equally furious. The friction began as follows.

The precedents for the conduct of the Committee were to be found in the proceedings of the Committee of 1892. That Committee, no doubt recognizing the absurdity of calling on distinguished artists to give their views before it, and then refusing to allow them to state their views except in nervous replies to such questions as it might suit members to put to them, allowed Sir Henry Irving and Sir John Hare to prepare and read written statements, and formally invited them to read them to the Committee before being questioned. I accordingly prepared such a statement. For the greater convenience of the Committee, I offered to have this statement printed at my own expense, and to supply the members with copies. The offer was accepted; and the copies supplied. I also offered to provide the Committee with copies of those plays of mine which had been refused a licence by the Lord Chamberlain. That offer also was accepted; and the books duly supplied.

As far as I can guess, the next thing that happened was that some timid or unawakened member of the Committee read my statement and was frightened or scandalized out of his wits by it. At all events it is certain that the majority of the Committee allowed themselves to be persuaded to refuse to allow any statement to be read; but to avoid the appearance of pointing this expressly at me, the form adopted was a resolution to adhere strictly to precedent, the Committee being then unaware that the precedents were on my side. Accordingly, when I appeared before the Committee, and proposed to read my statement "according to precedent," the Committee was visibly taken aback. The Chairman was bound by the letter of the decision arrived at to allow me to read my statement, since that course was according to precedent; but as this was exactly what the decision was meant to prevent, the majority of the Committee would have regarded this hoisting of them with their own petard as a breach of faith on the part of the Chairman, who, I infer, was not in agreement with the suppressive majority. There was nothing for it, after a somewhat awkward pause, but to clear me and the public out of the room and reconsider the situation *in camera*. When the doors were opened again I was informed simply that the Committee would not hear my statement. But as the Committee could not very decently refuse my evidence altogether, the Chairman, with a printed copy of my statement in his hand as "proof," was able to come to the rescue to some extent by putting to me a series of questions to which no doubt I might have replied by taking another copy out of my pocket, and quoting my statement paragraph by paragraph, as some of the later witnesses did. But as in offering the Committee my statement for burial in their Bluebook I had made a considerable sacrifice, being able to secure greater publicity for it by independent publication on my own account; and as, further, the circumstances of the refusal made it offensive enough to take all heart out of the scrupulous consideration with which I had so far treated the Committee, I was not disposed to give its majority a second chance, or to lose the opportunity offered me by questions to fire an additional broadside into the censorship. I pocketed my statement, and answered the questions *vive voce.** At the conclusion of this, my examination-in-chief, the Committee adjourned, asking me to present myself again for (virtually) cross-examination. But this cross-examination never came off, as the sequel will shew.

The refusal of the Committee to admit my statement had not unnaturally created the impression that it must be a scandalous document; and a lively demand for copies at once set in. And among the very first applicants were members of the majority which had carried the decision to exclude the document. They had given so little attention to the business that they did not know, or had forgotten, that they had already been supplied with copies at their own request. At all events, they came to me publicly and cleaned me out of the handful of copies I had provided for distribution to the press. And after the sitting it was intimated to me that yet more copies were desired for the use of the Committee: a demand, under the circumstances, of breath-bereaving coolness. At the same time, a brisk demand arose outside the Committee, not only among people who were anxious to read what I had to say on the subject, but among victims of the craze for collecting first editions, copies of privately circulated pamphlets, and other real or imaginary rarities. Such maniacs will cheerfully pay five guineas for any piece of discarded old rubbish of mine when they will not pay as many shillings for a clean new copy of it, because everyone else can get it for the same price too.

The day after the refusal of the Committee to face my statement, I transferred the scene of action to the columns of The Times,[8] which did yeoman's service to the public on this, as on many other occasions, by treating the question as a public one without the least regard to the supposed susceptibilities of the Court on the one side, or the avowed prejudices of the Free Churches or the interests of the managers or

* My evidence will be found in the Bluebook, pp. 46–53.

theatrical speculators on the other. The Times published the summarized conclusions of my statement, and gave me an opportunity of saying as much as it was then advisable to say of what had occurred. For it must be remembered that, however impatient and contemptuous I might feel of the intellectual cowardice shewn by the majority of the Committee face to face with myself, it was none the less necessary to keep up its prestige in every possible way, not only for the sake of the dignity and importance of the matter with which it had to deal, and in the hope that the treatment of subsequent witnesses and the final report might make amends for a feeble beginning, but also out of respect and consideration for the minority. For it is fair to say that the majority was never more than a bare majority, and that the worst thing the Committee did—the exclusion of references to particular plays—was perpetrated in the absence of the Chairman.

I, therefore, had to treat the Committee in The Times very much better than its majority deserved, an injustice for which I now apologize. I did not, however, resist the temptation to hint, good-humoredly, that my politeness to the Committee had cost me quite enough already, and that I was not prepared to supply the members of the Committee, or anyone else, with extra copies merely as collectors' curiosities.

Then the fat was in the fire. The majority, chaffed for its eagerness to obtain copies of scarce pamphlets retailable at five guineas, went dancing mad. When I presented myself, as requested, for cross-examination, I found the doors of the Committee room shut, and the corridors of the House of Lords filled by a wondering crowd, to whom it had somehow leaked out that something terrible was happening inside. It could not be another licensed play too scandalous to be discussed in public, because the Committee had decided to discuss no more of these examples of the Censor's notions of purifying the stage; and what else the Committee might have to discuss that might not be heard by all the world was not easily guessable.

Without suggestion that the confidence of the Committee was in any way violated by any of its members further than was absolutely necessary to clear them from suspicion of complicity in the scene which followed, I think I may venture to conjecture what was happening. It was felt by the majority, first, that it must be cleared at all costs of the imputation of having procured more than one copy each of my statement, and that one not from any interest in an undesirable document by an irreverent author, but in the reluctant discharge of its solemn public duty; second, that a terrible example must be made of me by the most crushing public snub in the power of the Committee to administer. To throw my wretched little pamphlet at my head and to kick me out of the room was the passionate impulse which prevailed in spite of all the remonstrances of the Commoners, seasoned to the give-and-take of public life, and of the single peer who kept his head. The others, for the moment, had no heads to keep. And the fashion in which they proposed to wreak their vengeance was as follows.

I was to be admitted, as a lamb to the slaughter, and allowed to take my place as if for further examination. The Chairman was then to inform me coldly that the Committee did not desire to have anything more to say to me. The members were thereupon solemnly to hand me back the copies of my statement as so much waste paper, and I was to be suffered to slink away with what countenance I could maintain in such disgrace.

But this plan required the active co-operation of every member of the Committee; and whilst the majority regarded it as an august and impressive vindication of the majesty of parliament, the minority regarded it with equal conviction as a puerile tomfoolery, and declined altogether to act their allotted parts in it. Besides, they did not all want to part with the books. For instance, Mr Hugh Law, being an Irishman, with an Irishman's sense of how to behave like a gallant gentleman on occasion, was determined to be able to assure me that nothing should induce him to give up my statement or prevent him from obtaining and cherishing as many copies as possible. (I quote this as an example to the House of Lords of the right thing to say in such emergencies.) So the program had to be modified. The minority could not prevent the enraged majority from refusing to examine me further; nor could the Chairman refuse to communicate that decision to me. Neither could the minority object to the secretary handing me back such copies as he could collect from the majority. And at that the matter was left. The doors were opened; the audience trooped in; I was called to my place in the dock (so to speak); and all was ready for the sacrifice.

Alas! the majority reckoned without Colonel Lockwood. That hardy and undaunted veteran refused to shirk his share in the scene merely because the minority was recalcitrant and the majority perhaps subject to stage fright. When Mr Samuel had informed me that the Committee had no further questions to ask me with an urbanity which gave the public no clue as to the temper of the majority; when I had jumped up with the proper air of relief and gratitude; when the secretary had handed me his little packet of books with an affability which effectually concealed his dramatic function as executioner; when the audience was simply disappointed at being baulked of the entertainment of hearing Mr Robert Harcourt cross-examine me; in short, when the situation was all but saved by the tact of the Chairman and secretary, Colonel Lockwood rose, with all his carnations blazing, and gave away the whole case by handing me, with impressive simplicity and courtesy, his two copies of the precious statement. And I believe that if he had succeeded in securing ten, he would have handed them all back to me with the most sincere conviction that every one of the ten must prove a crushing addition to the weight of my discomfiture. I still cherish that second copy, a little blue-bound pamphlet, methodically autographed "Lockwood B," among my most valued literary trophies.

An innocent lady told me afterwards that she never knew that I could smile so beautifully, and that she thought it shewed very good taste on my part. I was not conscious of smiling; but I should have embraced the Colonel had I dared. As it was, I turned expectantly to his colleagues, mutely inviting them to follow his example. But there was only one Colonel Lockwood on that Committee. No eye met mine except minority eyes, dancing with mischief. There was nothing more to be said. I went home to my morning's work, and returned in the afternoon to receive the apologies of the minority for the conduct of the majority, and to see Mr Granville-Barker, overwhelmed by the conscience-stricken politeness of the now almost abject Committee, and by a powerful smell of carnations, heading the long list of playwrights who came there to testify against the censorship, and whose treatment, I am happy to say, was everything they could have desired.

After all, ridiculous as the scene was, Colonel Lockwood's simplicity and courage was much more serviceable to his colleagues than their inept *coup de théâtre* would have been if he had not spoiled it. It was plain to everyone that he had acted in entire good faith, without a thought as to these apparently insignificant little books being of any importance or having caused me or anybody else any trouble, and that he was wounded in his most sensitive spot by the construction my Times letter had put on his action. And in Colonel Lockwood's case one saw the case of his party on the Committee. They had simply been thoughtless in the matter.

I hope nobody will suppose that this in any way exonerates them. When people accept public service for one of the most vital duties that can arise in our society, they have no right to be thoughtless. In spite of the fun of the scene on the surface, my public sense was, and still is, very deeply offended by it. It made an end for me of the claim of the majority to be taken seriously. . . . Under a college of cardinals, or bishops, or judges, or any other conceivable form of experts in morals, philosophy, religion, or politics, we should get little except stagnant mediocrity.

It only remains to say that public performances of The Shewing-up of Blanco Posnet . . . really a religious tract in dramatic form, . . . [were] prohibited in Great Britain by the Lord Chamberlain [in 1909]. An attempt was made to prevent even its performance in Ireland by some indiscreet Castle officials in the absence of the Lord Lieutenant. This attempt gave extraordinary publicity to the production of the play; and every possible effort was made to persuade the Irish public that the performance would be an outrage to their religion, and to provoke a repetition of the rioting that attended the first performances of Synge's Playboy of the Western World before the most sensitive and, on provocation, the most turbulent audience in the kingdom. The directors of the Irish National Theatre, Lady Gregory and Mr William Butler Yeats, rose to the occasion with inspiring courage. I am a conciliatory person, and was willing, as I always am, to make every concession in return for having my own way. But Lady Gregory and Mr Yeats not only would not yield an inch, but insisted, within the due limits of gallant warfare, on taking the field with every circumstance of defiance, and winning the battle with every trophy of victory. Their triumph was as complete as they could have desired. The performance exhausted the possibilities of success, and provoked no murmur, though it inspired several approving sermons. Later on, Lady Gregory and Mr Yeats brought the play to London and performed it under the Lord Chamberlain's nose, through the instrumentality of the Stage Society.[9]

After this, the play was again submitted to the Lord Chamberlain.

. . . The Lord Chamberlain handed it to his reader, Mr [George Alexander] Redford. He was a little puzzled by the play. It had a passage in it, "He is a mean one; he is a sly one." Mr Redford could not make out to whom the speaker was referring. I presume he asked someone in the office who was meant by the "mean one; the sly one." The reply must have been, "I am afraid he is alluding to God Almighty, because immediately afterwards, when someone asks who it is, he points upwards."

What could Mr Redford do? He could not allow God Almighty to be described on the stage as "a mean one; a sly one." He issued a license conditional on all references to God Almighty being cut out. The result was curious. I could not allow the play to be performed with these lines cut out, because without them it became a senseless, rowdy, blasphemous, coarse play—a horrible play, a thing I could not have my name connected with.

But you can imagine Mr Redford's astonishment when, on the first Sunday after the play was published, no less than three sermons were preached on the subject of the play. The clergy were delighted with it, and it has been the subject of . . . sermons since. When Lord Sandhurst became Lord Chamberlain he withdrew the ban, and the play is now licensed. Yet, if you had been in the position of Mr Redford you would have found it very hard, on coming to that passage, to see that the dramatic effect was no more blasphemous than the reproaches addressed by Job to his Maker in the Bible are blasphemous. The truth is, Mr Redford and the Lord Chamberlain were confronted with a task which, in itself, was impossible. . . .

There is, besides, a crushing material difficulty in the way of an enlightened censorship. It is not too much to say that the work involved would drive a man of any intellectual rank mad. Consider, for example, the Christmas pantomimes. Imagine a judge of the High Court, or an archbishop, or a Cabinet Minister, or an eminent man of letters, earning his living by reading through the mass of trivial doggerel represented by all the pantomimes which are put into rehearsal simultaneously at the end of every year. The proposal to put such mind-destroying drudgery upon an official of the class implied by the demand for an enlightened censorship falls through the moment we realize what it implies in practice.

Another material difficulty is that no play can be judged by merely reading the dialogue. . . . I remember the old days when . . . most music-hall songs were indecent songs. If you read those old songs you will find nothing indecent in them. I remember a case, I believe in Manchester, of a very popular young music-hall singer, the daughter of an even more popular lady in the same profession, who was prosecuted because of a certain song she sang. Her counsel had no difficulty in the matter before the magistrates. He simply took the song and read the words, which were perfectly innocent. They were silly, perhaps, but what harm was there in them? The magistrate was about to dismiss the case when the lady in question burst into tears and began to protest. She said, "He is spoiling my song; it is not the words, but the way I sing them." That gave away the whole show.

I remember one well-known comedian in a play which I had to criticize at a time when I got my living by criticizing plays instead of by writing them and being criticized. This comedian had to say to another lady on the stage, "Might I speak to you, miss?" Well, who could possibly object to such a line? Yet as spoken on the stage it became exceedingly indecent and offensive. You can read the play, but you cannot control the gesture made, and do not know what the play will be like when it comes to the performance.

. . . It is immorality, not morality, that needs protection: it is morality, not immorality, that needs restraint; for morality, with all the dead weight of human inertia and superstition to hang on the back of the pioneer, and all the malice of vulgarity and prejudice to threaten him, is responsible for many persecutions and many martyrdoms. . . . I deny that anybody has the right to demand more from me, over and above lawful conduct in a general sense, than liberty to stay away from the theatre in which my plays are represented. If he is unfortunate enough to have a religion so petty that it can be insulted (any man is as welcome to insult my religion if he can, as he is to insult the universe) I claim the right to insult it to my heart's content, if I choose, provided I do not compel him to come and hear me. . . . It is no more possible for me to do my work honestly as a playwright without giving pain than it is for a dentist. The nation's morals are like its teeth: the more decayed they are the more it hurts to touch them. Prevent dentists and dramatists from giving pain, and not only will our morals become as carious as our teeth, but toothache and the plagues that follow neglected morality will presently cause more agony than all the dentists and dramatists at their worst have caused since the world began.

5

Shavian Busts

IN MUNICH ONCE, when I was complimenting a German on the artistic activity of the place (whither I had come to see an enthusiastic but execrable performance of one of my own plays), he replied, "Do not be deceived: this city is a Capua. When an artist settles down here he produces no more art. Our art will be our ruin."

Some time before this, I had written to the greatest artist France or the world has produced for several centuries. I addressed the letter to Monsieur Auguste Rodin, Meudon. If, during one of his visits to London, I had addressed it to Rodin, England, the British Post Office, Philistine as it is, would have delivered it to him within twenty-four hours. It was returned to me by the French Post Office marked *Inconnu*. I naturally exclaimed "God has forgotten this people: they are hopeless." Rodin explained to me afterwards that as he was not a pupil of the Beaux Arts he was not counted as an artist in France, but only as a common mason. I then understood why Germany was the first country to recognize me as a considerable dramatic author, and why France will be the last. Not that I complain; . . . but I am so deplorably lacking in good taste as the French understand it as to know my own value (and perhaps a little more); and I affirm that Europe can be divided into barbarous countries and civilized countries by the simple test of the presence or absence of a Shaw vogue in the theatres.

In the year 1906 it was proposed to furnish the world with an authentic portrait-bust of me before I had left the prime of life too far behind. The question then arose: Could Rodin be induced to undertake the work? On no other condition would I sit, because it was clear to me that Rodin was not only the greatest sculptor then living, but the greatest sculptor of his epoch: one of those extraordinary persons who, like Michael Angelo, or Phidias, or Praxiteles, dominate whole ages as fashionable favorites dominate a single London season. I saw, therefore, that any man who, being a contemporary of Rodin, deliberately allowed his bust to be made by anybody else, must go down to posterity (if he went down at all) as a stupendous nincompoop.

Also, I wanted a portrait of myself by an artist capable of seeing me. Many clever portraits of my reputation were in existence; but I have never been taken in by my reputation, having manufactured it myself. A reputation is a mask which a man has to wear just as he has to wear a coat and trousers: it is a disguise we insist on as a point of decency. The result is that we have hardly any portraits of men and women. We have no portraits of their legs and shoulders; only of their skirts and trousers and blouses and coats. Nobody knows what Dickens was like, or what Queen Victoria was like, though their wardrobes are on record. Many people fancy they know their faces; but they are deceived: we know only the fashionable mask of the distinguished novelist and of the queen. And the mask defies the camera. When Mr Alvin Langdon Coburn[1] wanted to exhibit a full-length photographic portrait of me, I secured a faithful representation up to the neck by the trite expedient of sitting to him one morning as I got out of my bath. The portrait was duly hung before a stupefied public as a first step towards the realization of Carlyle's antidote to political idolatry: a naked parliament. But though the body was my body, the face was the face of my reputation. So much so, in fact, that the critics concluded that Mr Coburn had faked his photograph, and stuck my head on somebody else's shoulders.[2] For, as I have said, the mask cannot be penetrated by the camera. It is transparent only to the eye of a veritably god-like artist.

Rodin tells us that his wonderful portrait-busts seldom please the sitters. I can go further, and say that they often puzzle and disappoint the sitters' friends. The busts are of real men, not of the reputations of celebrated persons. Look at my bust, and you will not find it a bit like that brilliant fiction known as G.B.S. or Bernard Shaw. But it is most frightfully like me. It is what is really there, not what you think is there. The same with Puvis de Chavannes[3] and the rest of them. Puvis de Chavannes protested, as one gathers—pointed to his mirror and to his photographs to prove that he was not like his bust. But I am convinced that he was not only like his bust, but that the bust actually was himself as distinct from his collars and his public manners. Puvis, though an artist of great merit, could not see himself. Rodin could. He saw me. Nobody else has done that yet.

Troubetskoi[4] once made a most fascinating Shavian bust of me. He did it in about five hours, in Sargent's[5] studio. It was a delightful and wonderful performance. He worked convulsively, giving birth to the thing in agonies, hurling lumps of clay about with groans, and making strange, dumb movements with his tongue, like a wordless prophet. He covered himself with plaster. He covered Sargent's carpets and curtains and pictures with plaster. He covered me with plaster. And, finally, he covered the block he was working on with plaster to such purpose that, at the end of the second sitting, lo! there stood Sargent's studio in ruins, buried like Pompeii under the scoriae of a volcano, and in the midst a spirited bust of one of my reputations, a little idealized (quite the gentleman, in fact) but recognizable a mile off as the sardonic author of Man and Superman, with a dash of Offenbach, a touch of Mephistopheles, and a certain aristocratic delicacy and distinction that came from Troubetskoi himself, he being a prince. I should like to have that bust; but the truth is, my wife [could not] stand Offenbach-Mephistopheles; and I was not allowed to have the bust any more than I was allowed to have that other witty jibe at my poses, Neville Lytton's portrait of me as Velasquez's Pope Innocent.

Rodin worked very differently.[6] He plodded along exactly as if he were a river god doing a job of wall-building in a garden for three or four francs a day. When he was in doubt he measured me with an old iron dividers, and then measured the bust. If the bust's nose was too long, he sliced a bit out of it, and jammed the tip of it up to close the gap, with no more emotion or affection than a glazier putting in a window pane. If the ear was in the wrong place, he cut it off and slapped it into its right place, excusing the ruthless mutilations to my wife (who half expected to see the already terribly animated clay bleed) by remarking that it was shorter than to make a new ear. Yet a succession of miracles took place as he worked. In the first fifteen minutes, in merely giving a suggestion of human shape to the lump of clay, he produced so spirited a thumbnail bust of me that I wanted to take it away and relieve him from further labor. It reminded me of a highly finished bust by Sarah Bernhardt.[7] . . . But that phase vanished like a summer cloud as the bust evolved. I say evolved advisedly; for it passed through every stage in the evolution of art before my eyes in the course of a month. After that first fifteen minutes it sobered down into a careful representation of my features in their exact living dimensions. Then this representation mysteriously went back to the cradle of Christian art, at which point I again wanted to say: "For Heaven's sake, stop and give me that: it is a Byzantine masterpiece." Then it began to look as if Bernini had meddled with it. Then, to my horror, it smoothed out into a plausible, rather elegant piece of eighteenth-century work, almost as if Houdon had touched up a head by Canova or Thorwaldsen, or as if Leighton had tried his hand at eclecticism in bust-making. At this point Troubetskoi would have broken it with a hammer, or given it up with a wail of despair. Rodin contemplated it with an air of callous patience, and went on with his job, more like a river god turned plasterer than ever. Then another century passed in a single night; and the bust became a Rodin bust, and was the living head of which I carried the model on my shoulders. It was a process for the embryologist to study, not the aesthete. Rodin's hand worked, not as a sculptor's hand works, but as the Life Force works. What is more, I found that he was aware of it, quite simply. I no more think of Rodin as a celebrated sculptor than I think of Elijah as a well-known *littérateur* and forcible after-dinner speaker. His "Main de Dieu" is his own hand. That is why all the stuff written about him by professional art critics is such ludicrous cackle and piffle. I have been a professional art critic myself, and perhaps not much of one at that (though I fully admit that I touched nothing I did not adorn), but at least I knew how to take off my hat and hold my tongue when my cacklings and pifflings would have been impertinences.

Rodin took the conceit out of me most horribly. Once he shewed me a torso of a female figure; an antique. It was a beauty; and I swallowed it whole. He waited rather wistfully for a moment, to see whether I really knew chalk from cheese, and then pointed out to me that the upper half of the figure was curiously inferior to the lower half, as if the sculptor had taught himself as he went along. The difference, which I had been blind to a moment before, was so obvious when he pointed it out, that I have despised myself ever since for not seeing it. There never was such an eye for carved stone as Rodin's. To the average critic or connoisseur half the treasures he collects seem nothing but a heap of old paving stones. But they all have somewhere a scrap of modelled surface, perhaps half the size of a postage stamp, that makes gems of them. In his own work he shews a strong feeling for the beauty of marble. He gave me three busts of myself: one in bronze, one in plaster, one in marble. The bronze is me (growing younger now). The plaster is me. But the marble has quite another sort of life: it glows; and the light flows over it. It does not look solid: it looks luminous; and this curious glowing and flowing keeps people's fingers off it; for you feel as if you could not catch hold of it.

Busts outlive plays. In [a] copy of the Kelmscott Chaucer I wrote these lines:

I have seen two masters at work, Morris who made this book,
  The other Rodin the Great, who fashioned my head in clay:
I give the book to Rodin, scrawling my name in a nook
  Of the shrine their works shall hollow when mine are dust by the way.

I once wrote that at least I was sure of a place in the biographical dictionaries a thousand years hence as: "Shaw, Bernard: subject of a bust by Rodin: otherwise unknown."

6

Tree and a Potboiler

LIKE SHAKESPEAR I had to write potboilers until I was rich enough to satisfy my evolutionary appetite (or, as they say, give way to my inspiration) by writing what came to me without the least regard to the possibility of lucrative publication or performance. Like Shakespear again, I was a born dramatist, which means a born artist-biologist struggling to take biology a step forward on its way to positive science from its present metaphysical stage in which the crude facts of life and death, growth and decay, evolution and reversion, consciousness and unconsciousness, self-preservation and self-sacrifice, defy the methods of investigation we employ in our research laboratories, and have to be made apprehensible by fictions, pictures, and symphonies in which they are instinctively arranged in a manner which gives a mysterious pleasure to some of the readers, spectators, and listeners, and provokes others to passionate denial and persecution. When I am not potboiling for myself or others I am being driven by my evolutionary appetite to write these fictions. Even when I have the box office in view I am not free to choose the most lucrative sort of fiction. Evolution keeps creeping in. I write such shameless potboilers as Pygmalion, Fanny's First Play, and You Never Can Tell to oblige theatre managers or aspiring players; but at least I do not write detective stories to oblige publishers. I am clever enough at the tricks of my trade to be able to combine some worldly potboiling with my transcendental metabiology, but only up to an impassable boundary. If I could not do this, and had either to prosper as a stockholder or starve as a metabiologist I should starve, as Mozart and Beethoven very nearly did when they composed symphonies instead of sentimental drawingroom ballads.

Take Pygmalion, for example. In 1914 its extraordinary success in London was not the success of my Eliza and my Higgins, but of Mrs Patrick Campbell's Eliza and Beerbohm Tree's Higgins. . . . Tree was the despair of authors. His attitude towards a play was one of wholehearted anxiety to solve the problem of how to make it please and interest the audience.

Now this is the author's business, not the actor's. The function of the actor is to make the audience imagine for the moment that real things are happening to real people. It is for the author to make the result interesting. If he fails, the actor cannot save the play unless it is so flimsy a thing that the actor can force upon it some figure of his own fancy and play the author off the stage. This has been done successfully in several well-known, though very uncommon, cases. Robert Macaire and Lord Dundreary[1] were imposed by their actors on plays which did not really contain them. Grimaldi's clown[2] was his own invention. These figures died with their creators, though their ghosts still linger on the stage. Irving's Shylock was a creation which he thrust successfully upon Shakespear's play; indeed, all Irving's impersonations were changelings. His Hamlet and his Lear were to many people more interesting than Shakespear's Hamlet and Lear; but the two pairs were hardly even related. To the author, Irving was not an actor: he was either a rival or a collaborator who did all the real work. Therefore, he was anathema to master authors, and a godsend to journeymen authors, with the result that he had to confine himself to the works of dead authors who could not interfere with him, and, very occasionally, live authors who were under his thumb because they were unable to command production of their works in other quarters.

Into this tradition of creative acting came Tree as Irving's rival and successor; and he also, with his restless imagination, felt that he needed nothing from an author but a literary scaffold on which to exhibit his own creations. He, too, turned to Shakespear as to a forest out of which such scaffolding could be hewn without remonstrance from the landlord, and to foreign authors who could not interfere with him, their interests being in the hands of adapters who could not stand up against his supremacy in his own theatre. As far as I could discover, the notion that a play could succeed without any further help from the actor than a simple impersonation of his part never occurred to Tree. The author, whether Shakespear or Shaw, was a lame dog to be helped over the stile by the ingenuity and inventiveness of the actor-producer. How to add and subtract, to interpolate and prune, until an effective result was arrived at, was the problem of production as he saw it. Of living authors of eminence the two he came into personal contact with were Brieux[3] and Henry Arthur Jones; and I have reason to believe that their experience of him in no way contradicts my own. With . . . masters of the stage like Pinero and Carton,[4] in whose works the stage business is an integral part of the play, and the producer, when he is not the author in person, is an executant and not an inventor, Tree had never worked; and when he at last came upon the species in me, and found that, instead of having to discover how to make an effective histrionic entertainment on the basis of such scraps of my dialogue as might prove useful, he had only to fit himself into a jig-saw puzzle cut out by me, and just to act his part as well as he could, he could neither grasp the situation nor resist the impersonal compulsion of arrangements which he had not made, and was driven to accept only by the fact that they were the only ones which would work. But to the very end they bewildered him; and he had to go to the box office to assure himself that the omission of his customary care had not produced disastrous results.

Just before the production of my play we lunched together at the Royal Automobile Club. I said to him: "Have you noticed during the rehearsals that though you and I are no longer young, and have achieved all the success possible in our respective professions, we have been treating one another throughout as beginners?" To this, on reflection, he had to assent, because we actually were, relatively to one another, beginners. I had never had to deal with him professionally before, nor he with me; and he was quite unaccustomed to double harness, whilst I was so accustomed to every extremity of multiple harness, both in politics and in the theatre, that I had been trained to foresee everything and consider everybody. Now if I were to say that Tree foresaw nothing and considered nobody, I should suggest that he was a much less amiable man than he was. Let me therefore say that he never foresaw anything or considered anybody in cold blood. Of the foresight which foresees and faces entirely uninteresting facts, and the consideration which considers entirely uninteresting persons, he had as little as a man can have without being run over in the street. When his feelings were engaged, he was human and even shrewd and tenacious. But you really could not lodge an indifferent fact in his mind. This disability of his was carried to such a degree that he could not remember the passages in a play which did not belong to or bear directly upon his own conception of his own part: even the longest run did not mitigate his surprise when they recurred. Thus he never fell into that commonest fault of the actor: the betrayal to the audience that he knows what his interlocutor is going to say, and is waiting wearily for his cue instead of conversing with him. Tree always seemed to have heard the lines of the other performers for the first time, and even to be a little taken aback by them.

Let me give an extreme instance of this. In Pygmalion the heroine, in a rage, throws the hero's slippers in his face. When we rehearsed this for the first time, I had taken care to have a very soft pair of velvet slippers provided, for I knew that Mrs Patrick Campbell was very dexterous, very strong, and a dead shot. And, sure enough, when we reached this passage, Tree got the slippers well and truly delivered with unerring aim bang in his face. The effect was appalling. He had totally forgotten that there was any such incident in the play; and it seemed to him that Mrs Campbell, suddenly giving way to an impulse of diabolical wrath and hatred, had committed an unprovoked and brutal assault on him. The physical impact was nothing; but the wound to his feelings was terrible. He collapsed on the nearest chair, and left me staring in amazement, whilst the entire personnel of the theatre crowded solicitously round him, explaining that the incident was part of the play, and even exhibiting the prompt-book to prove their words. But his *moral* was so shattered that it took quite a long time, and a good deal of skilful rallying and coaxing from Mrs Campbell, before he was in a condition to resume the rehearsal. The worst of it was that as it was quite evident that he would be just as surprised and wounded next time, Mrs Campbell took care that the slippers should never hit him again, and the incident was consequently one of the least convincing in the performance.

This, and many similar scenes that are told of Tree, will not be believed by experienced men of business. They will say curtly that it is no use trying to stuff them with stories like that: that running a theatre like His Majesty's must have been a big business, and that no man could possibly have done it for so long without being too capable and wide awake to forget everything that did not amuse or interest him. But they will be quite wrong. Theatrical business is not like other business. A man may enter on the management of a theatre without business habits or knowledge, and at the end of forty years of it know less about business than when he began. The explanation is that a London West-End theatre is always either making such an enormous profit that the utmost waste caused by unbusinesslike management is not worth considering, or else losing so much that the strictest economy cannot arrest the process by a halfpenny in the pound. In an industrial concern the addition of a penny to the piece-work rate or the hourly time rate of wages, the slowing of a steam engine by a few revolutions, the retention of a machine two years out-of-date, or the loss of fifteen minutes' work in the day by unpunctuality, may make all the difference between profit and bankruptcy. The employer is held to rigid conditions by a stringent factory code enforced by a Government inspector on the one hand and by a jealous trade union on the other. He is the creature of circumstance and the slave of law, with so little liberty for sentiment and caprice that he very soon loses not only the habit of indulging them but even the sense of possessing them. Not so the manager of a theatre. Tree was accustomed to make two hundred per cent profit every day when he was in luck. With such a margin to play with, it was no more worth his while to economize or remember uninteresting things than it was to walk when there was a taxi at his beck. When his theatre was built for him, the equipment of its stage, apart from the electric lighting instalment, was exactly what it would have been a hundred years before, except that there were no grooves for side wings. If every employee on the premises had come an hour late every day and had received double wages, the difference in profit would have been hardly worth noticing. A theatre is a maddening place to a thrifty man of business, and an economic paradise to an artist, because there is practically no limit to the waste of time and money that may go on, provided the doors are open every night and the curtain up half an hour later. But for this necessity, and a few County Council by-laws, an actor-manager would be as unbridled as Nero, without even the Neronian check of a Praetorian Guard to kill him if he went beyond all bearing.

There is no denying that such conditions put a strain on human character that it can seldom sustain without injury. If Tree's caprices, and his likes and dislikes, had not been on the whole amiable, the irresponsibility and power of his position would have made a fiend of him. As it was, they produced the oddest results. He was always attended in the theatre by a retinue of persons with no defined business there, who were yet on the salary list. There was one capable gentleman who could get things done; and I decided to treat him as the stage manager; but until I saw his name in the bill under that heading I never felt sure that he was not some casual acquaintance whom Tree had met in the club or in the street and invited to come in and make himself at home. Tree did not know what a stage manager was, just as he did not know what an author was. He had not even made up his mind any too definitely what an actor was. One moment he would surprise and delight his courtiers (for that is the nearest word I can find for his staff and entourage) by some stroke of kindness and friendliness. The next he would commit some appalling breach of etiquette by utterly ignoring their functions and privileges, when they had any. It was amiable and modest in him not to know his own place, since it was the highest in the theatre; but it was exasperating in him not to know anyone else's. I very soon gave up all expectation of being treated otherwise than as a friend who had dropped in; so, finding myself as free to interfere in the proceedings as anyone else who dropped in would apparently have been, I interfered not only in my proper department but in every other as well; and nobody gainsaid me. One day I interfered to such an extent that Tree was moved to a mildly sarcastic remonstrance. "I seem to have heard or read somewhere," he said, "that plays have actually been produced, and performances given, in this theatre, under its present management, before you came. According to you, that couldn't have happened. How do you account for it?"

"I cant account for it," I replied, with the blunt good faith of a desperate man. "I suppose you put a notice in the papers that a performance will take place at half past eight, and take the money at the doors. Then you *have* to do the play somehow. There is no other way of accounting for it." On two such occasions it seemed so brutal to worry him, and so hopeless to advance matters beyond the preliminary arrangement of the stage business (which I had already done), that I told him quite cordially to put the play through in his own way, and shook the dust of the theatre from my feet. On both occasions I had to yield to urgent appeals from other members of the cast to return and extricate them from a hopeless mess; and on both occasions Tree took leave of me as if it had been very kind of me to look in as I was passing to see his rehearsals, and received me on my return as if it were still more friendly of me to come back and see how he was getting on. I tried once or twice to believe that he was only pulling my leg; but that was incredible: his sincerity and insensibility were only too obvious. Finally, I had to fight my way through to a sort of production in the face of an unresisting, amusing, friendly, but heartbreakingly obstructive principal.

We finally agreed that I should have been an actor and he an author; and he always sent me his books afterwards. As a matter of fact, he had a very marked literary talent, and, even as an amateur, achieved a finish of style and sureness of execution that was not always evident in his acting, especially when, as in the case of Pygmalion, he had to impersonate a sort of man he had never met and of whom he had no conception. He tried hard to induce me to let him play the dustman instead of the Miltonic professor of phonetics; and when he resigned himself to his unnatural task, he set to work to make this disagreeable and incredible person sympathetic in the character of a lover, for which I had left so little room that he was quite baffled until he lit on the happy thought of throwing flowers to Eliza in the very brief interval between the end of the play and the fall of the curtain.[5] If he had not been so amusing, so ingenious, and so entirely well-intentioned he would have driven me crazy. As it was, he made me feel like his grandfather. I should add that he never bore the slightest malice for my air of making the best of a bad job. A few days before his death,[6] when he was incredibly young and sanguine, and made me feel hopelessly old and grumpy, he was discussing a revival of Pygmalion as if it promised to be a renewal of the most delightful experience of our lives. The only reproach he ever addressed to me was for not coming to Pygmalion every night, which he thought the natural duty of an author. I promised to come on the hundredth night, adding rather unkindly that this was equivalent to not coming at all. The hundredth night, however, was reached and survived; and I redeemed my promise, only to find that he had contributed to my second act a stroke of comic business[7] so outrageously irrelevant that I solemnly cursed the whole enterprise, and bade the delinquents farewell for ever.

The fact that Tree could do and be done by thus without bloodshed, although he had all the sensitiveness of his profession, and all the unrestrained impulsiveness of a man who had succeeded in placing himself above discipline from the beginning of his adult life, shews that he was never quite unpardonable; and though this, to the world that knows nothing of the theatre, may seem more of an apology than a tribute, those who know the theatre best will understand its value. It has to be considered, too, that the statement that he did nothing unpardonable does not imply that he did nothing irreparable. Almost all the wrongs and errors of the West-End London theatre are like the wrongs and errors of the battlefield: they cannot be undone. If an actor's or an author's chance is spoilt, it is spoilt for years and perhaps for ever: neither play nor part gets a second chance. I doubt whether there is an actor-manager living who has not done both these wrongs more than once. Tree was no exception; but as the result, like that of the elephant sitting on the hen's eggs, was never intended, it was impossible to bear malice for long.

What Tree could do was always entertaining in some way or other. But, for better for worse, it was hardly ever what the author meant him to do. His parts were his avatars; and the play had to stand the descent of the deity into it as best it could. Sometimes, as in my case, the author understood the situation and made the best of it. Sometimes, no doubt, the author either did not understand the situation or would not make the best of it. But Tree could not act otherwise than as he did; and his productions represented an output of invention on his part that may have supplied many deficiencies in the plays.

One of his ambitions was to create a Tree Don Quixote. He used to discuss this with me eagerly as a project we might carry out together. "What I see," he said, "is a room full of men in evening dress smoking. Somebody mentions the Don. They begin talking about him. They wonder what he would make of our modern civilization. The back wall vanishes; and there is Piccadilly, with all the buses and cabs coming towards you in a stream of traffic; and with them, in the middle, a long tall figure in armor on the lean horse, amazing, foreign, incongruous, and yet impressive, right in the centre of the picture."

"That is really a very good idea," I would say. "I must certainly carry it out. But how could we manage the buses and things?"

"Yes," he would go on, not listening to me after my first words of approval: "there you see him going down the mountain side in Spain just after dawn, through the mist, you know, on the horse, and—"

"And Calvert as Sancho Panza on the ass," I would say. That always surprised him.

"Yes," he would say slowly. "Yes. Sancho, of course. Oh, yes." Though he had quite forgotten Sancho, yet, switching instantly over to his Falstaff line, he would begin to consider whether he could not double the two parts, as he doubled Micawber and Peggotty. For your true actor is still what he was in the days of Bottom: he wants to play every part in the comedy.

But the heart of the matter (which I have been coming to slowly all this time) is that the cure for the disease of actor-managership (every author must take that pathological view of it) is actor-author-managership: the cure of Molière, who acted his plays as well as wrote them, and managed his theatre into the bargain. And yet he lasted fifty-one years. Richard Wagner was author-composer-conductor-manager at Bayreuth: a much more arduous combination. Tree should have written his own plays. He could have done so. He had actually begun to do it as Shakespear and Molière began, by tinkering other men's plays. The conflict that raged between him and me at the rehearsals in his theatre would then have taken place in his own bosom. He would have taken a parental pride in other parts beside his own. He would have come to care for a play as a play, and to understand that it has powers over the audience even when it is read by people sitting round a table or performed by wooden marionettes. It would have developed that talent of his that wasted itself in *jeux d'esprit* and epigrams. And it would have given him what he was always craving from authors, and in the nature of the case could never get from them: a perfect projection of the great Tree personality. What did he care for Higgins or Hamlet? His real objective was his amazing self. That also was Shakespear's objective in Hamlet; but Shakespear was not Tree, and therefore Hamlet could never be to Tree what Hamlet was to Shakespear. For with all his cleverness in the disguises of the actor's dressing room, Tree was no mere character actor. The character actor never dares to appear frankly in his own person: he is the victim of a mortal shyness that agonizes and paralyzes him when his mask is stripped off and his cothurnus snatched from beneath his feet. Tree, on the contrary, broke through all his stage disguises: they were his robes of state; and he was never happier than when he stepped in front of the curtain and spoke in his own immensity to the audience, if not as deep calling unto deep (for the audience could not play up to him as splendidly as that), at least as a monarch to his courtiers. . . . It is my misfortune that I cannot do him justice, because, as author and actor, we two were rivals who regarded one another as usurpers. Happily, no bones were broken in the encounter; and if there is any malice in my description of it, I hope I have explained sufficiently to enable the reader to make the necessary allowance and correction.[8]

Pygmalion Higgins is not a portrait of [Henry] Sweet, to whom the adventure of Eliza Doolittle would have been impossible; still, . . . there are touches of Sweet in the play. With Higgins's physique and temperament Sweet might have set the Thames on fire. As it was, he impressed himself professionally on Europe to an extent that made his comparative personal obscurity, and the failure of Oxford to do justice to his eminence, a puzzle to foreign specialists in his subject. I do not blame Oxford, because I think Oxford is quite right in demanding a certain social amenity from its nurslings (heaven knows it is not exorbitant in its requirements!); for although I well know how hard it is for a man of genius with a seriously underrated subject to maintain serene and kingly relations with the men who underrate it, and who keep all the best places for less important subjects which they profess without originality and sometimes without much capacity for them, still, if he overwhelms them with wrath and disdain, he cannot expect them to heap honors on him.

Those who knew him will recognize in my third act the allusion to the patent shorthand in which he used to write postcards, and which may be acquired from a four-and-sixpenny manual published by the Clarendon Press. The postcards which Mrs Higgins describes are such as I have received from Sweet. I would decipher a sound which a cockney would represent by *zerr,* and a Frenchman by *seu,* and then write demanding with some heat what on earth it meant. Sweet, with boundless contempt for my stupidity, would reply that it not only meant but obviously was the word Result, as no other word containing that sound, and capable of making sense with the context, existed in any language spoken on earth. That less expert mortals should require fuller indications was beyond Sweet's patience. Therefore, though the whole point of his Current Shorthand is that it can express every sound in the language perfectly, vowels as well as consonants, and that your hand has to make no stroke except the easy and current ones with which you write *m, n,* and *u, l, p,* and *q,* scribbling them at whatever angle comes easiest to you, his unfortunate determination to make this remarkable and quite legible script serve also as a shorthand reduced it in his own practice to the most inscrutable of cryptograms. His true objective was the provision of a full, accurate, legible script for our noble but ill-dressed language; but he was led past that by his contempt for the popular Pitman system of shorthand, which he called the Pitfall system. The triumph of business organization: there was a weekly paper to persuade you to learn Pitman: there were cheap text-books and exercise books and transcripts of speeches for you to copy, and schools where experienced teachers coached you up to the necessary proficiency. Sweet could not organize his market in that fashion. He might as well have been the sibyl who tore up the leaves of prophecy that nobody would attend to. The four-and-sixpenny manual, mostly in his lithography handwriting, that was never vulgarly advertized, may perhaps some day be taken up by a syndicate and pushed upon the public as The Times pushed the Encylopaedia Britannica; but until then it will certainly not prevail against Pitman. I have bought three copies of it during my lifetime; and I am informed by the publishers that its cloistered existence is still a steady and healthy one. I actually learned the system two several times; and yet the shorthand in which I am writing these lines is Pitman's. And the reason is that my secretary cannot transcribe Sweet, having been perforce taught in the schools of Pitman. Therefore, Sweet railed at Pitman as vainly as Thersites railed at Ajax: his raillery, however it may have eased his soul, gave no popular vogue to Current Shorthand.

. . . When I became interested in the subject towards the end of the eighteen-seventies, the illustrious Alexander Melville Bell, the inventor of Visible Speech, had emigrated to Canada, where his son invented the telephone; but Alexander J. Ellis was still a London patriarch, with an impressive head always covered by a velvet skull cap, for which he would apologize to public meetings in a very courtly manner. He and Tito Pagliardini, another phonetic veteran, were men whom it was impossible to dislike. Henry Sweet, then a young man, lacked their sweetness of character: he was about as conciliatory to conventional mortals as Ibsen or Samuel Butler. His great ability as a phonetician (he was, I think, the best of them all at his job) would have entitled him to high official recognition, and perhaps enable him to popularize his subject, but for his Satanic contempt for all academic dignitaries and persons in general who thought more of Greek than of phonetics. Once, in the days when the Imperial Institute rose in South Kensington, and Joseph Chamberlain was booming the Empire, I induced the editor of a leading monthly review to commission an article from Sweet on the imperial importance of his subject. When it arrived, it contained nothing but a savagely derisive attack on a professor of language and literature whose chair Sweet regarded as proper to a phonetic expert only. The article, being libellous, had to be returned as impossible; and I had to renounce my dream of dragging its author into the limelight. When I met him afterwards, for the first time for many years, I found to my astonishment that he, who had been a quite tolerably presentable young man, had actually managed by sheer scorn to alter his personal appearance until he had become a sort of walking repudiation of Oxford and all its traditions. It must have been largely in his own despite that he was squeezed into something called a Readership of phonetics there.[9] . . . His pupils all swore by him; but nothing could bring the man himself into any sort of compliance with the university to which he nevertheless clung by divine right in an intensely Oxonian way. . . . He was, I believe, not in the least an ill-natured man: very much the opposite, I should say; but he would not suffer fools gladly.

Of the later generations of phoneticians I know little. Among them towers the Poet Laureate [Robert Bridges], to whom perhaps Higgins may owe his Miltonic sympathies, though here again I must disclaim all portraiture. But if the play makes the public aware that there are such people as phoneticians, and that they are among the most important people in England at present, it will serve its turn.

. . . For the encouragement of people troubled with accents that cut them off from all high employment, I may add that the change wrought by Professor Higgins in the flower-girl is neither impossible nor uncommon. The modern concierge's daughter who fulfils her ambition by playing the Queen of Spain in Ruy Blas at the Theatre Francais is only one of many thousands of men and women who have sloughed off their native dialects and acquired a new tongue. But the thing has to be done scientifically, or the last state of the aspirant

WITHDRAWN

may be worse than the first. An honest and natural slum dialect is more tolerable than the attempt of a phonetically untaught person to imitate the vulgar dialect of the golf club. . . .

The English have no respect for their language, and will not teach their children to speak it. They spell it so abominably that no man can teach himself what it sounds like. It is impossible for an Englishman to open his mouth without making some other Englishman hate or despise him. German and Spanish are accessible to foreigners: English is not accessible even to Englishmen. The reformer England needs today is an energetic phonetic enthusiast: that is why I have made such a one the hero of a popular play. There have been heroes of that kind crying in the wilderness for many years past. . . .

Pygmalion has been an extremely successful play all over Europe and North America as well as at home. It is so intensely and deliberately didactic, and its subject is esteemed so dry, that I delight in throwing it at the heads of the wiseacres who repeat the parrot cry that art should never be didactic. It goes to prove my contention that art should never be anything else.

7

War Madness

IN COMPILING this record of what I did with my pen in the Great War, as we called it, I have purposely made no attempt to trim it into an academic history or to brush the dust off my own clothes or anyone else's before coming up for judgment. . . . To appreciate the moral shock [I] produced it must be borne in mind that our morality is never a simple, single, perfectly homogeneous body of thought and sympathy, as we conventionally assume it to be. Like white light it may present that appearance at quiet times; but the prism of war splits it violently into a spectrum in which all the colours of the rainbow are contrasted. I had to deal with several moralities, writing in terms sometimes of one, sometimes of another, and thus shocking some moral section at every stroke of my pen. For I entirely refused Romain Rolland's invitation[1] to *planer au dessus de la mêlée* and survey the war from the empyrean of a morality which none of the combatants could possibly practice even if, like myself, they recognized that morality as their natural own, and regarded war with implacable horror and disgust. . . .

I have no ethical respect for modern Capitalist society, and therefore contemplated the British, German, and French sections of it with impartial disapproval. I felt as if I were witnessing an engagement between two pirate fleets, with, however, the very important qualification that as I and my family and friends were on board British ships I did not intend the British section to be defeated if I could help it. All the ensigns were Jolly Rogers; but mine was clearly the one with the Union Jack in the corner. . . . The Socialists and Trade Unionists who constituted the Proletarian movement were romantic novices in foreign policy, having always been too much preoccupied with industrial affairs at home to attend to it. They knew nothing of what was going on. It was one of their pet commonplaces that wars are caused by the Capitalist struggle for markets; and that, pending the abolition of the Capitalist system, the remedy (an impossible one) for war is a general strike. In the Liberal middle class echoes still lingered of the old comfortable assurances that diplomatic balancing of power is obsolete, and war between the great Powers of the west "unthinkable." I was not imposed on by either; but I also had been too preoccupied with my colleagues of the Fabian Society in working out the practicalities of English Socialism, and establishing a parliamentary Labour Party, to busy myself with foreign policy.

What woke me up was the effort of Count Harry Kessler to affirm an *entente cordiale* between England and Germany lest it should appear that the *entente* cultivated with France by Edward VII had exhausted England's stock of cordiality. Count Kessler proposed reciprocal manifestoes of friendship between London and Berlin; and I was asked to draft the London manifesto. Now nothing was easier than to draw up a string of eloquent references to the cultural bonds between Britain and Germany, to our common responsibility for the pioneering of modern civilization, to Shakespear and Goethe, Newton and Leibniz, London's love of Wagner's music and the like, on the lines of a Secretary of State for Foreign Affairs proposing the health of a distinguished German visitor at a civic banquet. But there was nothing in all this to prevent our signing it and going to war next day. Kessler was acting in good faith; and I felt that I could not be a party to humbugging him. I therefore introduced into my draft a test sentence which really meant something. It was to the effect that England, far from being jealous of the possession of a fleet by Germany, could regard it only as an additional guarantee of civilization.

I was taken aback by the completeness of the result of my test. I had expected that our thoroughgoing conquistadores would demur. But everybody demurred. Nobody would sign the manifesto with that sentence in it. Everybody would sign without it. The sentence was dropped; and everybody did sign—except myself. . . . In desperation I, as a private individual, suggested a line of action when Prince Lichnowsky was appointed German ambassador in London. Under the impression that well-known authors and sociologists enjoy the same consideration in England as in Germany, he invited me to visit him at the embassy, and even went so far as to say that a place should always be ready for me at his table. As it happened, I had just induced The Daily Chronicle to place its columns at my disposal for a proposed solution of the Franco-German difficulty.[2] I had urged that for the sake of averting war, England should, as the holder of the balance of power, reinforce her army, and declare, officially and unequivocally, that if Germany attacked France, England would throw in her sword on the side of France, balancing this threat by a counter assurance that if Germany were attacked by Russia or France or both, she would defend Germany. I pointed out that this would have the effect of producing a combination of England, France, and Germany to keep the peace of Europe; that the weaker Northern States, Belgium and Holland, Norway, Sweden, and Denmark, would immediately join it; that the United States would have every reason to do the same; and that the final result would be a combination of western democracy against war from the Carpathians to the Rocky Mountains.

Lichnowsky's reply, if equally candid, would have been that Germany too had its . . . alarmists . . . , and that sensible people did not worry about such things. So I could only ask him one day when lunching with him what he thought of my published proposal. He evidently did not consider that sort of thing my business, and dismissed it by telling me emphatically that Sir Edward Grey, our Foreign Secretary, was the best friend Germany had in the world, and that he would not be a party to any action that implied the slightest mistrust of him. I was too polite to exclaim *Sancta simplicitas!* And I could not contradict him. . . .

There was nothing more to be said. My wife had done her best in vain to shake the belief of her hostess that the danger of revolt in Ireland[3] made it impossible for England to go to war. After all, as Kessler knew what had happened about my test sentence, the position was as much before Lichnowsky as before me. When he at last realized the situation it was too late. . . . The dead silence which followed this proposal in the Press was inevitable; for as I was not a party politician, nor a famous cricketer, jockey, or glovefighter, neither the political columns nor the stunt columns of the British press were concerned with me: I might as well have been Fielding, Goldsmith, Blake, Dickens, Hardy, Wells, or Bennett for all the attention my political ideas received from the newspapers. But the newspapers have very little to do with diplomacy. . . .

The only comment reported to me on my proposal was that if I were in the Foreign Office, there would be a European war in a fortnight. As I was not in the Foreign Office, there was a European war in eighteen months. The policy of drift proved, even on its own shewing, no more pacific than the policy of action.

As to Mr Asquith, I doubt whether Mr Asquith ever really had any policy at all. His years of office were very prosperous and comfortable years for the governing class; and as he shared that comfort and prosperity, and was blessed with an easy disposition and a ready talent that could deal plausibly with a difficulty when it arose, but could neither anticipate it nor remember it for a single day, he took things as he found them and would have been content to leave them as he found them, if only all the sleeping dogs had been allowed to lie by less placid spirits. . . .

I made such attempts as an unofficial individual writer could to warn the country not to be righteous overmuch, as it was extremely unlikely that we should get through the war without having to violate neutrality ourselves. But in England nothing can resist the national love of lecturing other people on their moral behavior. . . . And so my proposal inevitably came to nothing. There was nothing to be done but drift along. . . .

England did not "muddle through" this time. The Serbs assassinated the Austrian heir apparent; Austria sent a furious ultimatum to Serbia; Russia rallied to the defence of the Slav and mobilized against Austria; and Germany, being Austria's ally, and well aware that France was the ally of Russia, dashed at France in the hope of smashing her before Russia could bring her cumbrous forces to bear effectively. Then the . . . binding engagement[4] between Britain and France . . . was unmasked at last. . . .

Knowing little about war, and less about diplomacy, we all went crazy. Editions of the daily papers were rushed out every hour and bought up feverishly. They were written mostly by astonished and excited journalists who, like their readers, knew nothing of what had been going on under their noses for ten years. Their vision had no historic perspective; and their notions of warfare had been picked up at the cinema. It is impossible to describe the public feeling. It was perfectly natural and perfectly absurd. . . . Romantic exaltation reached the heavens; and deluded ignorance plumbed the bottomless pit.

As for me, knowing enough to be greatly oppressed by my own ignorance, I collected all the documents I could get, and retired to Torquay, where I sunned myself on the roof of the Hydro Hotel for nearly two months, at the end of which I had produced my Common Sense About the War.[5] . . . It appeared as a supplement to The New Statesman on the 14th November 1914.

It is part of our Manichean tradition that though God is great and good, yet the devil is frightfully clever, subtle, powerful, and efficient. It was "pro-German" to tell the truth, certainly; but it was still more pro-German to express the smallest scepticism as to the superb efficiency of the Germans. Their perfect organization, the completeness of their preparation, the thoroughness of their education, the devotion with which they had consecrated themselves to this war and qualified themselves for its ruthless prosecution by forty years of study of the works of Bernhardi, Treitschke, and Nietzsche,[6] were articles of faith to question which was to risk being dragged to the Tower and shot as a manifest Prussian spy. Yet if this, or even a tithe of it, had been true, the Germans would have reached Paris in a fortnight, and plucked Calais like a daisy. They knew beforehand, as all the soldiers in Europe had known, exactly what they had to do to achieve that feat; and they had often described it to us over the walnuts and wine, or at bouts of the war game. And the allies had often described how they would stop them. . . . In short, military Europe, headed by the experts of Germany, was, in its imagination, its theory, and its romance, prepared for scientific warfare with a completeness which made it doubtful as to whether the world could survive the shock of Armageddon, and certain that the strain would be so terrific and the operations so swift and decisive that it would be all over in six weeks. And military imagination, theory, and romance naturally communicated themselves to the civilians who are great consumers of fiction.

The reality was not a bit like it. . . .

At the outbreak of the war I was at a hotel in Devon; and the first I heard of it when I came down in the morning was from a very ordinary and typical Englishman on the elderly side of forty, who, after a fairly successful attempt to say unconcernedly "I suppose we shall have to fight them" suddenly became spitefully hysterical and changed "them" into "those swine" twice in every sentence. . . .

Only those who have lived through a first-rate war, not in the field, but at home, and kept their heads, can possibly understand the bitterness of Shakespear and Swift, who both went through this experience. The horror of Peer Gynt in the madhouse, when the lunatics, exalted by illusions of splendid talent and visions of a dawning millennium, crowned him as their emperor, was tame in comparison. I do not know whether anyone really kept his head completely except those who had to keep it because they had to conduct the war at first hand. I should not have kept my own (as far as I did keep it) if I had not at once understood that as a scribe and speaker I too was under the most serious public obligation to keep my grip on realities; but this did not save me from a considerable degree of hyperaesthesia. There were of course some happy people to whom the war meant nothing: all political and general matters lying outside their little circle of interest. But the ordinary war-conscious civilian went mad, the main symptom being a conviction that the whole order of nature had been reversed. All foods, he felt, must now be adulterated. All schools must be closed. No advertisements must be sent to the newspapers, of which new editions must appear and be bought up every ten minutes. Travelling must be stopped, or, that being impossible, greatly hindered. All pretences about fine art and culture and the like must be flung off as an intolerable affectation; and the picture galleries and museums and schools at once occupied by war workers. The British Museum itself was saved only by a hairsbreadth.[7] The sincerity of all this, and of much more which would not be believed if I chronicled it, may be established by one conclusive instance of the general craziness. Men were seized with the illusion that they could win the war by giving away money. And they not only subscribed millions to Funds of all sorts with no discoverable object, and to ridiculous voluntary organizations for doing what was plainly the business of the civil and military authorities, but actually handed out money to any thief in the street who had the presence of mind to pretend that he (or she) was "collecting" it for the annihilation of the enemy. Swindlers were emboldened to take offices; label themselves Anti-Enemy Leagues! and simply pocket the money that was heaped on them.

In 1914, this abuse reached such a pass that young women had only to dress themselves presentably and parade the streets waving collecting boxes and artificial flowers to have pennies showered on them. At last the police had to interfere, as the public would not discriminate between authorized collectors and enterprising cadgers. Giving away money was an easy outlet for the sacrificial impulse; and rogues had nothing to do but hold their hats under the spout to enjoy a month's opulence. . . .

When war is declared we all go mad. We assume that all who are doing anything must stop doing it and do something else, and that wherever we are we must go elsewhere. We forget, if we ever knew, that a war is only a ripple of slaughter and destruction on the surface of the world's necessary work, most of which must carry on without a moment's intermission, war or no war.

. . . There is money to be made out of these insanities. In 1914, one of the first things that happened was that actors were asked to "do their bit" by accepting half salaries for their work; and many of them, in an ecstasy of patriotism, did so, to the handsome profit of their exploiters. It was such a paying game that the said exploiters presently approached me with the proposal that "of course" I would halve my fees for the duration. I replied that "of course" I must double them, as the war would not only increase my income tax heavily, but the inevitable inflation and consequent rise in the cost of living would make a corresponding increase in my income a matter of life and death for me. In consenting, as I actually did, to make no change, I claimed credit for a heroic sacrifice, only possible for an author with some settled property at the back of his royalties. The exploiters were deeply shocked by my lack of public spirit, and set me down as an arrant pro-German.

Now the final gainers in the theatre business are the two renters: the author and the theatre landlord. . . . During the war, when 80,000 soldiers were at home on leave every night, many of them having never been in a theatre in their lives, and all of them in a delirium of relief from the terror and boredom of the trenches in which they wildly applauded any sort of childish fooling, whilst their girl companions squealed like fillies, producing a noise never heard in the theatre before, rents shot up in a few days to figures possible only on the assumption that the house would be crowded to suffocation at every performance. Actors demanded and obtained monstrous salaries for tomfooleries and barn-stormings that could not be crude enough for the hearers in front. . . . The fortunate lessee who had a theatre for

£100 a week was offered £200 for it; and the new lessee was offered £300 before he had turned the corner. My first commercially produced play at the old Avenue Theatre in 1894 cost £80 a performance. £10 of that £80 was for the lessee. After the war a revival of the same play cost £50 a performance for rent alone. The principal actor who in 1894 accepted £18 a week (nominally £20) was succeeded by a star who received £250 a week, which was more than the most idolized leading lady had ever dreamt of demanding before. . . . Thus the higher drama, which has never really been a commercially sound speculation, now became an impossible one . . . , as far as the West End of London is concerned.

When the Germans bombed the Cathedral of Rheims the world rang with the horror of the sacrilege. When they bombed the Little Theatre in the Adelphi, and narrowly missed bombing two writers of plays[8] who lived within a few yards of it, the fact was not even mentioned in the papers. . . . I do not suppose many people care particularly. We are not brought up to care; and a sense of the national importance of the theatre is not born to mankind: the natural man, like so many of the soldiers at the beginning of the war, does not know what a theatre is. . . .

Happy were the fools and the thoughtless men of action in those days. The worst of it was that the fools were very strongly represented in parliament, as fools not only elect fools, but can persuade men of action to elect them too. . . . Most of the men of action, occupied to the last hour of their time with urgent practical work, had to leave to idler people, or to professional rhetoricians, the presentation of the war to the reason and imagination of the country and the world in speeches, poems, manifestoes, picture posters, and newspaper articles.

Common Sense grew so monstrously in the public patriotic imagination as its actual text was forgotten that those who read it now with any recollection of its reputation will be surprised and possibly disappointed to find in it nothing of the passionate pro-Germanism, Defeatism, and Pacifism which it came to be supposed to contain. It was not only badly received at first: in fact its relative sanity must have been an enormous relief after the surfeit of raving. But it had a shocking effect on the most amiable and innocent of our people. In spite of all possible glorifications and concealments war is so horrible that only by enormous overdoses of self-righteousness and moral indignation can such decent souls be drugged and maddened into enduring it. They must be made to believe that a savage attack has been made on a peaceful people by inhuman foreign monsters, whose daily occupation is the committal of revolting atrocities and obscenities. Their clamor for impassioned statements of England's case in these terms, and for evidence, however absurd, of the atrocities and obscenities, was like the clamor of an agonizingly wounded combatant for morphia. The cruellest use I have ever had to make of my pen was to treat the balance of power diplomacy of which the war was an incident as so completely unmoral and Machiavellian that such expressions as war guilt had no place nor meaning in it; it was a game at which we had outwitted the Germans instead of the Germans cheating us; that a Junker was not a fiend in a spiked helmet but the German equivalent of an English country gentleman; and so on: all of which, though the conquistadores despised the amiable people as silly sentimentalists for being shocked by it, was so unbearable that if the amiable people had not been too amiable to lynch me, I should have been lynched. I bore no malice; for the amiable people were sound at heart, and had my entire sympathy fundamentally. Balance of power diplomacy and war *are* villainous; and all that the amiable people lacked was the knowledge and strength of mind to face that fact and extirpate both instead of masking them as moral and patriotic duties and becoming the admiring accomplices of the diplomatists. But I could not indulge these innocents: they were being catered for by our journalists and war orators to the most extravagant excess with utter recklessness as to the reaction of their statements on foreign, and especially on American opinion; and my business, as one of the few writers whose words cross frontiers, was to clear our case of false claims and thus anticipate and disarm their inevitable exposure by the enemy. . . .

Through the accident of my having attained some international fame in the profession of Eschylus, Shakespear, Goethe, and Ibsen, not only in Germany and Austria, but in those very countries whose neutrality hung most precariously in the balance (Sweden and the United States of America), I had the ear of these countries and could say nothing about the war that was not likely to be quoted there. I had to consider the effect of every word I wrote on these countries; and this involved not considering their effect in England at all, except, at first, on one vital English activity: that of voluntary recruiting. I had plenty [of] reminders of the reach of my pen. . . .

Early in the war the German government, wishing to stir up a rebellion against the French in Morocco and Algeria, circulated a document written in very choice Arabic to the effect that I am a great prophet, and that I once told an American senator that the violation of Belgian neutrality was an incident of the war and not the cause of it. I am quite unable to follow that operation of the German mind which led to the conclusion that any Moorish sheikh could be induced to rush to arms because some dog of an unbeliever had made a statement that was neither interesting nor even intelligible in Morocco to some other dog of an unbeliever; but the Germans formed that conclusion and spent money on it. Thereupon a distinguished literary colleague of mine, A. E. W. Mason,[9] who had plunged into active service in the war, and was busy circumventing the Germans round the Mediterranean and thereabouts, came to me and asked me for "a concise and straightforward denial" of the implication that the great prophet Shaw was a pro-German. Having been among the Moors and spoken to sheikhs and marabouts myself, I had no difficulty in convincing Mason that conciseness is not a virtue in Barbary. Also, I am not the man to lose an opportunity of preaching at the utmost admissible length when I find myself installed as a great prophet. Mason and I were not men of letters for nothing. We combined the style of our Bible with that of Burton's Arabian Nights in a prophetic message which will, I hope, find a permanent place in Arab literature as an additional surah of the Koran. It was, I assume, duly translated and circulated; anyhow the Moors lay low and did nothing. It had every quality except that of conciseness.

I was specially concerned about the case of Belgium. The violation of Belgian neutrality by the Germans was the mainstay of our righteousness; and we played it off on America for much more than it was worth. I guessed that when the German account of our dealings with Belgium reached the United States, backed with an array of facsimiles of secret diplomatic documents discovered by them in Brussels, it would be found that our own treatment of Belgium was as little compatible with neutrality as the German invasion. We had told her that in the event of her being invaded we should send troops into Belgium with or without her consent, and that she must resist instead of taking the only reasonable course available for a small state threatened by an overwhelmingly big one . . . : that is, to submit under protest to superior force. . . . I set to work to clean the slate in this respect not only by assuring Senator Beveridge[10] . . . that there was nothing in the Belgian pretext, but by publishing an Open Letter to President Wilson[11] inviting him to intervene on Belgium's account without committing himself to any demonstration of sympathy with us, and arguing the point fiercely at home in a series of letters to the Press, all intended for quotation abroad.

The controversy proved superfluous after all; for . . . the sinking of the Lusitania by a German submarine not only removed the danger of America coming into the war on the German side, but practically forced her in on our side. My officiousness in the matter was therefore entirely wasted. . . .

I must now go back . . . to the 7th November, a week before the publication of Common Sense. The overwhelming sensation of the first months of the war was the devastation of Belgium not only by the German invasion, but by the Belgian and British defence. A multitude of Belgian refugees and wounded soldiers were dumped on these shores, and received rashly, but very honorably, into the households of British patriots, most of whom could ill afford to keep them, and soon became pressingly anxious to get rid of them. But those of us who kept our heads saw that the support of the refugees could not be left to private hospitality; and a prodigious begging on their behalf set in, stimulated by the stories of atrocities which the refugees brought, and which they soon had to supplement liberally from their imagination, so great was the demand for them. In my own neighborhood in the country a young Belgian warrior, convalescing from his wound, described how a beautiful woman, with her hands chopped off at the wrists, had held up the bleeding stumps and said, "Avenge me, brother." He assumed the rank of Count, and was made much of at shooting parties in the country before returning to his native land to resume his normal career as a tailor's cutter. I mention his case, not as typical of the behavior of his countrymen, but as illustrating the boundless credulity of which he took humorous advantage. . . .

Sir Hall Caine[12] was asked by The Daily Telegraph to edit a book of gratuitous contributions by leading authors and composers, to be sold for the benefit of the Belgians. He asked me for a contribution; and I duly furnished it. But The Daily Telegraph of that day, being still under its old traditional management as a bourgeois paper, obliged, as such, to keep twenty years behind the times in domestic politics whilst being otherwise breezily up to date, was terrified by Common Sense, and absolutely refused to allow my name to be connected with its book. Hall Caine, always chivalrous in his sense of personal obligation, declared that he owed it to me to resign the editorship; but I dissuaded him, pointing out that nothing mattered at the moment but getting the money for the Belgians, and that the omission of my contribution would not make a penny difference to them or to anyone else, whereas his resignation might spoil the book's *début*. He had his revenge immediately; for on the question of an appeal to America coming up, the Belgians surprised The Daily Telegraph considerably by insisting that I should draft it, which I accordingly did. The explanation of their unexpected preference is to be found in [my] . . . Open Letter to President Wilson, which had appeared in The Nation a week before the publication of Common Sense. I was apparently the only publicly articulate person in London who could conceive that the Belgians had any case distinct from the British case. . . .

The editor to whom it was addressed was . . . H. W. Massingham, who, though he felt as a very English Englishman about the war, carried on with extraordinary courage and independence all through, refusing any kind of censorship, and receiving every instalment of official intelligence with blunt assurances that he did not desire any, and would pay no attention to it. He supported me valiantly when I ceased to address my polemics to The New Statesman, which, edited by Mr Clifford Sharp, had had the courage to publish Common Sense and several subsequent sallies of mine. But I had a proprietary interest[13] in The New Statesman. This made it improper for me to make use of it when the sinking of the Lusitania raised the temperature of the war fever on the home front to danger point. Thenceforth I felt that I must depend for publicity on editors who were either conspicuously hostile to my views or at least absolutely independent of my personal goodwill.

The idea that civilians as such are exempt from the risks of war, and are inviolable as to their persons, lasted so long, and is still so inveterate, that I myself came up against it when the first Zeppelin raids in London occurred. . . . I wrote a letter to The Times urging the authorities to provide bomb-proof shelters for the defenceless citizens, especially in the playgrounds of the elementary schools, so that the children might have a familiar refuge. I pointed out that the airplane and the dirigible had at last enabled military forces to overleap the defensive hedge of the army and make war on the civil population at first hand. To my amazement the editor of The Times indignantly refused to publish a communication countenancing the monstrous doctrine that civilians are not sacred, and that the soldier who would raise his hand to a fellow creature in mufti, save in the way of kindness, is not unworthy the name of Briton. I could only gasp out *"Sancta simplicitas!"* and send my letter to the leading Liberal London daily, then edited by one of the ablest journalists in the country. To my double amazement he also said that he had never expected to agree with the editor of The Times, but that in this matter he did so most heartily, and that it would be impossible to publish my letter in any civilized country. But for Mr Massingham, the editor of The Nation, it would not have been published at all. It had hardly appeared when the Germans rudely awakened the shocked editors from their dream by a fresh shower of explosive iron rain which spared neither age, sex, nor condition, with the exception of the soldiers home on leave, who, having no illusions on the subject, made for the nearest underground railway station at the first sound of an aircraft gun. No American civilian who stayed in his own country during the war can have any adequate conception of how completely every town in England within reach of the air raids was converted to the view that in the next war the only safe people would be the soldiers in their dug-outs. The authorities lied like Cretans to hide the extent of the damage and danger; for it is one of the necessities of war that from the moment the first shot is fired nobody dare tell the truth on any subject whatever. Not until long after the Armistice, when the claims for compensation from the East Coast towns came before Parliament, did the few people who read Hansard[14] learn that four reported casualties meant four hundred actual ones; that a couple of houses slightly damaged meant a street wrecked; and that a futile and contemptible exhibition of German incompetence and spite, followed by an ignominious flight meant a daring and successful bombardment.

. . . Most people could not comprehend these sorrows. There was a frivolous exultation in death for its own sake, which was at bottom an inability to realize that the deaths were real deaths and not stage ones. Again and again, when an air raider dropped a bomb which tore a child and its mother limb from limb, the people who saw it, though they had been reading with great cheerfulness of thousands of such happenings day after day in their newspapers, suddenly burst into furious imprecations on "the Huns" as murderers, and shrieked for savage and satisfying vengeance. At such moments it became clear that the deaths they had not seen meant no more to them than the mimic deaths of the cinema screen. Sometimes it was not necessary that death should be actually witnessed: it had only to take place under circumstances of sufficient novelty and proximity to bring it home almost as sensationally and effectively as if it had been actually visible.

For example, in the spring of 1915 there was an appalling slaughter of our young soldiers at Neuve Chapelle and at the Gallipoli landing. I will not go so far as to say that our civilians were delighted to have such exciting news to read at breakfast. But I cannot pretend that I noticed either in the papers, or in general intercourse, any feeling beyond the usual one that the cinema show at the front was going splendidly, and that our boys were the bravest of the brave. Suddenly there came the news that an Atlantic liner, the Lusitania, had been torpedoed, and that several well-known first class passengers, including a famous theatrical manager[15] and the author of a popular farce,[16] had been drowned, among others. The others included Sir Hugh Lane;[17] but as he had only laid the country under great obligations in the sphere of the fine arts, no great stress was laid on that loss.

Immediately an amazing frenzy swept through the country. Men who up to that time had kept their heads now lost them utterly. "Killing saloon passengers! What next?" was the essence of the whole agitation; but it is far too trivial a phrase to convey the faintest notion of the rage which possessed us. To me, with my mind full of the hideous cost of Neuve Chapelle, Ypres, and the Gallipoli landing, the fuss about the Lusitania seemed almost a heartless impertinence, though I was well acquainted personally with the three best-known victims, and understood, better perhaps than most people, the misfortune of the death of Lane. I even found a grim satisfaction, very intelligible to all soldiers, in the fact that the civilians who found the war such splendid British sport should get a sharp taste of what it was to the actual combatants. I expressed my impatience very freely, and found that my very straightforward and natural feeling in the matter was received as a monstrous and heartless paradox. When I asked those who gaped at me whether they had anything to say about the holocaust of Festubert,[18] they gaped wider than before, having totally forgotten it, or rather, having never realized it. They were not heartless any more than I was; but the big catastrophe was too big for them to grasp, and the little one had been just the right size for them. I was not surprised. Have I not seen a public body for just the same reason pass a vote for £30,000 without a word, and then spend three special meetings, prolonged into the night, over an item of seven shillings for refreshments?

Nobody will be able to understand the vagaries of public feeling during the war unless they bear constantly in mind that the war in its entire magnitude did not exist for the average civilian. He could not conceive even a battle, much less a campaign. To the suburbs the war was nothing but a suburban squabble. To the miner and navvy it was only a series of bayonet fights between German champions and English ones. The enormity of it was quite beyond most of us. Its episodes had to be reduced to the dimensions of a railway accident or a shipwreck. . . .

My anxiety as to neutral foreign opinion, including German opinion in the United States, brought me into sharp conflict with the recklessness of our patriotic agitators, who were unable to conceive that any other point of view than their own, except that of the enemy, could exist. Their attacks on me did not matter: they were part of the sport of controversy; and I easily found stunning counters for all their blows. But their extravagances were mischievous abroad; for there is nothing so repulsive to a foreigner as self-righteous patriotism. . . . I began pleading more or less directly to the overseas jury without regard to the feelings of the thoughtless ranters who, before compulsory service became inevitable, spent their days in Trafalgar Square trying to persuade their audiences to enlist. Naturally, I infuriated some of them to such an extent that an American wit described the war as a struggle between the British Empire and Bernard Shaw. This simplification brought the business within their mental range, I suppose. But such trifling with wholesale death and destruction strained my good humor to breaking point and occasionally beyond.

By the way, I interfered once in the Trafalgar Square business. Passing by one day, I found some ferociously bellicose clergymen tearing their throats out in denunciation of the villainy of the Germans and the dastardly cowardice of all the young men present who did not enlist on the spot. Their eloquence had produced only two recruits; and these two, duly posted on the plinth of Nelson's monument as heroic examples to British youth, were a couple of deplorable down-

and-outs so obviously untouchable that it was plain to me that no decent young man would be seen in their company. I went home and wrote to Lord Derby, who was in command of the recruiting, urging him to dress up his smartest young soldiers as civilians, with instructions to spend their days in the square joining up ostentatiously again and again as really attractive examples, care being taken at the same time to hurry away all unpleasant looking heroes to barracks before their appearance could act as a deterrent. Lord Derby at once offered me the post of Trafalgar Square stage manager; but I had other fish to fry, and had to excuse myself from this job: the only one offered me in those days of voluntary service.[19]

. . . When I said that the violation of Belgian neutrality as an excuse for the war would not impose on neutral diplomatists, and had better be dropped, it was immediately assumed that I had the mentality of the German General Staff, and was an ardent ally of the Kaiser and an ungrateful traitor to England, out of whose playgoers I was shamelessly making a huge fortune. . . . It was gravely stated in a Viennese paper that I had shut myself up in my house, put sentries at my doors, and could shew myself in public only on pain of immediate assassination by the infuriated patriotic London mob. At that time our own newspapers took it for granted that England was one solid roar of execration against Keir Hardie, and that the name Ramsay MacDonald was to British patriotism what the name of Judas Iscariot is to Christendom.[20] Never were evil reputations more firmly and unanimously established, as far as the Press went.

What were the facts? Keir Hardie died, neither unwept, unhonored, nor unsung. His funeral was like the funeral of Nelson; and his obituary notices stand unparalleled for eulogy since the Royalist obituaries of Charles I. Mr MacDonald was addressing crowded meetings throughout the country, with such standings-up, and singings of "For He's a Jolly Good Fellow," and salvos of cheers, as Mr Asquith himself can hardly elicit by the most dramatic repetitions of his famous stunt about the terms of which we will sheathe the sword. As for me, I was addressing large open public meetings in London every week, inviting and answering questions from all comers about the war or anything else, without a sign of hostility, and rather more than my usual need of applause (the questions were mostly about the allowances to the wives of the absent soldiers);[21] and I was receiving resolutions strongly approving my Common Sense from the provinces every day.

. . . In private I had to deal with a few cases of people who had been persuaded by their papers that I was arranging a victory for the Kaiser; and when these cases were complicated by war hysteria to the extent of being clearly pathological, like the delirium of fever, they gave me some special opportunities of observing this disease. But on the whole, the vituperation of the Press did not bring upon me as much resentment as I had incurred in the past by criticizing Shakespear, or pointing out that Brahms, compared to Beethoven and Wagner, had no brains. . . .

I could multiply these instances of the planting out of fools' paradises by the London Press. And I could add some examples of the reversal of the process. For instance, a play denouncing the alleged drunkenness and selfishness of the slackers who were supposed to be responsible for the shortage in shells had such a huge success in transpontine London that its proprietors thought they had acquired a gold mine. In the provinces it had to be withdrawn at once. And when Mr Lloyd George tried his magic spell over the working classes on the Clyde, he could not secure even a hearing until he had claimed to be a friend of Mr MacDonald, and the Socialists had appealed to the audience to give him fair play.

I am not here concerned with the merits of these cases. It may be that Mr Lloyd George ought to have been carried shoulder-high in triumph through Scotland; that Keir Hardie ought to have been buried at the cross-roads and a stake driven through him; that my works should have been burnt in the Stock Exchange as the Daily Mail was when that newspaper beloved of patriots first confessed a doubt as to whether we shall certainly beat the Germans if only we lie hard enough to one another. . . .

In 1916 came compulsory military service,* and with it the end of all the need for limiting discussion in the interest of voluntary re-

* Early in the war we were all registered. I still have my ticket, with its number. The people were numbered like the people in the Bible. There was some uneasy suspicion that this must be a preliminary to Conscription. Accordingly, the Prime Minister hastened to make a speech, in which he assured the nation that not the slightest idea of such a violation of British liberty had ever entered into the minds of the Government, the registration being a mere question of rationing. I forget the exact number of days—I think it was inside a week—which elapsed between that statement and the announcement of Conscription. But nobody noticed any sort of discrepancy between the speech and the announcement.

cruiting, and of young women presenting young civilians with white feathers and singing, "Oh we dont want to lose you; but we think you ought to go," which had a specially irritating effect on its cockney form of "Ow wee downt wornt—te le-oose yew—bat we thinkew orter gow." I remember making a private note that in war time only the most perfect speakers should be allowed to sing war songs.

The change went far deeper than that. It brought the war literally home to the nation. It made an end of the rhetoric about individual liberty with which the British have doped themselves for so many centuries. I can speak of the nineteenth at first hand. No article of faith was better established then than that Englishmen would never stand conscription, whatever spiritless Frenchmen and Germans might put up with. In the twentieth we had to put up with it as helplessly as sheep have to put up with the shambles. Englishmen might have been galley slaves, for all their vaunted Democracy could do for them. They were torn from their farms, their businesses, their practices, their studios, with as little resistance as from the fields and factories in which they had no interest except their week's wages. I say nothing about their being torn away from their homes; for some of their homes were so unhappy that the man found the army a welcome change, whilst his wife revelled in her freedom and in her separation allowance: an undreamt-of luxury. But all the homes were not like that: in many of them the separation and the dread of the always possible telegram of death made compulsory soldiering a calamity which neither man nor wife would have endured if they had had the smallest choice in the matter. The war songs did not include the old one which promised that Britons never never shall be slaves: it was now too evident that they had never been anything else.

But the old pretence was kept up by a clause in the Act which reserved the liberty of the Briton to refuse to serve if he had a conscientious objection to war. Only, lest all those who had not enlisted under the voluntary system should nullify compulsion by giving a conscientious complexion to their reluctance to serve, the authorities took care to make the lot of the Conshy, as he was called, much less eligible than that of the soldier. He was vigorously persecuted. When his maltreatment in prison resulted in his death, patriotic coroners' juries exonerated everyone concerned effusively. The local "competent" military authorities who had to decide in cases where exemption was claimed were sometimes men of intelligence and culture, sometimes insolent snobs, impenetrable blockheads, or both. In the west country a well-known opera composer[22] was hustled contemptuously to barbacks, where, however, he was promptly and sensibly made bandmaster. In the north country a youth who had once composed a waltz was exempted with a respect which would have left Handel nothing to complain of.

In my own case the question of conscientious objection did not arise: I was past military age. I did not counsel others to object, and should not have objected myself if I had been liable to serve; for intensely as I loathed the war, and free as I was from any illusions as to its character, and from the patriotic urge (patriotism in my native country taking the form of an implacable hostility to England), I knew that when war is once let loose, and it becomes a question of kill or be killed, there is no stopping to argue about it: one must just stand by one's neighbors and take a hand with the rest. If England had adopted me, as some of my critics alleged in their attempts to convict me of gross ingratitude, I could have pleaded that she must take the consequences without claiming any return; but as I had practically adopted England by thrusting myself and my opinions on her in the face of every possible rebuff, it was for me to take the consequences, which certainly included an obligation to help my reluctant ward in her extremity as far as my means allowed. Nevertheless I could not feel, as so many English people felt, that the conscientious objector was a criminal for whom no punishment was too cruel. As to calling him a coward and a slacker because he was facing martyrdom and standing out against a whole nation of men who were letting themselves be driven like sheep into the trenches, that was a little too much for my sense of humor; for as far as the question was one solely of courage the Conshy was the hero of the war; and the man who would not enlist until he was forced was the coward. But the war knocked all such old romantic pretences out of us. It was, I think, the first war in which everyone confessed himself a coward: at least I have not met a single soldier who does not admit without the slightest shame that he suffered a good deal from acute funk from time to time. There was some feeling on the part of the soldiers against the men who had to be kept at home in civil employment at high wages: indeed in Italy this feeling rose to such a pitch of fury at the end of the war that it carried Signor Mussolini to Rome and made him dictator; but in England this sort of jealousy did not affect the Conshy: the soldier rather admired him for doing something that many a soldier would have liked to do but dared not; and he had certainly no good luck to envy. Nobody could deny that his conduct passed the Kantian "if everybody did as I am doing" test triumphantly. Indeed in my Common Sense I had myself begun by telling all the soldiers, friends and foes alike, that if they were not fools they would go home and mind their own business, leaving diplomatists to fight out their quarrels as best they could, and that it was only because it was plain that they would not take this sensible advice that I had to accept the war as imposed on us by human folly and pugnacity. It is not surprising, then, that I soon felt obligated to intervene with my pen[23] in protesting against cases of gross maltreatment or outrageously severe sentences.

It was a delicate business; for the objectors were a very mixed lot. They ranged from shirkers who had no self-respect to fanatical Protestants who would submit their private judgment to no external authority, and who, in their determination to be martyrs, deliberately created situations in which their military persecutors had either to do their worst or confess themselves beaten. I began by giving evidence at a court-martial which I must not attempt to describe, as the proceedings were so funny that no one would believe them possible, and also because, though I told the exact truth and nothing but the truth, my evidence convinced and was meant to convince the court that the prisoner was an Evangelical fanatic, whereas he was as a matter of fact a Freethinker. His case was quite genuine as a case of conscience; but a military court would not have held that a Freethinker could have a conscience; consequently it was necessary in the interests of justice to produce the evidence of fanaticism, of which there was plenty, and leave the court to infer that a fanatic must be a hyperpious Quaker. ...I had already made an attempt to induce the Government to think a little about what they were doing before letting themselves be driven into handing over the nation to military slavery without a single precaution against its abuse. It had no effect, because when war breaks out Governments have neither time nor energy nor daring to spare for thinking: they have to take the military law as they find it. . . .

During the first days of the war I was passing through Gower Street when a company of young volunteers who had rushed to the colors came swinging along. To my utter scandal I was seized with a boyish impulse to join them. Men technically as superannuated as myself did so: A. E. W. Mason, who had played for me in Arms and the Man twenty years earlier, was certainly more than, as he alleged, twenty-two; and when C. E. Montague's hair turned white in a single night in the trenches, it was not shell shock, but the impossibility of procuring relays of hair dye, which produced the phenomenon.[24] I had to remind myself that I could be of much more use with my pen than with a bayonet, and that the courage of my own profession was likely to be tested at home quite as severely as the courage of the military profession (to which I make no pretension) before I felt quite safe from making a fool of myself. How then could I have disparaged the ardor of Cecil Chesterton, my junior by a generation, whose soul I had saved from Materialism by my Quintessence of Ibsenism?

Cecil Chesterton, then one of the brightest and cleverest of our young author-journalists, . . . a younger brother of the great Gilbert, was on the most cordial personal terms with me, and remained so until his death from trench fever,[25] one of those events which so often brought home with a personal stab the fundamental waste and folly of the whole miserable business. The Chestertons were by far the most striking examples of the anti-Prussian fury of the amiable people, because in their case innocence and amiability were combined with extraordinary literary ability and public spirit. Their fury was romantic and fundamentally playful, expressing itself mostly in splendidly readable pen-pictures of an absurdly fictitious conflict of Prussian paganism with a profound and elementary Christianity and sanity in the French peasantry, the moral being that it was our most sacred duty to help the French farmers to exterminate the Baltic heathen in defence of the Christendom they were menacing with destruction. It was interesting, ingenious, and very well written: in fact nothing was wrong with it except that it was obviously a Quixotic version which could have been fitted on to any pair of nations on earth.

The congenitally friendly Chestertons, conscientiously acting their parts as haters to the death, gave what was to me a ludicrously unconvincing, but on that account entirely pardonable performance. Cecil, I think, enjoyed it more than Gilbert. When he visited me for the last time he was in khaki, a sturdy, jolly, deeply sunburnt, hopelessly unsoldierlike figure. Military discipline insists on smartness of dress and elegance of carriage; but Cecil, void of vanity, was incorrigibly careless as to what he wore or how he wore it; and his easy personality defied the sumptuary laws of the British barracks. The word camouflage was in everyone's mouth then; and though it was quite heartbreaking to think of his talent being risked under real gunfire, my unruly imagination instantly presented me with a picture of Cecil camouflaging himself as a beetroot on a sack of potatoes by simply standing stock still. "I have come here to tell you," he said, "that it is not true that I have given up beer. I am told that beer will shorten my life by ten years; and I am prepared to pay that price cheerfully." It is impossible to describe what I used to feel on such occasions. It was hard enough to see any young man thrown into the common heap of cannon fodder with only the inhuman military excuse that there were plenty of the same sort to replace him; but when the young man, possessing a rare and highly valuable talent, was not replaceable, one's hatred of the war bit fiercely in. However, there was nothing to be done but to keep his spirits up and my own wrath down, and to console myself with his statistical chances of coming back safe and sound. I wished he had left the job of being a military hero to the poor fellows who were not clever enough to be heroic at anything else; but it was not a point on which I could interfere with another man's conscience. So we parted gaily; and the next I heard of him was that he was dead of the war pestilence against which he was so ill fortified by his anti-Puritan contempt for my vegetarian diet.

8

Joy Riding at the Front

EARLY IN 1917 I received an invitation from the British Commander-in-Chief, then Sir Douglas Haig, to visit the front and say my say about it. I felt this as a call, which I was not free to refuse, to such service as I was able to perform in the way of my profession. . . . Thus I had occasion to spend some days in procuring the necessary passports and other official facilities for my journey. It happened just then that the Stage Society gave a performance of . . . Augustus Does His Bit.[1] . . . It opened the heart of every official to me. I have always been treated with distinguished consideration in my contacts with bureaucracy during the war; but on this occasion I found myself *persona grata* in the highest degree. There was only one word when the formalities were disposed of; and that was "We are up against Augustus all day." The shewing-up of Augustus scandalized one or two innocent and patriotic critics who regarded the prowess of the British army as inextricably bound up with Highcastle prestige. But our Government departments knew better: their problem was how to win the war with Augustus on their backs, well-meaning, brave, patriotic, but obstructively fussy, self-important, imbecile, and disastrous.

Save for the satisfaction of being able to laugh at Augustus in the theatre, nothing, as far as I know, came of my dramatic reduction of him to absurdity. Generals, admirals, Prime Ministers, and controllers, not to mention Emperors, Kaisers, and Tsars, were scrapped remorselessly at home and abroad, for their sins or services, as the case might be. But Augustus stood like the Eddystone in a storm, and stands so to this day. He gave us his word that he was indispensable; and we took it.

. . . I equipped myself with a pair of trench boots and a tunic and breeches of khaki, in which I looked neither like a civilian nor a soldier, but in which I was supposed to be invisible to the enemy's marksmen. H. V. Massingham warned me that he had been almost turned back and sent home because the black of his civilian clothes shewed for an inch beneath his khaki trench overcoat. H. G. Wells told me to take waders, as I should have to walk kneedeep through the Flanders mud.

When I arrived on the field of battle I found that these precautions were entirely wasted. Flanders was virgin white in its mantle of snow. The temperature averaged about 17°F.; and I came home without a speck of mud on the trench boots.

The chateau for distinguished visitors at which I was billeted was run with first rate tact and efficiency by an officer named Roberts, whom I should unhesitatingly have appointed Commander-in-Chief on his merits. I spent an evening at another chateau, where all the war correspondents were, among them Beach Thomas,[2] who surprised me by saying that the British soldier could beat any soldier on earth. This was . . . out of tune with the prevailing disparagement of everybody except the enemy.

At the Chateau where the army entertained the rather mixed lot who, being nondescript, were classified as Distinguished Visitors, I met Montague.[3] . . . I was glad to learn that he was to be my bear-leader on my excursions. Except on three occasions, when he was relieved, once by Tomlinson,[4] once by Philip Gibbs,[5] and once during my visit to Robert Loraine's flying camp, we spent all the time together.

The standing joke about Montague was his craze for being under fire, and his tendency to lead the distinguished visitors, who did not necessarily share this taste (rare at the front), into warm corners. Like most standing jokes it was inaccurate, but had something in it. War is fascinating even to those who, like Montague, have no illusions about it, and are not imposed on by its boasting, its bugaboo, its desperate attempts to make up for the shortage of capable officers by sticking tabs and brass hats on duffers, its holocausts of common men for nothing, its pretences of strategy and tactics where there is only bewilderment and blundering, its vermin and dirt and butchery and terror and foul-mouthed boredom. None of these things were lost on a man so critical as Montague any more than they were lost on me. But neither of us ever asked the other, "And what the devil are *you* doing in this galley?" Both of us felt that, being there, we were wasting our time when we were not within range of the guns. We had come to the theatre to see the play, not to enjoy the intervals between the acts like fashionable people at the opera.

We had, nevertheless, no great excitements. On the Somme battlefield, which was the favourite military show at that moment, I found the British army blazing away industriously at imaginary Germans. . . . The guns that were banging away my taxes so strepitously were only making holes in the ground and not filling them up again. As we walked up towards the windmill at Pozières a solitary German shell exploded harmlessly half a mile ahead of us. Montague stopped dead, and surveyed a Roumanian general who was with us, wearing a gorgeous uniform. "I ought not to take you up to the windmill," said Montague; "You are not in khaki. They may see you and have a shot at you. And I am responsible for you." General Giorgescu grinned: "Let me point out, gentlemen," he said, contemplating our careful khaki with amused contempt, "that as the whole country is frozen white, you are much more likely to be conspicuous than I." This was obviously true. . . . Montague shrugged his shoulders; and we went on. The Germans must, I think, have left behind them one of the patent scarecrows advertized in [Army and Navy] Stores catalogues, which fire a shot automatically every fifteen minutes; for they did send over one more aimless shell, which impressed the general sufficiently to make him insist on a young friend of his who was also present retiring behind a knocked-out tank. And this was all the satisfaction Montague got that day out of the battle of the Somme. Ypres, where the smell of powder was distinctly stronger, was better from this point of view.

Montague was a typical daredevil; that is, a quiet, modest-looking, rather shy elderly man with nothing of the soldier about him except his uniform. He would have been a hopeless failure on the stage as Captain Matamore.[6] He had something of the Tolstoyan bitterness and disillusion that war produces at close quarters, less by its horrors, perhaps, than by its wastes and futilities. But to this he gave no intentional expression: his conversation and manner were entirely kindly. He said nothing of the exploits for which he was mentioned in despatches. . . .

By that time Montague was a captain, and, being a man of conspicuous civil capacity without military ambitions, was needed to run the show much more than to stop projectiles in the firing line. Hence, I presume, his efforts to get back into it occasionally as escort to distinguished sightseers and joy-riders.

As Montague stuck to the provinces after the war I never saw him again. I liked him so well that I once or twice wrote to him to see how we could renew contact; but it somehow never came off.

. . . The battle seemed to me unaccountably onesided. Our guns worked away industriously, the heavenrending energy of the guns and whizzing rush of the shells contrasting quaintly with the languid boredom of the gunners as they screwed in the fuses, hoisted the shells into the guns and pulled the string, letting another steel comet loose in space without a pretence of conviction that it would arrive anywhere in particular or of concern as to whether it did or not. At first I expected their efforts to provoke a thundering retaliative connonade from the embattled central empires, an expectation which gained a mild thrill from the possibility that their first efforts to find the range might land on my epigastrium; but no: our bombardment did not elicit a single remonstrance: it was like the imaginary battles of my childhood, in which I was always victorious and the enemy fell before my avenging sword without getting in a single blow. I demanded explanations. The first reply was, "Oh, they have not been doing much counter battery work lately." Another was, "They will start firing on Albert at three o'clock." Nobody knew the truth, which was that the Germans had retreated quietly to the Hindenburg line and left us to waste our ammunition on their empty trenches. In short, the Somme battlefield was very much safer than the Thames Embankment with its race of motors and trams. Only in Ypres and perhaps in Arras could I flatter myself that I was to any perceptible extent under fire. I did not see yellow as Goethe did on the field of Valmy and Wagner in the Dresden insurrection. I suffered much more from funk during the air raids in London, where I was too lazy to leave my bed and take refuge in the cellars or the nearest underground railway station, as the more energetic citizens did.

. . . When I last met Richard Strauss we were standing in the courtyard of a London house, listening to a band of strange instruments from Barcelona which set our midriffs vibrating with their terrific *fortissimo;* and our cry was, "Louder, louder." But the thundering batteries on the Somme were still better than the Barcelona orchestra; and I found myself wishing that Strauss were with me to enjoy it; for at the front you do not hate your enemy, though it may be your lot to fight him and kill him. Hating is one of the things you can do better at home. And you generally stay at home to do it.

The artillery major who obligingly blew half a field to bits for me to shew me how it is done, assured me that he was doubling the value of the farmer's land by a super-ploughing which no farmer could afford. "But," said I, "how are these pits to be filled up and smoothed over for the tillage?"

"I could shove them together with a few charges of dynamite," he said. . . .

War is frightfully expensive and frightfully destructive: it results in a dead loss as far as money is concerned. And everything has to be paid for on the nail; for you cannot kill Germans with promissory notes or mortgages or national debts: you must have actual stores of food, clothing, weapons, munitions, fighting men, and nursing, car driving, munition making women of military age. When the army has worn out the clothes and eaten up the food, and fired off the munitions, and shed its blood in rivers, there is nothing eatable, drinkable, wearable, or livable-in left to shew for it: nothing visible or tangible but ruin and desolation. For most of these military stores the Government in 1914–18 went heavily into debt. It took the blood and work of the young men as a matter of course, compelling them to serve whether they liked it or not, and breaking up their businesses, when they had any, without compensation of any kind. But being a Capitalist government it did not take all the needed ready money from the capitalists in the same way. It took some of it by taxation. But in the main, it borrowed it.

It is sometimes said that the capitalists who lent the Government the money for the war deserve the hire of it because they made sacrifices. As I was one of them myself I can tell you without malice that this is sentimental nonsense. They were the only people who were not called on to make any sacrifice: on the contrary, they were offered a gilt-edged investment of five per cent when they would have taken four. The people who were blinded, maimed, or killed by the war were those really sacrificed; and those who worked and fought were the real saviors of the country; whilst the people who did nothing but seize the national loaf that others had made, and take a big bite out of it (they and their servants) before passing on what they left of it to the soldiers, did no personal service at all. . . .

. . . Though still a superannuated civilian, I was in khaki, like everybody else, by way of camouflage. . . . On my way I discarded my cap, and, like Don Quixote, donned the helmet of Mambrino.[7] And I stuck into my ears a pair of seeming black collar-studs, which did not prevent my hearing anything, but did prevent my overdoing it. Everything was different. The weather was again bright, but intensely cold. The language of the country was English in all its dialects. The farmhouses and villas had no roofs, no floors, large holes in the walls, and no inhabitants. The trees were chipped and scarred, and here and there broken off short.

A man lying by the roadside was not a tramp taking a siesta, but a gentleman who had lost his head. There was no Belgian carillon, but plenty of German music: an imposing orchestration in which all the instruments were instruments of percussion. I cannot honestly say I disliked it: the big drum always excites me. I was not yet in the town; but I was unmistakably in the Ypres salient; and the Boche was "sending them over" as persistently as the gentleman next door to Mrs Nickleby sent cucumbers and marrows over the garden wall. I was reminded of him by the fact that in the whole countryside there was an extraordinary prevalence of gas and gaiters. Boom! whizzzzzz!!! Boom! whizzzzzz!!! Boom! whizzzzzz!!!—all *fortissimo diminuendo;* then, *crescendo molto subito,* Whizzzzzz-bang clatter! In such a bang and clatter had the gentleman by the roadside lost his head. Well, in time of peace he might have lost it much more painfully and mischievously. There are worse ways of ending one's walk in life.

Stimulated by the orchestration the car develops an extra 10 h.p.; and presently I am again in Ypres. Its houses are standing like the villas and farmhouses, and, like them, have no roofs, no floors, nothing but walls to hide behind, the Germans having with exemplary perseverance converted a city of comfortable homes for friendly people into effective cover for any troops that may see fit at any time to use the town for anti-German military proceedings. Thus is the Boche on the warpath mocked by the Demon of the Unintended, who has a glorious time of it when the drums begin to beat. Everything is arranged at the front with military precision and order; but nothing ever happens as it was arranged. Out of a hundred orders, ninetynine ended in "Wash out": the poetic formula which cancels. Even the visitor is soon shaken out of his civilian routine of order and punctuality. In the morning the captain proposes: in the afternoon the general disposes: mostly by a very agreeable invitation which is joyfully treated as an order.

Ypres, then, delended and done in as to its hearths, its floors, its roofs, and its domestic amenities, still rears its walls undaunted to the sky, and still provokes the German artillery to "send over" and give an interest to a tour of its streets that was lacking in the happy season of the noonday carillon. An aeroplane flew across above me: a British aeroplane (as it happened, I did not see a single Boche in the air during my eight-day visit); and presently the sky about him flowered into puff-balls. He sailed on triumphantly; and I had an extraordinary lapse of patriotism, and indeed of decency; for when the puff-balls and the bang-bang of the aircraft guns stopped, apparently discouraged, I, forgetting that the warrior in the sky might easily be one of my own personal friends, demanded why the guns did not keep it up. It seemed to me intolerably perfunctory of them to give in so soon. It was explained to me that the guns would have to be relaid to bring them on a target that was travelling at a hundred miles an hour. As a person of my intelligence ought to have known this without having to be told, I was somewhat abashed, and also a little horrified on reflection by the discovery of myself in the character I have so often reprobated: that of a sportsman.

My guide took no interest in the artillery beyond enabling me to circumvent certain soldiers whose duty it was to keep people out of the more dangerous parts of the town, and insisting on full speed across the square and past the shattered tower and the twenty or thirty yards sample of facade that was once the Cloth Hall. He was a gigantic officer, an Irishman of the south, full of the historic interest of Ypres, apparently knowing every stone of it, and not giving a dump for the bombardment except as an additional chapter for his book on it. He took me up to a pinnacle and shewed me Ypres beneath me as if it were all the kingdoms of the earth. "Go flat on your face if anything comes over," he remarked. In my youth I had learnt, by sedulously imitating the pantaloons in the harlequinades, to drop flat on my face instantly and then produce the illusion of being picked up neatly by the slack of my trousers and set on my feet again. I had a wild hope that Brer Boche would send over something that would give me an excuse for exhibiting this accomplishment to my new friend. But nothing came over just then; and I left Ypres with my dignity unimpaired.

When our car had left the town far behind, and I took the collar-studs out of my ears and exchanged the helmet of Mambrino for a cloth cap, I found the world suddenly duller. From this I infer that Ypres and its orchestra had been rather exciting, though I had not noticed it at the time.

Of Arras, I will say little, except that in my opinion . . . the British bombardment of Dublin beat it hollow;[8] but I resisted the temptation to say this just then. . . . The cathedral, a copy of a copy, looked better as a ruin than when it was intact. The Town Hall, like the Cloth Hall of Ypres, is now only a subject of gentle regret; and the houses round it are a sample of what might have happened to the whole town if the Boches had thought it worth some more ammunition. . . . Those who have seen the Somme front hardly notice the damage. A gas alert was conspicuously announced; but nothing in that line happened, except that I talked a great deal to Mr Special Correspondent Tomlinson, who came round with me.

From St Eloi, Philip Gibbs and I surveyed the battlefields of the Vimy ridge. It was a landscape like any other landscape. The silence of the cold winter evening after sunset was threatened rather than broken by the booming of the guns that never cease now in this devoted countryside. A solitary shell burst in Neuville St Vaast. Gibbs, a man of a fine Irvingesque melancholy, seemed to meditate on the Ruins of Empires, but was probably reflecting on the chances of our being frozen during the journey back to our quarters. We were. The Poles have no terrors for me now. But my spirits always rise as the thermometer falls below freezing. Snow is beautiful to me; I hate mud, of which I did not encounter a single gob. . . .

The Somme front in the snow and brilliant sunshine was magnificent. The irony of the signposts was immense. "To Maurepas"; and there was no Maurepas. "To Contalmaison"; and there was no Contalmaison. "To Pozières"; and there was no Pozières. I went to the windmill of Pozières, and saw a little mound on which the windmill may have stood. Trones Wood was a cocoanut shy with no cocoanuts on the sticks: our guns had scooped what the enemy guns had left. On the road to Ypres the trees had stood, an unbroken Old Guard lining the road, with hardly a gap in their ranks. But here! With every limb shot to bits, beheaded, halved, cut off at the shins or torn out of the earth and flung prostrate, these woods seemed to scud with bare poles or broken jury-masts before the wind as our car passed, all their rigging blown and shot away. Of houses, except in one strangely-spared place, not a trace. And I knew from what I had seen in Ypres that this meant that almost every square yard of brick had received a separate smashing hit. As to the ground, you cannot find enough flat earth in a square mile to play marbles on. The moon seen through a telescope, or a slice of Gruyère cheese, is a tennis lawn by comparison. From the small pit made by the funny little Stokes gun that spits out shells as fast as you drop them in, to the dew-pond made by the medium trench mortar, culminating in the incredible crater made by the subterranean mine, the land is humped and hollowed continuously everywhere. Such ploughing and harrowing was never seen before on earth. . . .

I spent a week in the survey of all this ruin, with the booming and whizzing of its unresting progress continually in my ears. And I am bound to state plainly, as a simple fact to be exploited by devils or angels, according to its true nature, that I enjoyed myself enormously and continuously, in spite of exposures and temperatures that finally gave me my first taste of frostbite.

. . . The Commander-in-Chief, with whom I spent a very pleasant afternoon, was good enough to take me to witness a series of experiments with certain terrifying methods of destruction. . . . I did not ask Sir Douglas Haig or Sir Henry Rawlinson whether they sympathized with Quaker Stephen Hobhouse or with fire-eating Admiral Fisher: not because it would have been indiscreet—for they put me extremely at my ease by their frankness and hospitality—but because it did not matter.

The Commander-in-Chief had taken me with him to see a great display of the latest contrivances in flame projection, incendiary showers of thermite, and poison gas discharge. The thermite shower was produced by firing from Stokes guns a cloud of shells packed with it. I was standing with Haig amid an imposing group of officers on a highway, beside which the ground dropped straight down to an emplacement seven or eight feet below, on which were ranged the Stokes guns; so that they were right under our noses. Their first volley was a wonder of pyrotechny: it produced a vast curtain of white incandescence of dazzling brilliancy, and—at least so we were assured—of such incredibly high temperature that hell itself would have shrivelled up in it. This sounded impressive; but the older officers were contemptuous, declaring that the stuff cooled so suddenly that you could pick it up when it touched ground and put it in your pocket "like a fourpenny bit" (a coin I had not seen since early childhood) with perfect impunity. Nevertheless the military love of display insisted on a second volley; and this time one of the guns immediately beneath us, instead of hurling its fiery shell joyously into the skies, gave a sickly cough and tossed it about twenty feet up, from which eminence it began returning to the toes of the gunner, where it seemed inevitable that it must explode and consume us all like stubble.

Now on the evidence of my own senses I am prepared to swear that neither I nor any of that dignified group of commanding officers budged an inch. Our *tenue* was splendidly undisturbed: the example we set of heroic imperturbability in danger was perfect. Only, I noticed that we were now all at the other side of the road. On the evidence of that fact we must have scuttled like rabbits. On the evidence of my own consciousness I had not flinched; and the others certainly looked as if they had stood like statues. Fortunately the shell had not exploded: it was a dud. I can only hope that I did not head the retreat.

The flame projection was very horrible: the contents of a huge array of barrels of kerosene swept through a half circle of about eighty feet radius, devouring everything there in an ugly stinking rush of smoke and murky fire. But as it must have taken at least twenty-four hours to build up the contrivance, which was a clumsy affair after all, I privately concluded that it was neither practicable in the face of an active enemy nor worthwhile. The portable flame throwers, about which recent German experiments had made Haig anxious, were obviously first attempts, hopeless except as instruments for self-cremation. Even the poison gas shewed its most obvious limitation when an officer came up to Haig and apologized for having exhibited only two clouds of it (they were white and visible) his excuse being that any more would be a little hard on the two friendly villages towards which they were drifting.

The danger of these infernal machines is real and appalling enough; but it cannot seek its foe as a man does. At Ypres, when the gas scattered one regiment, and its victims lined the road, coughing their lungs out in torment, another regiment, undaunted by the spectacle, went right through them up towards the gas and carried on. No doubt these miracles can be explained; but they certainly occur; and the moral is, do not be in a hurry to bid the devil good morning. Life is very uncertain at the front; but so is death. The inevitable does not always come off.

I enjoyed my tour of the Flanders front all the more because modern war is so appallingly tedious that a person of any conversational powers (and I am an incorrigible talker) is more welcome than he could ever be anywhere else. I talked and talked and talked until poor Montague, in whose charge I was, must have learnt all my conversational stunts by heart. But his patience was inexhaustible. When I would apologize after repeating the very same string of sallies and pseudo-impromptus and stories and dicta on the war at the fourth or fifth mess table he would assure me affectionately that it always sounded fresh. I did not come across any of the drunken foulmouthed colonels who figure in recent war books; and I doubt if any such men could have imposed on me by a mask of company manners. I took away a favorable impression of the colonels who entertained me. As to my intercourse with the high command, I thought it would be limited to lunching with Haig and accompanying him on the afternoon expedition to the pyrotechnic display; but he insisted on my seeing Rawlinson,[9] with whom I had a long talk on the following day.

I was aware that scrupulous discretion would be necessary in dealing with anything they might say to me, and that it was therefore possible that they might say very little, and that little of the most banal kind. But they put no apparent restraint on their war-intensified communicativeness. Though they must have known, if they had bothered to think about it, that no censorship could muzzle me effectively, they talked with a freedom reckless enough to make it impossible for me to report a single word of their conversation. Haig, surfeited with illustrious visitors, was interested only in Mr Ben

Tillett,[10] whom he had found the best company of them all. He was clearly uneasy about the influence of Lord Northcliffe, one of whose correspondents . . . had in an article given away the position of an English battery. The Germans promptly wiped it out; yet Haig had not been able to get rid of him. Northcliffe's latest feat at that moment had been the shelving of Kitchener;[11] and when I said that however necessary that operation may have been it was appalling that it should have been in the power of an irresponsible commercial adventurer like Northcliffe, and of Northcliffe alone, to perform it, Haig did not demur.

He seemed to me a first rate specimen of the British gentleman and conscientiously studious soldier, trained socially and professionally to behave and work in a groove from which nothing could move him, disconcerted and distressed by novelties and incredulous as to their military value, but always steadied by a well-closed mind and an unquestioned code. Subject to these limitations he was, I should say, a man of chivalrous and scrupulous character. He made me feel that the war would last thirty years, and that he would carry it on irreproachably until he was superannuated.

Rawlinson, whom he evidently cherished, was as unlike him as it is possible for one British officer to be unlike another. Rawlinson's mind, as far as it went (and it was quite a lively one), was open and unstiffened. He was frank; his manners were his own; and he had no academic illusions about the situation, which was not then a very rosy one; for the recent Somme offensive had come to nothing but a very superfluous demonstration of the homicidal uselessness of sending waves of infantry to attack barbed wire defended by machine guns, even after the costliest bombardments and minings.

In the active sectors I saw no officers whom I could guess as incompetent: no doubt they had been weeded out by that time. At the training camp at Etaples I had momentary glimpses of elderly dug-outs hurrying round with an earnest sense of their duty to their country, easily mistaken by the looker-on for mere self-importance. Their chief occupation seemed to be to present themselves urgently at the staff offices for interviews with the chiefs, and to be put off on all sorts of pretexts by agreeable subalterns. They meant well, and sincerely believed they were helping to win the war; but from that point of view they had better have stayed at home. At Etaples I saw, too, the sergeants instructing circles of recruits in the use of the bayonet, with comments intended to inspire them with blood lust, but more effective in maintaining a grinning good humor among the novices, many of whom, in civilian dress and spectacled, imparted a bank holiday air to the proceedings. I was taken through a trench in which a tear shell had been exploded, and came out weeping profusely. But there was no thrill about Etaples, or indeed in any place out of earshot of the guns.

I overstayed my permit to spend a day with Sir Almroth Wright[12] at Wimereux and in Boulogne, where in the hospital wounded men were being operated on in all sorts of odd corners, and those who had been attended to and were safe in bed seemed so glad to be there and not in the trenches that nothing that the operating surgeons could do could dispel the general cheerfulness. Wright was, as usual, extraordinarily interesting; but when I congratulated him on the success of his famous saline treatment of wounds he opened my eyes by a single opening of his own to the folly of supposing that the wholesale butcheries of war leave time for delicately scientific novelties in surgery. . . .

At night at Robert Loraine's flying camp, which seemed to me an obvious and completely exposed mark for the German aces, passed in perfect peace. . . . At that station the commanding officer, in pointing out to me an alarum horn which meant "Huns!" accidentally touched the button and sounded it. Before he could explain that it was a false alarm a knight errant sprang into the air and spent the next hour searching for an imaginary foeman. For the credit of one of my own profession let me add that this commanding officer was a famous actor.[13] That he handled a flying squadron without effort was easy for me to understand. To a man who has produced a modern comedy, a campaign is child's play.

My professional instincts were all against an actor of Robert's mark being a crude real colonel running real risks and receiving real wounds instead of artistically simulated ones. I needed him for something more important. I missed my boat next morning, purposely as he thought, but really because the excitement and novelty of a journey to a fighting section made it seem less than quarter of its real distance and duration: it was always ten miles there and thirty or forty back.

When I was home again and had presented my trench boots to a clergyman, I had to consider how to fill a dozen columns of The Daily Chronicle with an account of my experiences which would tell the enemy nothing that he did not know already better than I, and that would help the general reader, by this time badly discouraged by the duration of the war and the absence of any prospect of its ending, to stick it. The appallingly slaughterous British offensives that just stopped short of getting there; the bombarded coast towns about which our authorities lied so heroically; the holocausts of British youth sacrificed in holding the ground for French offensives that never came off; the air raided cities and torpedoed ships; the Red Cross vans with their loads of mutilated men; the "combing out" of the civilians as the need for more cannon fodder made the medical examinations for fitness less and less fastidious and the tribunals more and more inflexible: above all, the reaction of unreasoning patriotic enthusiasm into equally unreasoning disillusion: all this could easily have been exploited to rub in Pacifist and anti-Imperialist morals, or conversely, to harden the public temper in the opposite direction. Neither of these opportunities appealed to me.

What I actually said can be ascertained from . . . the text of my three articles [in *The Daily Chronicle*].[14] I may add that I did my own censoring so effectually that only two objections were raised by the authorities. One led me to change a word which had a technical military sense with which I had been unacquainted. The other was a description of some German prisoners which suggested that they had been set to work. A change of another word or two got over that. The rest was unchallenged.

The following may serve as postscript. I cut it from the parliamentary report in The Times.

MR. BERNARD SHAW'S VISIT TO THE FRONT

(From The Times, 9th May 1917)

Replying to Major Hunt (Shropshire, Ludlow, U.), Mr Macpherson (Ross and Cromarty, L.) said 'It is the accepted policy to ask distinguished publicists and authors to visit our front. These invitations are issued by the Department of Information and General Headquarters. In accordance with this policy Mr George Bernard Shaw recently visited the British Front in France.'

Major Hunt asked whether the hon. member was aware

that Mr Bernard Shaw was the gentleman who advised British soldiers to shoot their officers, as reported in the San Francisco Bulletin of November 2, 1914, and whether he thought that this was the sort of man who ought to be allowed to go to the front.

Mr Macpherson. 'I was not aware of that particular fact; but I have always found that when any gentleman visits the front in France he comes back with an added desire to help the British Army and is proud of it.' (Cheers.)

Mr. Arnold White had already called the War Office to account for sending me out. He received the following reply.

War Office. Whitehall S.W. March 24.

Dear Sir,

I am directed to acknowledge the receipt of your letter of the 6th March 1917, and to inform you that the case has been investigated, and that nothing is known against this Officer.

I am, Sir, your obedient servant,

E. W. ENGLEHEART, S.C.

(For Lieutenant-General, Military Secretary).

9

Crash of an Epoch

THE WAR dragged on; and I sedulously assured everyone who discussed it with me that it would last thirty years; for the war of attrition, as it was called, attrited both sides impartially, the great offensives always petering out just before their consummation, and the momentary successes producing no more decisive result than the tediously protracted failures. In spite of my knowledge of the fact that Capitalism destroys the habit of self-support in nations so completely that when the necessity arises they do not know how to set about it, I could not believe that a region so vast and fertile as that covered by the central empire could be starved by blockade if, under the terrible pressure of war, its rulers organized its production effectively. As it proved, Capitalism had left Germany without knowledge of or belief in any other methods than capitalistic methods. Capitalistic bookkeeping is useless for vital as distinguished from commercial balance sheets; and in the end Germany and Austria had to surrender as being at the end of their resources when they were hardly at the beginning of them, as their plunderers soon found. In 1917, however, their artificial exhaustion was still a secret, even from most of their own people; and there seemed no reason to believe that if both sides cut their military coat according to their monetary cloth they could not prolong the game of Kilkenny cats for ever.

Suddenly came the cataclysm. It was the crash of an epoch. . . .

Reference to the parliamentary report quoted at the end of the preceding chapter will remind you that in Common Sense About the War I had said that if the soldiers had any sense they would go home and attend to their own affairs. There was nothing new enough in this to be very startling: it was only a variation on the theme of Carlyle's well-known apologue of Dumdrudge. The parliamentary questioner, narrowed by his patriotism, did not grasp its full scope: he thought I had confined my advice to British soldiers. At all events he expressed no objection to its application to enemy soldiers. With the general reader it had passed as a pious and wellworn commonplace, of no importance because there was no apparent possibility of its being acted on.

In 1917 the Russian soldiers acted on it. They went home. . . .

In 1918 the war collapsed. The German commanders informed the civil authorities, with regret, that effective military defence against the Allies was no longer practicable. The Kaiser withdrew into Holland, and instead of receiving a vote of thanks from Europe for that very sensible and considerate step was reviled for it, apparently because he had not rushed on the enemy sword in hand and perished gloriously, like Byron's vision of the Duke of Brunswick at Waterloo. From which it is clear that even four years of sanguinary disillusion had not quite cured our romantic civilians of enjoying the war as a cinema show.

I shewed less sense than the Kaiser; for in spite of the obvious fact that nobody was paying the slightest attention to my criticisms and proposals, I was still self-important enough to offer my views to the impending Versailles Conference in a *brochure* published in 1919. . . . This utterance of mine[1] had about as much effect on the proceedings at Versailles as the buzzing of a London fly has on the meditations of a whale in Baffin's Bay. . . . The extent to which the war had frightened us was shewn by the fact that the controversies it raised were much more furious after the Armistice than during the firing. The Treaty of Versailles, which was perhaps the greatest disaster of the war for all the belligerents, and indeed for civilization in general, left nothing to be done in foreign affairs but face the question of the next war. . . .

As for myself, why, it may be asked, did I not write two plays about the war instead of two pamphlets on it? The answer is significant. You cannot make war on war and on your neighbor at the same time. War cannot bear the terrible castigation of comedy, the ruthless light of laughter that glares on the stage. When men are heroically dying for their country, it is not the time to shew their lovers and wives and fathers and mothers how they are being sacrificed to the blunders of boobies, the cupidity of capitalists, the ambition of conquerors, the electioneering of demagogues, the Pharisaism of patriots, the lusts and lies and rancors and bloodthirsts that love war because it opens their prison doors, and sets them in the thrones of power and popularity. For unless these things are mercilessly exposed they will hide under the mantle of the ideals on the stage just as they do in real life.

And though there may be better things to reveal, it may not, and indeed cannot, be militarily expedient to reveal them whilst the issue is still in the balance. Truth telling is not compatible with the defence of the realm. . . . That is why comedy, though sorely tempted, had to be loyally silent; for the art of the dramatic poet knows no patriotism; recognizes no obligation but truth to natural history; cares not whether Germany or England perish; is ready to cry with Brynhild, *"Lass' uns verderben, lachend zu grunde geh'n"* sooner than deceive or be deceived; and thus becomes in time of war a greater military danger than poison, steel, or trinitrotoluene. That is why I had to withhold Heartbreak House from the footlights during the war; for the Germans might on any night have turned the last act from play into earnest,[2] and even then might not have waited for their cues.

Heartbreak House is not merely the name of the play. . . . It is cultured, leisured Europe before the war. When the play was begun not a shot had been fired;[3] and only the professional diplomats and the very few amateurs whose hobby is foreign policy even knew that the guns were loaded. A Russian playwright, Tchekov, had produced four fascinating dramatic studies of Heartbreak House, of which three, The Cherry Orchard, Uncle Vanya, and The Seagull, had been performed in England. Tolstoy, in his Fruits of Enlightenment, had shewn us through it in his most ferociously contemptuous manner. Tolstoy did not waste any sympathy on it: it was to him the house in which Europe was stifling its soul; and he knew that our utter enervation and futilization in that overheated drawing-room atmosphere was delivering the world over to the control of ignorant and soulless cunning and energy, with the frightful consequences which have now overtaken it. . . . Tchekov, more of a fatalist, had no faith in these charming people extricating themselves. They would, he thought, be sold up and sent adrift by the bailiffs; therefore he had no scruple in exploiting and even flattering their charm.

Tchekov's plays, being less lucrative than swings and roundabouts, got no further in England, where theatres are only ordinary commercial affairs, than a couple of performances by the Stage Society. We stared and said, "How Russian!" They did not strike me in that way. Just as Ibsen's intensely Norwegian plays exactly fitted every middle and professional class suburb in Europe, these intensely Russian plays fitted all the country houses in Europe in which the pleasures of music, art, literature, and the theatre had supplanted hunting, shooting, fishing, flirting, eating, and drinking. The same nice people, the same utter futility. The nice people could read; some of them could write; and they were the only repositories of culture who had social opportunities of contact with our politicians, administrators, and newspaper proprietors, or any chance of sharing or influencing their activities. But they shrank from that contact. They hated politics. They did not wish to realize Utopia for the common people: they wished to realize their favorite fictions and poems in their own lives; and, when they could, they lived without scruple on income which they did nothing to earn. . . .

The alternative to Heartbreak House was Horseback Hall, consisting of a prison for horses and with an annex for the ladies and gentlemen who rode them, hunted them, talked about them, bought them and sold them, and gave nine tenths of their lives to them, dividing the other tenth between charity, churchgoing (as a substitute for religion), and conservative electioneering (as a substitute for politics). It is true that the two establishments got mixed at the edges. Exiles from the library, the music room, and the picture gallery would be found languishing among the stables, miserably discontented; and hardy horsewomen who slept at the first chord of Schumann were born, horribly misplaced, into the garden of Klingsor; but sometimes one came upon horsebreakers and heartbreakers who could make the best of both worlds. As a rule, however, the two were apart and knew little of one another. . . .

Heartbreak House was quite familiar with revolutionary ideas on paper. It aimed at being advanced and freethinking, and hardly ever went to church or kept the Sabbath except by a little extra fun at week-ends. When you spent a Friday to Tuesday in it you found on the shelf in your bedroom not only the books of poets and novelists, but of revolutionary biologists and even economists. Without at least a few plays by myself and Mr Granville-Barker, and a few stories by

Mr H. G. Wells, Mr Arnold Bennett, and Mr John Galsworthy, the house would have been out of the movement. You would find Blake among the poets, and beside him Bergson, Butler, Scott Haldane, the poems of Meredith and Thomas Hardy, and, generally speaking, all the literary implements for forming the mind of the perfect modern Socialist and Creative Evolutionist. It was a curious experience to spend Sunday in dipping into these books, and on Monday morning to read in the daily paper that the country had just been brought to the verge of anarchy because a new Home Secretary or chief of police, with an idea in his head that his great-grandmother might not have had to apologize for, had refused to "recognize" some powerful trade union, just as a gondola might refuse to recognize a 20,000-ton liner.

In short, power and culture were in separate compartments. The barbarians were not only literally in the saddle, but on the front bench in the House of Commons, with nobody to correct their incredible ignorance of modern thought and political science but upstarts from the countinghouse, who had spent their lives furnishing their pockets instead of their minds. Both, however, were practised in dealing with money and with men, as far as acquiring the one and exploiting the other went; and although this is as undesirable an expertness as that of the medieval robber baron, it qualifies men to keep an estate or a business going in its old routine without necessarily understanding it, just as Bond Street tradesmen and domestic servants keep fashionable society going without any instruction in sociology. . . .

The Heartbreak people neither could nor would do anything of the sort. With their heads as full of the Anticipations[4] of Mr H. G. Wells as the heads of our actual rulers were empty even of the anticipations of Erasmus or Sir Thomas More, they refused the drudgery of politics, and would have made a very poor job of it if they had changed their minds. Not that they would have been allowed to meddle anyhow, as only through the accident of being a hereditary peer can anyone in these days of Votes for Everybody get into parliament if handicapped by a serious modern cultural equipment; but if they had, their habit of living in a vacuum would have left them helpless and ineffective in public affairs. Even in private life they were often helpless wasters of their inheritance, like the people in Tchekov's Cherry Orchard. Even those who lived within their incomes were really kept going by their solicitors and agents, being unable to manage an estate or run a business without continual prompting from those who have to learn how to do such things or starve. . . . Nature gave us a very long credit; and we abused it to the utmost. But when she struck at last she struck with a vengeance. For four years she smote our firstborn and heaped on us plagues of which Egypt never dreamed. They were all as preventible as the great Plague of London. . . .

It is difficult to say whether indifference and neglect are worse than false doctrine; but Heartbreak House and Horseback Hall unfortunately suffered from both. . . . Heartbreak House, in short, did not know how to live, at which point all that was left to it was the boast that at least it knew how to die: a melancholy accomplishment which the outbreak of war presently gave it practically unlimited opportunities of displaying. Thus were the firstborn of Heartbreak House smitten; and the young, the innocent, the hopeful expiated the folly and worthlessness of their elders.

The mess made of Europe by the Treaty of Versailles was kept in countenance by the mess made of our home affairs the moment the strain on us was relaxed by the Armistice. It is impossible to contemplate it without being tempted to declare that only under fire will Englishmen listen to reason or think of anything outside their immediate profits and pleasures. Such a remark is invidious only in view of the fact that the other belligerents did no better, except in Italy and Russia, where the disbanded soldiers destroyed the existing forms of government. Currency inflation, which raged throughout the continent, was comparatively mild with us: prices at worst only doubled. In Germany they soared to such astronomical altitudes that commerce finally had to be conducted with American dollars, a practical alternative which forced the German government, and indeed all the bankrupt Governments, to stabilize their currencies on pain of having them superseded by American gold. The Germans boldly and sensibly stabilized. . . . I remember Germany owed me about 200,000 marks, and paid me handsomely with a note for a million marks, worth a few pence as a museum curiosity. Mr Lloyd George called this "making Germany pay"; but as a matter of fact the German government, by the trick of inflation, made me pay.

10

Burglars

THE BURGLAR in . . . Heartbreak House, who makes his living by breaking into people's houses, and then blackmailing them by threatening to give himself up to the police and put them to the expense and discomfort of attending his trial and giving evidence after enduring all the worry of the police enquiries, is not a joke: he is a comic dramatization of a process that is going on every day. As to the black sheep of respectable families who blackmail them by offering them the alternative of making good their thefts and frauds, even to the extent of honoring their forged cheques, or having the family name disgraced, ask any experienced family solicitor.

I blush when I recall the shifts by which I succeeded in shirking jury service until I was superannuated, my best excuse being that our way of dealing with criminals by retributive punishment and deterrent example is in my opinion so wrong that I should be impossible as a juryman. . . . Besides the chances of not being prosecuted, there are the chances of acquittal; but I doubt whether they count for much except with very attractive women. Still, it is worth mentioning that juries will snatch at the flimsiest pretexts for refusing to send people who engage their sympathy to the gallows or to penal servitude, even on evidence of murder or theft which would make short work of a repulsive person.

Take my own experience as probably common enough. Fifty years ago a friend of mine, hearing that a legacy had been left him, lent himself the expected sum out of his employers' cash; concealed the defalcation by falsifying his accounts; and was detected before he could repay. His employers angrily resented the fraud, and had certainly no desire to spare him. But a public exposure of the affair would have involved shock to their clients' sense of security, loss of time and consequently of money, an end to all hope of his ever making good the loss, and the unpleasantness of attendance in court at the trial. All this put any recourse to the police out of the question; and my friend obtained another post after a very brief interval during which he supported himself as a church organist. This, by the way, was a quite desirable conclusion, as he was for all ordinary practical purposes a sufficiently honest man. It would have been pure mischief to make him a criminal; but that is not the present point. He serves here as an illustration of the fact that our criminal law, far from inviting prosecution, attaches serious losses and inconveniences to it.

It may be said that whatever the losses and inconveniences may be, it is a public duty to prosecute. But is it? Is it not a Christian duty not to prosecute? A man stole £500 from me by a trick. He speculated in my character with subtlety and success; and yet he ran risks of detection which no quite sensible man would have ventured on. It was assumed that I would resort to the police. I asked why. The answer was that he should be punished to deter others from similar crimes. I naturally said, "You have been punishing people cruelly for more than a century for this kind of fraud; and the result is that I am robbed of £500. Evidently your deterrence does not deter. What it does is to torment the swindler for years, and then throw him back upon society, a worse man in every respect, with no other employment open to him except that of fresh swindling. Besides, your elaborate arrangements to deter me from prosecuting are convincing and effective. I could earn £500 by useful work in the time it would take me to prosecute this man vindictively and worse than uselessly. So I wish him joy of his booty, and invite him to swindle me again if he can." Now this was not sentimentality. I am not a bit fonder of being swindled than other people; and if society would treat swindlers properly I should denounce them without the slightest remorse, and not grudge a reasonable expenditure of time and energy in the business. But to throw good money after bad in setting to work a wicked and mischievous routine of evil would be to stamp myself as a worse man than the swindler, who earned the money more energetically, and appropriated it no more unjustly, if less legally, than I earn and appropriate my dividends.

I must however warn our thieves that I can promise them no immunity from police pursuit if they rob me. Some time after the operation just recorded, an uninvited guest came to a luncheon party in my house. He (or she) got away with an overcoat and a pocketful of my wife's best table silver. But instead of selecting my overcoat, he took the best overcoat, which was that of one of my guests. My guest was insured against theft; the insurance company had to buy him a new overcoat; and the matter thus passed out of my hands into those of the police. But the result, as far as the thief was concerned, was the same. He was not captured; and he had the social satisfaction of providing employment for others in converting into a strongly fortified obstacle the flimsy gate through which he had effected an entrance, thereby giving my flat the appearance of a private madhouse.[1]

On another occasion a drunken woman obtained admission by presenting an authentic letter from a soft-hearted member of the House of Lords. I had no guests at the moment; and as she, too, wanted an overcoat, she took mine, and actually interviewed me with it most perfunctorily concealed under her jacket. When I called her attention to it she handed it back to me effusively; begged me to shake hands with her; and went her way.

Now these things occur by the dozen every day, in spite of the severity with which they are punished when the thief is dealt with by the police. I daresay all my readers, if not too young to have completed a representative experience, could add two or three similar stories. What do they go to prove? Just that detection is so uncertain that its consequences have no really effective deterrence for the potential offender, whilst the unpleasant and expensive consequences of prosecution, being absolutely certain, have a very strong deterrent effect indeed on the prosecutor. In short, all the hideous cruelty practised by us for the sake of deterrence is wasted: we are damning our souls at great expense and trouble for nothing.

When I was a boy in my teens in Dublin I was asked by an acquaintance of mine who was clerk to a Crown Solicitor, and had business in prisons, whether I would like to go through Mountjoy Prison, much as he might have asked me whether I would like to go through the Mint, or the cellars at the docks. I accepted the invitation with my head full of dungeons and chains and straw pallets and stage gaolers:

in short, of the last acts of Il Trovatore and Gounod's Faust, and of the Tower of London in Richard III. I expected the warders to look like murderers, and the murderers like heroes. At least I suppose I did, because what struck me most was that the place was as bright and clean as whitewash and scrubbing and polish could make it, with all the warders looking thoroughly respectable, and all the prisoners ruffianly and degenerate, except one tall delicate figure tramping round in the exercise ring, a Lifer by the color of his cap, who had chopped up his family with a hatchet, and been recommended to mercy on account of his youth. I thought, and still think, imprisonment for life a curious sort of mercy. My main impression of the others, and the one that has stuck longest and hardest, was that as it was evidently impossible to reform such men, it was useless to torture them, and dangerous to release them.

I have never been imprisoned myself; but in my first years as a public speaker I had to volunteer for prison martyrdom in two Free Speech conflicts with the police. As my luck would have it, on the first occasion the police capitulated on the eve of the day on which I had undertaken to address a prohibited meeting and refuse to pay a fine; and on the second a rival political organization put up a rival martyr, and, on a division, carried his election over my head, to my great relief.[2] These incidents are not very impressive now; but the fact that my acquaintance with the subject . . . began with the sight of an actual prison, and that twice afterwards I was for a week or so firmly convinced that I was about to spend at least a fortnight and possibly a month in the cells, gave me an interest in the subject less perfunctory than that of the ordinary citizen to whom prison is only a reference in the police news, denoting simply a place where dishonest and violent people are very properly locked up.

This comfortable ignorance, by the way, is quite commonly shared by judges. A Lord Chief Justice of England, grieved at hearing from a lady of social importance that her son had been sent to prison as a Conscientious Objector, told her that he hoped she would get to see him often, and keep up his spirits with frequent letters, and send him in nice things to eat. He was amazed to learn from her that he might just as well have suggested a motor ride every afternoon and a visit to the opera in the evening. He had been sentencing people all through his judicial career to terms of imprisonment, some of them for life, without knowing that it meant anything more than being confined to the house and wearing a dress with broad arrows all over it. No doubt he thought, quite rightly, that such confinement was bad enough for anybody, however wicked.

I had no such illusions about prison life. My political activities often brought me into contact with men of high character and ability who had been victims of modern forms of persecution under the very elastic headings of treason, sedition, obstruction, blasphemy, offences against press laws, and so forth. I knew that Karl Marx had declared that British prisons were the cruellest in the world; and I thought it quite probable that he was right. I knew Prince Peter Kropotkin, who after personal experience of the most villainous convict prisons in Siberia and the best model prison in France, said that they were both so bad that the difference was not worth talking about. What with European "politicals" and amnestied Irish Fenians, those who, like myself, were in the way of meeting such people could hardly feel easy in their consciences about the established methods of handling criminals.

Also I was in occasional touch with certain efforts made by the now extinct Humanitarian League, and by a little Society called the Police and Public Vigilance Society, to call attention to the grievances of prisoners. The League dealt with punishments: the Society, which was really an agitation conducted by one devoted man with very slender means, the late James Timewell, tried to obtain redress for people who alleged that they had been the victims of petty frame-ups by the police. But the witnesses on whose testimony these two bodies had to proceed were mostly either helpless creatures who could not tell the truth or scoundrels who would not tell it. The helpless creatures told you what they wanted to believe themselves: the scoundrels told you what they wanted you to believe. . . . Neither the Humanitarian League nor Mr Timewell could rouse general public compunction with such testimony, or attract special subscriptions enough to enable them to conduct a serious investigation. And John Galsworthy had not then arisen to smite our consciences with such plays as The Silver Box and Justice.[3]

This situation was changed by the agitation for Votes for Women and the subsequent war of 1914–18, both of which threw into prison an unprecedented number of educated, critical, public-spirited, conscientious men and women who under ordinary circumstances would have learnt no more about prisons than larks learn about coal mines. They came out of prison unembittered by their personal sufferings: their grievance was the public grievance of the whole prison system and its intense irreligiousness. In prison they had been capable of observing critically what they saw; and out of prison they were able to describe it. The official whitewash of the Prison Commissioners could not impose on them. They and their friends had money enough to take an office and engage a secretarial staff, besides supplying some voluntary educated labor. They formed a committee with Lord Olivier as chairman, which investigated the condition of English prisons and incidentally read some interesting reports of American ones. Eventually they issued their report as a volume entitled English Prisons Today, edited by Stephen Hobhouse and Fenner Brockway, who had both been in prison during the war. I was a member of that committee. . . .

. . . My friends Sidney and Beatrice Webb were just then reinforcing the work of the committee by issuing the volume of their monumental history of English Local Government which deals with prisons. By . . . my preface[4] to their book I was able to secure . . . publicity for it. . . . However, the matter did not stop with the issue of Mr and Mrs Webb's Prisons Under Local Government. Fortunately, my preface to it attracted the attention of the Department of Christian Social Service of the National Council of the Protestant Episcopal Church in the United States. That body put it into general circulation in America.

Imprisonment as it exists today is a worse crime than any of those committed by its victims: for no single criminal can be as powerful for evil, or as unrestrained in its exercise, as an organized nation. Therefore, if any person is addressing himself to . . . this dreadful subject in the spirit of a philanthropist bent on reforming a necessary and beneficent public institution, I beg him to . . . go about some other business. It is just such reformers who have in the past made the neglect, oppression, corruption, and physical torture of the old common gaol the pretext for transforming it into that diabolical den of torment, mischief, and damnation, the modern model prison.

11

A Member by Baptism

SO FAR I have not been imprisoned, as poorer men have been in my time, for blasphemy or apostasy. I am not technically an apostate, as I have never been confirmed; and my godparents are dead. But having torn some of the Thirtynine Articles to rags, I should have been pilloried and had my ears cropped had I lived in the days of the British Inquisition called the Star Chamber. Nowadays nonconformity and agnosticism are far too powerful electorally for such persecution. But the Blasphemy Laws are still available and in use against obscure sceptics, whilst I suffer nothing worse than incessant attempts to convert me. All the religions and their sects, Christian or Moslem, Buddhist or Shinto, Jain or Jew, call me to repentance, and ask me for subscriptions. I am not so bigoted as to dismiss their experiences as the inventions of liars and the fancies of noodles. They are evidence like any other human evidence; and they force me to the conclusion that every grade of human intelligence can be civilized by providing it with a frame of reference peculiar to its mental capacity, and called a religion. . . . If I were asked to fill up an ordinary official form containing a column for my religion I should probably save the officials trouble by writing The Episcopal Church of Ireland, of which I am a member by baptism. . . .

When my affairs do not oblige me to be in London, I live in a little village of 130 scattered inhabitants.[1] It has a church and a rector. My own house was for a long time the rectory; and my tenancy of it endowed the church. When the churchwardens apply to me at the usual seasons I contribute; and when the hat goes for special expenses for repairs to the building, I pay my share of what may be necessary to keep it standing. I am on intimate terms with the Rector. I am, in short, a local pillar of the Church; and I visit it occasionally. But I have never attended a service there.

Whether from defect or excess of intellect, I cannot use the Church of England ritual either as spiritual food or to express and demonstrate my religion. The last time I tried it was when my mother died. She was not a Church of England ritualist; but she had no prejudices nor bigotries; and she would have agreed with me that when there was a chaplain attached to the crematorium, it would have been a little shabby to save his fee and consign her body to the fire without any ceremony at all. And so the Church of England burial service was read. But I found it morbid and heathenish. It was all wrong for my mother and wrong for me. . . .[2]

Our indifference to one another's deaths marked us as a remarkably unsentimental family. . . . [My sister] Lucy, away from home, was everybody's darling: she broke many hearts, but never her own. When she was middle-aged, she married: why, I cannot tell you. My best guess is that she liked her husband's family, who were pillars of the Irvingite Church and highly respectable solid people. Her mother-in-law had discovered that the pleasantest place to live is in bed, where she remained for fifteen years or so until she died. Lucy had always fought shy of the opportunities her good looks and her singing gave her of getting into feudal society: she knew that she had neither the money nor, as a professional singer, the social standing to be comfortable there, so she very wisely kept among people who looked up to her and petted her rather than those who looked down their noses at her. She had no use for the Shaw pretensions, nor for the country-gentility of her maternal stock. Yet she hated Bohemianism and was ashamed of it. Her bedridden mother-in-law saw what was the matter, and set herself to give Lucy the social training she bitterly needed; for my mother, herself tyrannically over-trained, left us all to train ourselves; and Lucy, who had always resented this, was greatly relieved when her new mother won her eternal gratitude by teaching her how to behave herself.

Lucy had literary faculty enough to have one or two stories, written in the style of Rhoda Broughton,[3] accepted by the old Family Herald. In middle life she perpetrated a book[4] of which one of her admirers, who happened to be a publisher, brought out an edition. It is supposed to be a series of letters addressed by an old woman to a young one, advising her as to her conduct in life. It was so cynical that it revolted my mother, and almost shocked even me.

Her husband was a little dumpling of an ex-insurance clerk whose pretty face seemed to be carved on a bladder of lard. His one ambition was to be a leading tenor in light opera. His clerkship in the colonies enabled him to save £50; and with this sum he bribed the manager of a touring light opera company to allow him to sing the principal tenor part for one night. After this, I suppose, they could not very well turn him into the street. He sang with difficulty; but still he could sing a bit; and his tastes made him quite at home in the theatre. He was addicted to gambling and to women. In the theatre he met Lucy and married her.[5] She soon got tired of him and banished him, resuming her way of living as a free spinster. This had gone on for some years when she learnt accidentally that at the time of her marriage he had been attached to another woman. In a burst of fury she came to me and said she must have a divorce. As she had already practically divorced him I suggested that the operation was superfluous; but she was determined to be legally rid of him; and he was quite willing to leave her petition undefended if all claims for alimony or damages were waived. Accordingly, the divorce went through; and Lucy resumed her spinster name.

Then came the Shavian touch. Later on he turned up again, lonely and at a loss for somewhere to spend his evenings. Lucy immediately tolerated him as a waif and stray, though as a husband she had found him unbearable. So he became her frequent visitor until he died, when his place was taken by his very capable brother, who was manager of one of London's monster multiple shops. Lucy survived them all without shedding a tear. Our parents had been dead a long time. I was the only immediate relative left; and I visited her only at very long intervals when we had some business to discuss. One afternoon, when her health was giving some special anxiety, I called at her house and found her in bed. When I had sat with her a little while she said: "I am dying."

I took her hand to encourage her and said, rather conventionally, "Oh no; you will be all right presently." We were silent then; and there was no sound except from somebody playing the piano in the nearest house (it was a fine evening and all the windows were open) until there was a very faint flutter in her throat. She was still holding my hand. Then her thumb straightened. She was dead.

The doctor came in presently; and, as I had to register the death, I asked him what cause of death he would put in the certificate, adding that I supposed it was tuberculosis, from which she had suffered for many years following an attack of pneumonia which had ended her stage career. He said no: her tuberculosis had been completely cured. I said, "What then?"

He replied: "Starvation." I remonstrated, assuring him that I had provided for her better than that. He then told me that since the 1914–18 war he had never been able to make her eat enough. During the air raids an anti-aircraft gun, planted just outside her garden, had broken all the windows and crockery in her house, and shellshocked her badly. They had taken her away to Devon, out of range of the German bombers; but she never recovered her appetite.

Not knowing her circle of friends I did not invite anyone to her cremation at Golders Green; . . . and she left a will in which she expressly barred any ritual. But there I found myself up against a religious need. When I found myself in the chapel of the crematorium surrounded by her friends, many of them suffering from a distress that needed some recognition and expression, I found that it was not possible to order the officials to dispose of the remains that still had my sister's shape as if they were a scuttleful of coals. I had to improvise a ceremony which was none the less a funeral ceremony because it consisted of an address by myself in my own words. . . . I delivered a funeral oration, and finished by reciting the dirge from Cymbeline because

> Fear no more the lightning-flash,
> Nor the all-dreaded thunder-stone

so nearly fitted what the doctor told me.[6]

. . . This was possible for me: I am a practised public speaker, and by profession an author. But of the relatives of those who die not one in a thousand could compose a suitable address, or dare utter it in public if he or she could. For the vast majority there must be a form of words provided and a professional speaker to utter them impressively. To bury without a word or gesture would be to them to bury "like a dog." How then could I possibly live in a village and refuse my share in the provision of a ceremony to my neighbours merely because the ceremony did not fit my own case, and I was able to supply one for myself? It would be the act not merely of a bigot, but of a curmudgeon.

Later still a friend of mine induced me to go to the nuptially famous London church of St George's, Hanover Square, to see him married. Here my feelings were quite decisive. I felt that I would live and die celibate rather than take part in such a ceremony and thereby seem to assent to its unwholesome and nonsensical comparison of my mating to the mystical union of Christ with the Church, and to that very disingenuous reference to St Paul by which the authors of the Prayer Book tried to make the best of what they evidently considered (as he did) a rather questionable business. I congratulated myself on having had the alternative of civil marriage open to me. . . .

The chapel may find its attitude of moral superiority to the theatre, and even to the public-house, hard to maintain, and may learn a little needed charity. We all need to be reminded of the need for temperance and toleration in religious emotion and in political emotion, as well as in sexual emotion. But . . . [do] not conclude that I want to close up all places of worship: on the contrary, I preach in them. I do not even clamour for the suppression of political party meetings, though nothing more foolish and demoralizing exists in England today. . . . I live and let live. As long as I am not compelled to attend revival meetings, or party meetings, or theatres at which the sexual emotions are ignored or reviled, I am prepared to tolerate them on reciprocal terms; for though I am unable to conceive any good coming to any human being as a set-off to their hysteria, their rancorous bigotry, and their dullness and falsehood, I know that those who like them are equally unable to conceive any good coming of the sort of assemblies I frequent; so I mind my own business. . . .

It may seem that between a Roman Catholic who believes devoutly in Confession and a modern freethinking scientist there can be neither sympathy nor co-operation. Yet there is no essential difference between Confession and modern psychotherapy. The post-Freudian psychoanalyst relieves his patient of the torments of guilt and shame by extracting a confession of their hidden cause. What else does the priest do in the confessional, though the result is called cure by one and absolution by the other? What I, a freethinker, call the Life Force, my pious neighbors call Divine Providence: in some respects a better name for it. Bread and wine are changed into living tissue by swallowing and digestion. If this is not transubstantiation what *is* transubstantiation? I have described the surprise of a Fabian lecturer on being asked to open a political meeting with [a] prayer. When I was invited to address the most important secular society in England I found that I had to supply the sermon in a ritual of hymns and lessons in all respects like a religious Sunday service except that the lessons were from Browning and the hymns were aspirations to "join the choir invisible." Later on, when I attended a church service in memory of my wife's sister, and was disposed to be moved by it, the lesson was the chapter from the Bible which describes how the Israelites in captivity were instructed by a deified Jonathan Wild[7] to steal the jewellry of the Egyptians before their flight into the desert. The Leicester atheists were in fact more pious than the Shropshire Anglicans.

Once, when I was a guest in a Manchester club, I was insulted by one of the members so offensively that I had to lecture him severely on his breach of club manners, and warn him that my host might complain to the Committee. What annoyed him was not my uncompromising refusal to accept Jehovah as a god, but that I had denied the omniscience and infallibility of Shakespear. On another occasion I was present at a meeting addressed by a gentleman who was devoting his life to combating the modern heresy that the earth is globular, and maintaining that it is flat. The debate that followed was quite the funniest I have ever attended. Opposition such as no atheist could have provoked assailed him; and he, having heard their arguments hundreds of times, played skittles with them, lashing the meeting into a spluttering fury as he answered easily what it considered unanswerable. When he was asked whether he had ever watched a ship through a telescope and seen it sink beneath the horizon he blandly inquired whether the questioner had ever used a telescope in this manner. Apparently nobody present except myself and the lecturer ever had. The lecturer went on, "I have myself witnessed this interesting illusion. My questioner, though he admits he has spoken from hearsay about the ship, has no doubt often stood on a railway bridge and seen the two parallel tracks converge and meet in the distance. May I ask him whether he believes that the two lines do actually converge and meet as they seem to him to do?"

Thereupon another questioner, boiling with rage, rose and shouted,

"Can you deny that if you start from Liverpool and keep travelling due west or east you will find yourself in Liverpool again?"

"Of course you do," said the lecturer, and traced a circle on the flat table top with his finger.

The next questioner, confident that he was cornering the lecturer this time, played his ace of trumps with, "In an eclipse the shadow of the eclipsing body is round: how do you account for that?"

"So is the shadow of a griddle, which is the flattest thing on earth," was the reply.

I joined in the debate to declare that the lecturer had answered and silenced all his opponents, who had only picked up and parroted a string of statements they had never thought out nor verified. I added, however, that having followed the lecturer's argument closely, I thought it led to the conclusion that the earth is in shape a cylinder.

For the rest of the week the Everymans showered comminatory letters on me, renouncing friendship with me, and demanding my expulsion from all societies of advanced thinkers and even of decent people. They assumed that I believed the earth to be flat, and concluded that this indicated not only gross ignorance of science, but abhorrent moral delinquency. It was evident that the writers would have seen me, if not burnt at the stake, at least imprisoned for a year, with entire satisfaction. I might have written the leading article in The Freethinker for twenty years without provoking a single abusive postcard. Mr Everyman is often as credulous and bigoted in his modern scientific scepticism as his grandfather was in his Evengelicalism.

I was present once at the induction of a rector into a Church of England living. Although I knew beforehand that the bishop would have to ask the postulant a question to which the answer would be a deliberate lie, known to be such to both of them, and was prepared to admit that they were both doing this under duress, having to do it or have their vocations closed to them, it was none the less shocking to see and hear it actually done. The best brain among our Church dignitaries has given it to us in writing that if the Thirtynine Articles (the subject of the lie) were taken seriously the Church would be staffed exclusively by fools, bigots, and liars. Until we have a Church and a Government righteous enough and strong enough to discard the Articles, rewrite the Prayer Book, and put the Bible in its proper place, we shall not get our civilization out of the murderous mess in which it is at present staggering. . . . The popular notion that one of the two must be all right and the other all wrong is what I call Soot-or-Whitewash reasoning: it is not reasoning at all, but thoughtless unobservant jumping at conclusions. Both our science and our religion are gravely wrong; but they are not all wrong; and it is our urgent business to purge them of their errors and get them both as right as possible. If we could get them entirely right the contradictions between them would disappear: we should have a religious science and a scientific religion in a single synthesis. Meanwhile we must do the best we can instead of running away from the conflict as we are cowardly enough to do at present.

Anthropomorphic Deism will remain for long as a workable hypothesis not only for children but for many adults. Prayer consoles, heals, builds the soul in us; and to enact a Prohibition of Prayer, as some Secularists would if they had the power, would be as futile as it would be cruel. But there are all sorts of prayers, from mere beggars' petitions and magic incantations to contemplative soul building, and all sorts of divinities to pray to. A schoolboy who witnessed a performance of my play Saint Joan told his schoolmaster that he disliked Jesus and could not pray to him, but that he could pray to Joan. An Ulster Orange schoolmaster would probably have given him an exemplary thrashing to make a proper young Protestant of him; but this schoolmaster was wiser: he told the boy to pray to Joan by all means: it is the prayer and not the prayee that matters. To the Franciscan, Francis and not Jesus is the redeemer; and to countless Catholics and not a few Anglicans Our Lady is the intercessor. To the Jains God is Unknowable; but their temple in Bombay is full of images of all sorts of saints, from nameless images of extraordinary beatific peace to crude elephant-headed idols. As a Protestant child I was taught that my Roman Catholic fellow countrymen would all go to hell because they said, "Hail, Mary!" At the same time my English contemporary Arthur Conan Doyle was being taught at Stonyhurst that I should be damned for not saying it. I have lived to see modern Germany discard "Hail, Mary!" and substitute "Heil, Hitler!"; and for the life of me I cannot bring myself to regard the change as an improvement. . . . Still, I think the Church of England wrong in imposing Jesus, whom many people dislike as my schoolboy devotee of Joan did, as the sole form in which God can be prayed to. Every Church should be a Church of All Saints, and every cathedral a place for pure contemplation by the greatest minds of all races, creeds, and colors.

12

Back to Methuselah

IF ANYONE had told me . . . that I should one day write a cycle of plays as far beyond all possibility of performance in the beaten way of trade as Wagner's Ring was in Germany in 1866, and that this theatrical monstrosity would be first performed, and promptly performed, in Birmingham, I should have marked off that prophet as the most extravagant lunatic in the world. But . . . when the childish follies of our statesmen culminated in the orgy of slaughter and destruction, death and damnation, which called itself the war to end war . . . , I wrote not only one play but a cycle of five[1] entitled Back To Methuselah. In this, six years before Pavlov's treatise on Conditioned Reflexes[2] was translated into English, I took up the subject of reflexes and carried it so far as to forecast a more highly evolved people amusing themselves in their childhood by manufacturing and playing with dolls who could spout romantic poetry and formulate Athanasian creeds, seeming to be as alive as our own statesmen, poets, politicians, and theologians when they were really only "shuddering through a series of reflexes." This was going farther than Weismann,[3] who was a reflexo-maniac, or than Pavlov dared; but as I worded it all in common vernacular speech, and set it in a framework of aggressively vitalist creative evolution, it missed fire in the laboratories.

. . . If Darwin had really led the world at one bound from the book of Genesis to Heredity, Modification of Species by Selection, and to Evolution, he would have been a philosopher and a prophet as well as an eminent professional naturalist, with geology as a hobby. The delusion that he had actually achieved this feat did no harm at first, because if people's views are sound, about evolution or anything else, it does not make two straws difference whether they call the revealer of their views Tom or Dick. . . . But they must not, like the cruder sectarian missionaries, shove all their doctrines, relevant or irrelevant, down the throats of their converts as the Truth. Let me illustrate. Suppose I am in an Irish village with growing peasant girls to convert. They grow up between gentle nuns and learned priests called holy fathers who offer them for their guidance faith in Our Lady of Good Counsel. She is "the Seat of Wisdom, the Bride of the Holy Ghost, the Mother of Fair Love and of Knowledge and of Holy Hope. Her beautiful soul reflects the image of the Most Holy Trinity as a crystal mirror, and no shadow of sin or imperfection has ever darkened her understanding. For thirty years she lived in closest intercourse with the Son of God made Man. She drank in every utterance of His, and kept all His words in her heart. She is therefore the perfect counsel for us in this vale of tears."

What sort of fool should I be if, blind and deaf to the beauty of this vision and its fitness to the childish mind and imagination of the growing maid, I were to crash in with denunciations of it as a romantic fiction, and insist on the substitution of the preface and postscript to my Back to Methuselah, with its postulate of a Life Force which makes terrible blunders like cancer, osteitis, and epilepsy, and lets loose upon us unsatisfactory old experiments like the tiger and the anaconda? Our Lady of Good Counsel could nurse her growing mind and make a good girl of her. Creative Evolution, mentally beyond her reach, could only destroy her faith in anything and make her behaviour incalculable and uncivilized. . . .

In writing Back to Methuselah I threw over all economic considerations, and faced the apparent impossibility of a performance during my lifetime. When a professional manager of whom I had never heard (though his name, by the way, was Barry Jackson, and he was already famous in the Midlands) approached me with a view to a performance, I asked him whether he had no regard for his wife and family. He replied that he was not married, and that he kept a theatre out of his private means as other similarly endowed plutocrats kept racehorses or steam yachts. In short, he was doing it to gratify his evolutionary appetite and could afford the cost. So I gave him my blessing and a performing licence; and he went ahead and produced the Methuselah cycle at his Birmingham Repertory Theatre,[4] where he had made theatrical history by many notable experiments and revivals while London was barely marking time. When I asked him what he had lost by the Methuselah adventure he said with every appearance of satisfaction, "Only £2500." Later on, when he repeated it in London and I repeated my question, he answered exultantly "I have not lost: I have made twenty pounds." The twenty pounds did not give him a dock laborer's wages for his trouble; but it left him none the poorer, and my conscience all the lighter. Clearly then, Back to Methuselah was not a commercial job: it came straight from the Life Force operating as an *élan vital* through myself and Barry Jackson. . . .

A classic author has to consider how far he dare go; for though he is writing for the enlightenment of mankind he may not be willing to venture as far as martyrdom for its sake. Descartes burnt one of his books to escape being burnt for having written it. Galileo had to deny what he believed to escape the same fate. The priests forced these alternatives on them not because they did not agree with them, but because they had to govern the people, and the people could be governed only by fictions and miracles, not by the latest steps in science. If the people will not obey their rulers unless they see the blood of St Januarius liquefy,[5] then the priests must work that miracle for them or let them run wild. As long as civilization seems to stand or fall with the belief that God stopped the movement of the sun in its orbit to oblige Joshua as casually as the driver of a tramcar stops his vehicle to pick up a passenger, popes and emperors must take care that no physicist is allowed to tell the mob that it is the earth that moves round the sun and not the sun round the earth, even when they are entirely convinced that the physicist is right. When I was a municipal councillor I had to connive at bogus miracles, pretending that tubs of soap and water were as magical as the cauldron of Macbeth's witches, because my constituents believed in magic, not in soap and sunshine. It is useless to parrot the old saying that the blood of the martyrs is the seed of the Church, and expect scientific heretics to die to advertize their heresies rather than recant to save their lives. Descartes, when he burnt his book, knew that its truths would inevitably be rediscovered and became familiar, and that this would only be retarded by his being burnt for publishing them. As for me I can write safely on the assumption that Galileo and Descartes knew much more about physics than Moses. . . .

. . . It is fairly safe for me personally to fill my books and plays with heresies and even be accepted as a world classic on the strength of them. . . . The moral of this is that heretical teaching must be made irresistibly attractive by fine art if the heretics are not to starve or burn. I have to make my heresies pleasing as plays to extract the necessary shillings from those to whom they are also intensely irritating. Back to Methuselah, having begun its stage career by extracting £2500 from the pocket of Sir Barry Jackson, presently enabled him to extract a surplus of £20 from the pockets of his audiences.

When I contributed my Utopia in a batch of plays entitled Back To Methuselah, in which mind reigned as irresistibly over muscle as Prospero over Caliban, I also had to . . . conceive a society in which the power of men to kill one another was . . . held in check . . .; but I could not be satisfied with an imaginary one, as that would have taken me no further towards possibility and credibility than the older Utopians. There is no real hope in impossible Utopias. I had to resort to a power which, as it exists and is in daily operation, can easily be conceived as capable of evolutionary intensification.

This power is called Awe. It enables a head master to control masses of schoolboys who could mob him and tear him to pieces as de Witt was torn by a Dutch mob in 1672[6] if they were not restrained by Awe. The statesman has to exploit it because he has to give authority not only to superior persons who naturally inspire it, but to ordinary Yahoos who can be made to produce an illusion of superiority by unusual robes, retinues and escorts, magnificent liveries and uniforms: in short, by making animated idols of them. Uniforms, vestments, robes, maces, diadems, retinues, pageants, processions, cannon salutes, and codes of etiquette are artificial Awe producers to give authority to persons who are not natural Awe producers.

The reaction against this factitious Awe has produced that Roundhead, the British Quaker, and the American diplomat who appears at court among costumed peers and royalties in coat and trousers instead of in breeches, swordless and plain Mister; but these iconoclasts are powerless against the genuine natural awe inspirer. I am as irreverent and even derisive as any sane thinker can be; but I can remember an occasion (I was over twenty at the time) on which I was so overawed by a Jewish rabbi that I could hardly speak to him. There was no reason for this: we had never met before, and had less than five minutes conversation on an ordinary matter of business which gave no occasion for embarrassment on either side of any sort; but he terrified me by some power in him, magnetic or mesmeric or hypnotic or whatever you like to call it, which reduced me to a subjection which I had never experienced before, and have never experienced since. I was simply discouraged by him. Since then my observation, and the stories I read about the dying-out of primitive tribes at the impact of civilized invaders, have convinced me that every living person has a magnetic field of greater or less intensity which enables those in whom it is strong to dominate those in whom it is relatively weak, or whose susceptibility to its influence, called shyness, is excessive. I have ranked this as a scientific fact in the fourth part of Back to Methuselah; [7] but it will not be accepted as such by the professional biologists until one of them has succeeded in making a guinea pig overawe a dog in a laboratory. Some day an intelligent biophysicist will perhaps find out how to measure this force as we now measure electricity. Meanwhile there is no denying that it exists and must be recognized and even exploited by every practical ruler.

In my Utopia I therefore fell back on Awe, both natural and artificial, as a means by which my Coming Race kept the Yahoos in subjection. And as age has to be naturally impressive so as to secure the necessary submission of children to their parents and guardians, I made my Coming Race exempt from natural death, in this following Weismann, who suggested that death is only Nature's remedy for overcrowding, and that men might be as immortal as amoebas if there were as much room for them on earth.

And so, without introducing any magic, I made it possible to accept a story in which by evolutionary development of purely natural forces wisdom had become awful to the extent of becoming lethal. For Awe operates through discouragement; and discouragement in the last degree is death.

Our villagers, contemplating the mischief and horror of the Four Years war in 1917, said, "Well, I suppose there must be a God; but what *is* He thinking of to let all this go on?" Not to admit that God can err, or that He is powerless in any particular, is to deprive Him of the attributes that qualify Him as God; but it is a very healthy admission for the strongminded. It increases our sense of responsibility for social welfare, and is radiant with boundless hopes of human betterment. Our will to live depends on hope; for we die of despair, or, as I have called it in the Methuselah cycle, discouragement. What damns Darwinian Natural Selection as a creed is that it takes hope out of evolution, and substitutes a paralysing fatalism which is utterly discouraging. As Butler put it, it "banishes Mind from the universe." The generation that felt nothing but exultant relief when it was delivered from the tyranny of an Almighty Busybody by a soulless Determinism has nearly passed away, leaving a vacuum which Nature abhors.

. . . It was a remark by Weismann that set me on the track of Methuselah. He suggested that death is a result of Natural Selection, not "natural" in the ordinary sense, lifetimes varying in duration from the immortality of the eternally splitting amoeba to the brief span of the drosophila fly. Immortality is natural, death only an artifice to make it bearable as a burden and get rid of its garments of flesh as they wear out. The legend of Methuselah is neither incredible nor unscientific. Life has lengthened considerably since I was born; and there is no reason why it should not lengthen ten times as much after my death.

This possibility came to me when history and experience had convinced me that the social problems raised by millionfold national populations are far beyond the political capacity attainable in three score and ten years of life by slow-growing mankind. On all hands as I write the cry is that our statesmen are too old, and that Leagues of Youth must be formed everywhere to save civilization from them. But despairing ancient pioneers tell me that the young are worse than the old; and the truth seems to be that our statesmen are not old enough for their jobs. Life is too short for the experience and development needed to change romantic schoolboys and golfing sportsmen, or even prematurely forced Quakers, into wise senators. . . .

Considering . . . that I have lived . . . longer than twice as long as Mozart or Mendelssohn, and that within my experience men and women, especially women, are younger at fifty than they were at thirty in the middle of the nineteenth century, it is impossible to resist at least a strong suspicion that the term of human life cannot be fixed at seventy years or indeed fixed at all. If we master the art of living instead of digging our graves with our teeth as we do at present we may conceivably reach a point at which the sole cause of death will be the fatal accident which is statistically inevitable if we live long enough. In short, it is not proved that there is such a thing as natural death; it is life that is natural and infinite.

How long, then, would it take us to mature into competent rulers of great modern States instead of, as at present, trying vainly to govern empires with the capacity of village headmen. In my Methuselah cycle I put it at three hundred years: a century of childhood and adolescence, a century of administration, and a century of oracular senatorism.

. . . Physically I am failing: my senses, my locomotive powers, my memory, are decaying at a rate which threatens to make a Struldbrug of me if I persist in living; yet my mind still feels capable of growth; for my curiosity is keener than ever. My soul goes marching on; and if the Life Force would give me a body as durable as my mind, and I knew better how to feed and lodge and dress and behave, I might begin a political career as a junior civil servant and evolve into a capable Cabinet minister in another hundred years or so.

I started as a biologist in 1906 by a lecture on Darwin, which was the basis of my preface to Methuselah nearly twenty years later.

Science was then neo-Darwinian, and still obsessed and blinded by the reaction against Fundamentalism. But it has slowly come round to my way—until the essays of Joseph Needham[8] (like me, the son of a musical mother) and in Alexis Carrel's[9] Man the Unknown and Maurice Ernest's The Longer Life,[10] my view has become orthodox and reached even the Rockefeller Foundation.

When Methuselah was new, its reviewers persisted in describing my immortals as surviving by a conscious exertion of the will to live. But in Methuselah the advocates of longer life all die; and the survivors find it just happening to them, to their own puzzlement and surprise, in spite of their incredulity. . . .

We are only just discovering that there is such a thing as wishful thinking; but the Creative Evolutionist knows that all thinking is wishful, and that we cannot think until our wishes or fears or cupidities or curiosities create what we call attention. I have known this since my childhood, when somebody shewed me that if I held up my two forefingers in a line from my eyes, I could see two of the nearest when I looked at the farthest, or vice versa, because I had on my two retinas two separate images of everything in sight except the thing I wanted to see. Yet I was conscious of them only when I co-ordinated them. Later on, when I threw over my childish belief in the infallibility of the Bible on discovering that much of it is obsolete or wicked, what struck me most was that the obsolescences and wickednesses had never been hidden from me: they had been staring me in the face all the time. I had simply not thought about them. There must have been an evolutionary growth in my mind which directed my attention to them. Attention is the first symptom of thought. John the Evangelist would have worded it so, had he been born a Victorian.

Civilization is at present an imposture; we are a crowd of savages on whom a code of makeshift regulations is forced by penalties for breaking them. They are never explained to us. When I was sent to school I was confronted by a new set of rules and made aware that if I broke them I should be punished. As no other reason for obeying them was given to me I concluded naturally that I could break them without the slightest loss of self-respect, and indeed with some pride in my independence and cleverness, as long as I was not found out. My hero in fiction was the rebel, not the goodygoody citizen, whom I despised. This attitude became a habit which I have never been able to shake off quite completely. . . .

. . . Civilization means stabilization; and creative evolution means change. As the two must operate together we must carefully define their spheres, and co-ordinate them instead of quarrelling and persecuting as we do at present. We must not stay as we are, doing always what was done last time, or we shall stick in the mud. Yet neither must we undertake a new world as catastrophic Utopians, and wreck our civilization in our hurry to mend it. . . . The history of modern thought now teaches us that when we are forced to give up the creeds by their childishness and their conflicts with science we must either embrace Creative Evolution or fall into the bottomless pit of an utterly discouraging pessimism. This happened in dateless antiquity to Ecclesiastes the preacher, and in our own era to Shakespear and Swift. "George Eliot" (Marian Evans) who, incredible as it now seems, was during my boyhood ranked in literature as England's greatest mind, was broken by the fatalism that ensued when she discarded God. In her most famous novel, Middlemarch, which I read in my teens and almost venerated, there is not a ray of hope: the characters have no more volition than billiard balls: they are moved only by circumstances and heredity. "As flies to wanton boys are we to the gods: they kill us from their sport," was Shakespear's anticipation of George Eliot. Had Swift seen men as creatures evolving towards godhead he would not have been discouraged into the absurdity of describing them as irredeemable Yahoos enslaved by a government of horses ruling them by sheer moral superiority. Even Ibsen, though his characters, like Shakespear's, reek with volition, perpetrated a tragedy called Ghosts, in which an omnipotent god is discarded for an inevitable syphilis. One of the masters of comedy among my playwright colleagues[11] drowned himself because he thought he was going his father's way like Oswald Alving. . . . Discouragement does in fact mean death; and it is better to cling to the hoariest of the savage old creator-idols, however diabolically vindictive, than to abandon all hope in a world of "angry apes," and perish in despair like Shakespear's Timon. Goethe rescued us from this horror with his "Eternal Feminine that draws us forward and upward" which was the first modern manifesto of the mysterious force in creative evolution.

That is what made Faust a world classic. If it does not do the same for this attempt of mine, throw the book into the fire; for Back to Methuselah is a world classic or it is nothing.

13

How to Write a Play

IT IS QUITE TRUE that my plays are all talk, just as Raphael's pictures are all paint, Michael Angelo's statues all marble, Beethoven's symphonies all noise. . . . It is never safe to take my plays at their suburban face value: it ends in your finding in them only what you bring to them, and so getting nothing for your money. . . .

Now a playwright's direct business is simply to provide the theatre with a play. When I write one with the additional attraction of providing the twentieth century with an up-to-date religion or the like, that luxury is thrown in gratuitously; and the play, simply as a play, is not necessarily either the better or the worse for it. What, then, is a play simply as a play?

Well, it is a lot of things. Life as we see it is so haphazard that it is only by picking out its key situations and arranging them in their significant order (which is never how they actually occur) that it can be made intelligible. The highbrowed dramatic poet wants to make it intelligible and sublime. The farce writer wants to make it funny. The melodrama merchants want to make it as exciting as some people find the police news. The pornographer wants to make it salacious. All interpreters of life in action, noble or ignoble, find their instrument in the theatre; and all the academic definitions of a play are variations of this basic function.

Yet there is one function hardly ever alluded to now, though it was made much too much of from Shakespear's time to the middle of the nineteenth century. As I write my plays it is continually in my mind and very much to my taste. This function is to provide an exhibition of the art of acting. A good play with bad parts is not an impossibility; but it is a monstrosity. A bad play with good parts will hold the stage and be kept alive by the actors for centuries after the obsolescence of its mentality would have condemned it to death without them. A great deal of the British Drama, from Shakespear to Bulwer Lytton, is as dead as mutton, and quite unbearable except when heroically acted; yet Othello and Richelieu can still draw hard money into the pay boxes; and The School for Scandal revives again and again with unabated vigor. Rosalind can always pull As You Like It through in spite of the sententious futility of the melancholy Jaques; and Millamant, impossible as she is, still produces the usual compliments to the wit and style of Congreve, who thought that syphilis and cuckoldry and concupiscent old women are things to be laughed at. An artistic presentment must not condescend to justify itself by a comparison with crude nature; and I prefer to admit that in this kind my *dramatis personae* are, as they should be, of the stage stagey, challenging the actor to act up to them or beyond them, if he can. The more heroic the overcharging, the better for the performance.

In dragging the reader thus for a moment behind the scenes, I am departing from a rule which I have hitherto imposed on myself so rigidly that I never permit myself, even in a stage direction, to let slip a word that could bludgeon the imagination of the reader by reminding him of the boards and the footlights and the sky borders and the rest of the theatrical scaffolding,[1] for which nevertheless I have to plan as carefully as if I were the head carpenter as well as the author. But even at the risk of talking shop, an honest playwright should take at least one opportunity of acknowledging that his art is not only limited by the art of the actor, but often stimulated and developed by it. No sane and skilled author writes plays that present impossibilities to the actor or to the stage engineer. If, as occasionally happens, he asks them to do things that they have never done before and cannot conceive as presentable or possible (as Wagner and Thomas Hardy have done, for example), it is always found that the difficulties are not really insuperable, the author having foreseen unsuspected possibilities both in the actor and in the audience, whose will-to-make-believe can perform the quaintest miracles. Thus may authors advance the arts of acting and of staging plays. But the actor also may enlarge the scope of the drama by displaying powers not previously discovered by the author. If the best available actors are only Horatios, the authors will have to

Shaw and Harley Granville Barker in 1901, at the beginning of their relationship.

Shaw in an informal pose by Coburn. (Photo courtesy George Eastman House)

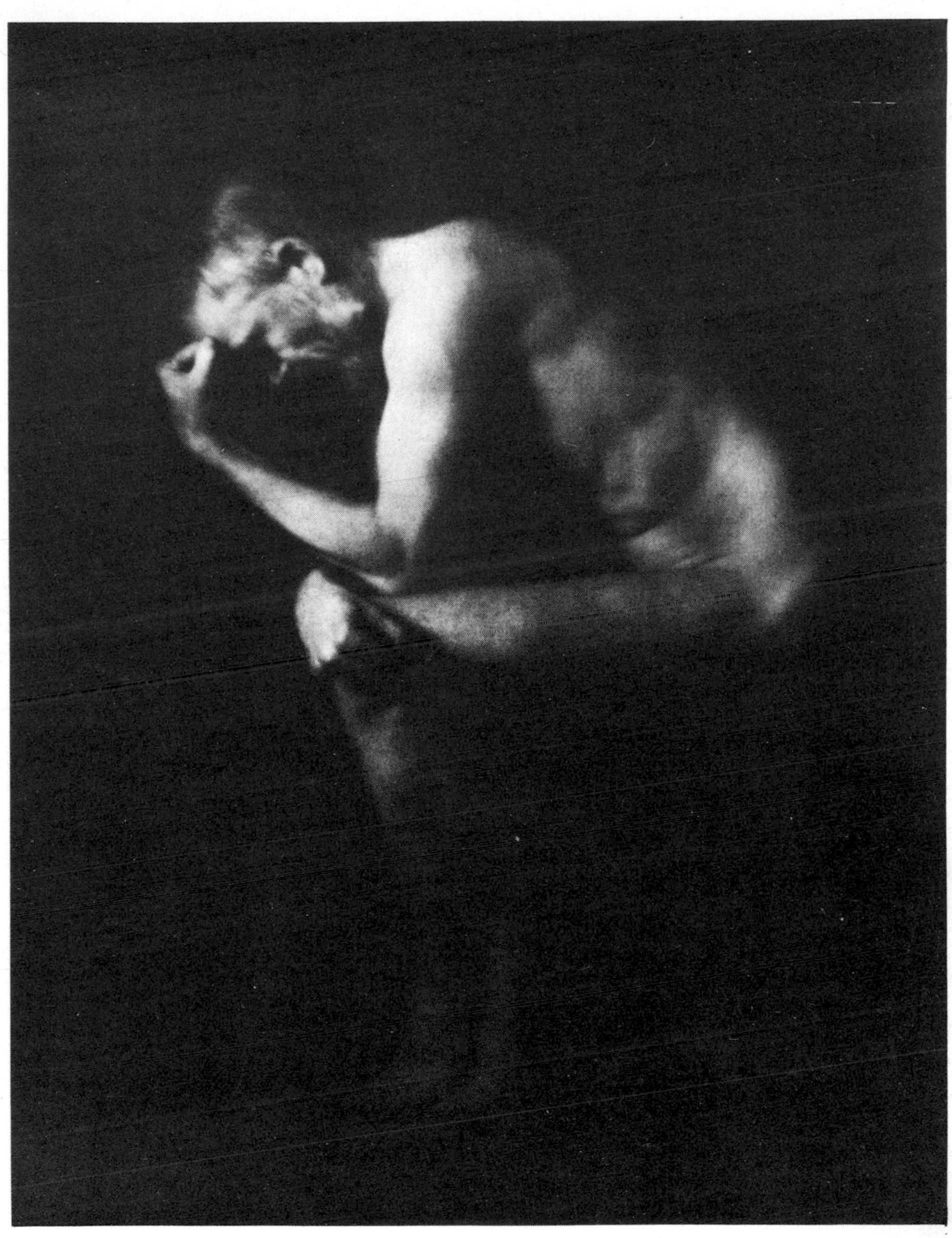

Shaw in 1906, in the nude, striking the famous Rodin pose. Exhibited by photographer Alvin Langdon Coburn as "Le Penseur." (Photo courtesy George Eastman House)

Shaw and H. G. Wells before the breakup of the Fabian alliance.
(Photo courtesy George Eastman House)

Four playwrights—James Barrie, John Galsworthy, Shaw and Barker—
photographed by Coburn in 1909. (Photo courtesy George Eastman House)

"Men of the Day" sketch by "Ruth" from *Vanity Fair,* December 28, 1905.

Shaw rehearsing Lillah McCarthy and Granville Barker in *Androcles* in 1913.
(Photo courtesy George Eastman House)

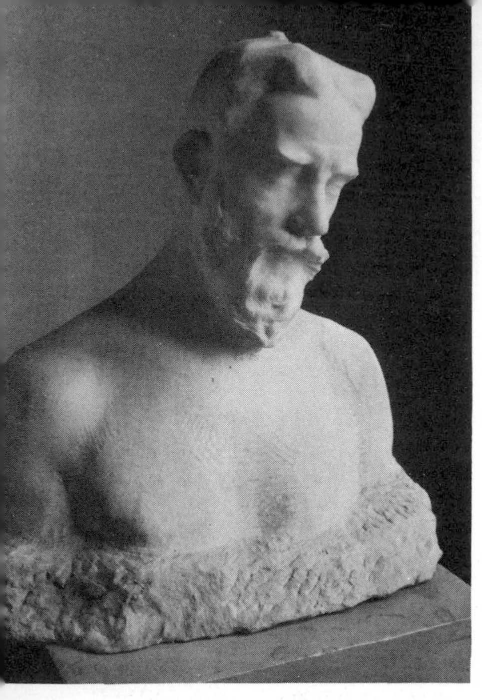

The Rodin bust of Shaw (1906), from the Musée Rodin, Paris — captioned by Shaw, "Plaster Saint." (© S.P.A.D.E.M. Paris)

Shaw addressing a crowd of dockyard men in an election campaign for Alderma Sanders. (Stephen Cribb, Southsea)

Shaw taking notes at rehearsal. (Collection of LaFayette Butler)

Interior of study at Shaw's Corner, Ayot St. Lawrence. (National Trust photograph)

Exterior of house at Shaw's Corner. (National Trust photograph)

A pre-World War I portrait photograph by Elliott and Fry.

The church clock strikes the second quarter.

HIGGINS [*hearing in it the voice of God, rebuking him for his Pharisaic want of charity to the poor girl*] A reminder. [*He raises his hat solemnly; then throws a handful of money into the basket and follows Pickering*].

THE FLOWER GIRL [*picking up a half-crown*] Ah-ow-ooh! [*Picking up a couple of florins*] Aaah-ow-ooh! [*Picking up several coins*] Aaaaaah-ow-ooh! [*Picking up a half-sovereign*] Aaaaaaaaaaaah-ow-ooh!!!

FREDDY [*springing out of a taxicab*] Got one at last. Hallo! [*To the girl*] Where are the two ladies that were here?

THE FLOWER GIRL. They walked to the bus when the rain stopped.

FREDDY. And left me with a cab on my hands! Damnation!

THE FLOWER GIRL [*with grandeur*] Never mind, young man. I'm going home in a taxi. [*She sails off to the cab. The driver puts his hand behind him and holds the door firmly shut against her. Quite understanding his mistrust, she shews him her handful of money*]. ~~Eightpence~~ [A taxi fare] aint no object to me, Charlie. [*He grins and opens the door*]. ~~Angel Court, Drury Lane, round the corner of Micklejohn's oil shop. Lets see how fast you can make her hop it.~~ ~~[*She gets in and pulls the door to with a slam as the taxicab starts*].~~

~~FREDDY. Well, I'm dashed!~~

Here. What about the basket?

THE TAXIMAN. Give it here. Tuppence extra.

ELIZA. No: I dont want nobody to see it. [*She crushes it into the cab and gets in, continuing the conversation through the window*] Goodbye, Freddy.

FREDDY [*dazedly raising his hat*] Goodbye

TAXIMAN. Where to?

ELIZA. Bucknam Pellis [*Buckingham Palace*].

TAXIMAN What d'ye mean — Bucknam Pellis?

ELIZA. Dont you know where it is? In the Green Park, where the King lives. Goodbye, Freddy. Dont let me keep you standing there. Goodbye.

FREDDY. Goodbye. [*He goes*].

TAXIMAN. Here. Whats this about Bucknam Pellis? What business have you at Bucknam Pellis?

ELIZA. Of course I havnt none. But I wasnt going to let him know that. You drive me home

TAXIMAN. And wheres home?

ELIZA. Angel Court, Drury Lane, next Meiklejohn's oil shop.

TAXIMAN. That sounds more like it, Judy. [*He drives off*].

Shaw's alterations to *Pygmalion* (1912) for the screen version produced by Gabriel Pascal in 1941. Shaw collected an Academy Award for his screenplay.

Shaw and Lady Astor at a reception for them in Moscow in 1931. From left to right in the front row are Karl Radek, A. V. V. Lunacharsky, Lady Astor, Shaw, and A. Khalatove. (Wide World Photo)

The Yousuf Karsh portrait of Shaw as he neared ninety. (© Karsh of Ottawa)

Shaw broadcasting on the BBC in the early 1930s. (Courtesy BBC)

WITHDRAWN

leave Hamlet out, and be content with Horatios for heroes. Some of the difference between Shakespear's Orlandos and Bassanios and Bertrams and his Hamlets and Macbeths must have been due not only to his development as a dramatic poet, but to the development of Burbage as an actor. Playwrights do not write for ideal actors when their livelihood is at stake: if they did, they would write parts for heroes with twenty arms like an Indian god. Indeed the actor often influences the author too much; for I can remember a time (I am not implying that it is yet wholly past) when the art of writing a fashionable play had become very largely the art of writing it "round" the personalities of a group of fashionable performers of whom Burbage would certainly have said that their parts needed no acting. Everything has its abuse as well as its use.

It is also to be considered that great plays live longer than great actors, though little plays do not live nearly as long as the worst of their exponents. The consequence is that the great actor, instead of putting pressure on contemporary authors to supply him with heroic parts, falls back on the Shakespearean repertory, and takes what he needs from a dead hand. In the nineteenth century, the careers of Kean, Macready, Barry Sullivan, and Irving ought to have produced a group of heroic plays comparable in intensity to those of Eschylus, Sophocles, and Euripides; but nothing of the kind happened: these actors played the works of dead authors, or, very occasionally, of live poets who were hardly regular professional playwrights. Sheridan Knowles, Bulwer Lytton, Wills, and Tennyson produced a few glaringly artificial high horses for the great actors of their time; but the playwrights proper, who really kept the theatre going, and were kept going by the theatre, did not cater for the great actors: they could not afford to compete with a bard who was not of any age but for all time, and who had, moreover, the overwhelming attraction for the actor-managers of not charging author's fees. The result was that the playwrights and the great actors ceased to think of themselves as having any concern with one another: Tom Robertson, Ibsen, Pinero, and Barrie might as well have belonged to a different solar system as far as Irving was concerned; and the same was true of their respective predecessors.

Thus was established an evil tradition; but I at least can plead that it does not always hold good. If Forbes Robertson had not been there to play Caesar, I should not have written Caesar and Cleopatra. If

Ellen Terry had never been born, Captain Brassbound's conversion would never have been effected. The Devil's Disciple, with which I won my *cordon bleu* in America as a potboiler, would have had a different sort of hero if Richard Mansfield had been a different sort of actor, though the actual commission to write it came from . . . William Terriss, who was assassinated before he recovered from the dismay into which the result of his rash proposal threw him. For it must be said that the actor or actress who inspires or commissions a play as often as not regards it as a Frankenstein's monster, and will have none of it. That does not make him or her any the less parental in the fecundity of the playwright.

To an author who has any feelings of his business there is a keen and whimsical joy in divining and revealing a side of an actor's genius overlooked before, and unsuspected even by the actor himself. When I snatched Mr Louis Calvert from Shakespear, and made him wear a frock coat and silk hat on the stage for perhaps the first time in his life, I do not think he expected in the least that his performance would enable me to boast of his Tom Broadbent as a genuine stage classic. Mrs Patrick Campbell was famous before I wrote for her, but not for playing illiterate cockney flower-maidens.

It is not the whole truth that if we take care of the actors the plays will take care of themselves; nor is it any truer that if we take care of the plays the actors will take care of themselves. There is both give and take in the business. I have seen plays written for actors that made me exclaim, "How oft the sight of means to do ill deeds makes deeds ill done!" But Burbage may have flourished the prompt copy of Hamlet under Shakespear's nose at the tenth rehearsal and cried, "How oft the sight of means to do great deeds makes playwrights great!" I say the tenth because I am convinced that at the first he denounced his part as a rotten one; thought the ghost's speech ridiculously long; and wanted to play the king. Anyhow, whether he had the wit to utter it or not, the boast would have been a valid one. The best conclusion is that every actor should say, "If I create the hero in myself, God will send an author to write his part." For in the long run the actors will get the authors, and the authors the actors, they deserve.

The art of all fiction, whether made for the stage, the screen, or the bookshelf, is the art of story-telling. My stock-in-trade is that of Scheherazade and Chaucer no less than of Aristophanes and Shakespear. I am quite aware that the jig-saw puzzle business, the working out of a plot, is necessary in detective stories, and helpful to playwrights who have talent enough to put their clockwork mice through amusing tricks, and hold their audiences effectively by jury-box suspenses. When I read a couple of acts of my first play to Henry Arthur Jones, all he said was, "Where's your murder?" But I needed no murder: I could get drama enough out of the economics of slum poverty: I scorned the police news and crude sexual adventures with which my competitors could not dispense. Clearly I had nothing to learn from Henry Arthur: he had something to learn from me, and did.

In writing a play you start anywhere you can. You may even have a plot, dangerous as that is. At the other extreme you may even not see a sentence ahead of you from the rise of the curtain to its fall. You mostly start with what is called a "situation," and write your play by leading up to it and taking its consequences. The situation may be a mere incident, or it may imply a character or conflict of characters. That is, it may be schoolboyishly simple or sagely complex. Even a repartee may be the seedling of a play. . . . Heartbreak House . . . began with an atmosphere and does not contain a word that was foreseen before it was written. Arms and the Man, The Devil's Disciple, and John Bull's Other Island grew around situations. The first fragment of Man and Superman that came into being was the repartee: "I am a brigand: I live by robbing the rich: I am a gentleman: I live by robbing the poor," though it afterwards developed into a thesis play, which is always a Confession of Faith or a Confession of Doubt on the author's part. The Philanderer began with a slice of life; most of the first act really occurred.[2] Back to Methuselah is prophecy, in the scriptural, not the race tipster's, sense.

A play with one big scene is like a farce with one joke. Where is the big scene in Lear or Hamlet? They are all big scenes from end to end. The Merchant of Venice has a big scene—the trial scene—from the nature of the story, but A Midsummer Night's Dream has none. Sometimes the grand scene is left out when you come to it. That happened in Pygmalion; the only person who spotted it was Barrie. You can amuse yourself by guessing what the scene was.[3]

Caesar and Cleopatra and St Joan are, of course, chronicles. They are all big scenes, with climaxes. The only play I ever planned and plotted was Captain Brassbound's Conversion, which was neither the better nor the worse for that perfunctory preliminary, and the *scène à faire* stands out so little that nobody but an expert could say which it is. That shows how little it matters what starts a play: what is important is to let it take you where it wants without the least regard to any plans you have formed. The more unforeseen the development the better. Nobody knows or cares about your plans and plots, and if you try to force your play to conform to them you will distort your characters, make the action unnatural, and bore and frustrate the audience. Trust your inspiration. If you have none, sweep a crossing. No one is compelled to write plays.

If you want to flatter me you must not tell me that I have saved your soul by my philosophy. Tell me that, like Shakespear, Molière, Scott, Dumas, and Dickens, I have provided a gallery of characters which are realer to you than your own relations and which successive generations of actors and actresses will keep alive for centuries as their *chevaux de bataille*. . . . Characters have to grow and define themselves as they go on: they may begin as mere dolls or even golliwogs. Falstaff began as a knockabout comedian or circus clown, drunken, cowardly, telling ridiculously extravagant lies, not pretending to be a real person, and I am sorry to say that it is only in this phase that he is popular on the stage; the second part of Henry IV does not please the public. Pickwick and Don Quixote were no more to their creators at first than an elderly gentleman at whose hat an impudent street boy throws a snowball. Dick Swiveller began as a repulsive melodramatic villain whom the heroine was to be forced by her selfish relatives to marry. All four developed in the author's hands in spite of him. Two of them wiped out characters which were meant to be more important: Poins and that futile relative of Little Nell's whose very name it is impossible to remember.

Fictitious characters often have to go through a sort of childhood during which it is impossible to guess how they will turn out, and sometimes they will emerge from this childhood, seize the center of the stage, and dominate the whole work. I can neither draw them or paint them. My sense of them is not a visual one; if it were I should be another Hogarth. My sense of my characters is one of the unspecified senses. It has nothing to do with sight, sound, taste, smell, or touch. Two intimate friends of mine have just died. I knew them both for forty years. But I cannot tell you the colour of their eyes.

. . . The use one makes of the living model varies from recognisable portraiture to suggestions so overloaded with fiction that the most ingenious detective could not penetrate the disguise. Among well-known people of whom I have made use are Mrs Besant, Cunninghame Graham, Gilbert Murray, the late Countess of Carlisle, Sidney Webb, Sir Almroth Wright, Stopford Brooke, Bishop Creighton, and Lord Haldane, to say nothing of A. B. Walkley, Mr Asquith, Mr Lloyd George, and the Kaiser.[4]

In one cast I thought I was using a certain public man as a model, but I became conscious years later that I had really used another. Cokane, in Widowers' Houses, was a man I had never seen, but my mother told me stories about him, and her father's solicitor was never tired of imitating him. Sartorious was an Irish stationer to whom I never spoke; his imposing manner suggested his character. Bohun in You Never Can Tell is a variation on Jaggers in Dickens's Great Expectations. The critic in The Philanderer was Clement Scott, the sentimentalist of The Daily Telegraph. I omit cases of writing parts for particular performers. Sometimes my imaginary characters turn up later in real life. But all this part of my business is very fanciful. The chief use of models is to correct or prevent too much family likeness between one's characters and excessive mannerism in drawing them. Real people often suggest people wildly unlike themselves—possibly unrealised selves.

Theatre technique begins with the circus clown and ringmaster and the Greek tribune, which is a glorified development of the pitch from which the poet of the market place declaims his verses, and, like Dickens's Sloppy or a modern playwright reading his play to the players, reads all the parts "in different voices." On any fine Sunday in Ceylon the street poet may still be seen declaiming his works and taking round his hat: I have seen him do it.

But you need not go so far as Ceylon to see this primitive performance. Wherever there is a queue waiting for the doors of a theatre to open you may see some vagabond artist trying to entertain it in one way or another; and that vagabond may be an incipient Shakespear or Garrick. Nor need you go to the doors of a theatre to witness this parturition of pavement art. In Hyde Park I have seen an elderly man, dressed in black, (his best, but old and seedy), step aside to the grass and address the empty air with the exordium "Ah, fahst EEbrews is very campfitn." Presently people stopped to listen to him; and he had a congregation. I myself have done the same on Clapham Common, and collected sixteen shillings in my hat at the end for the Socialist cause. I have stopped on the Thames Embankment; set my back to the river wall; and had a crowd listening to me in no time. . . .[5]

My first play was a crude affair in some ways; but it held to the end an audience half of whom had come intending to hoot it off the stage. You see, they always wanted to hear what was coming next; and so the end was reached before they thought their moment had come: and then there was nothing for it but to hoot *me*. Now I could teach a beginner as much as I have learned technically since that evening in 1892: I daresay it would all go on half a sheet of notepaper. But why should I teach, seeing that he can find it out for himself, and that I have something better to do?

All the instruction that was offered to me was either wrong absolutely or wrong for me. All the books that profess to show how to write plays are wrong from beginning to end, and should be labelled How Not To Do It. There is a great deal to be learnt on the stage as to stage execution; but it must be learnt by watching the masters at work to see how they do it, and watching the duffers to find out why and where they failed, also by practising public speaking and learning thereby how to "put it across." But teachers who are not practitioners and never have been are no use; and professors are the very devil, only duller. If you cant write a play without being taught, dont.

The born playwright has "theatre sense" and bears the . . . mechanical limitations of the stage . . . in mind automatically. They do not hamper his imagination, because all human faculties accept the limits of possibility without protest if they are conscious of them: that is, in this case, if they have theatre sense. For instance, no writer feels trammelled because his hero may have only one head and two legs, and cannot be in two places at once. In the same way the genuine playwright does not feel trammelled because he has to work under the conditions which are not imposed on the novelist. . . . It would be great fun to make a novelist work out all his scenes on a stage. He would be amazed at the number of physical impossibilities he would encounter. That is why all playwrights feel that any fool can write a novel.[6] What is there to hinder him when he is working on a plane where he is absolutely fancy free—where there is no real time, space, dimension, or gravitation? Both the playwright and the actor have to produce the illusions of this free plane within the limitations of a material framework in which there is inexorable time and very little of it, and a narrow space which is far more cramping than space in general, because though it has three dimensions it has only one aspect, and is therefore halfway between ordinary space and the space of one dimension with which the painter has to be content. . . .

. . . In writing a play you must keep within those limitations or your play will not be playable. The odd thing is that the limitations are natural to the born playwright, whereas they paralyse the novelist, making it impossible for him to take the stage seriously. The gravest novelists begin to tomfool the moment they try to write for the stage, unless they have theatre sense as well, like Galsworthy.

. . . Side by side, strangely enough, in order to restore that balance which Nature always appears to have in view, there arises the other sort of man, who is born with a tremendous desire to be laughed at and who will undergo the most extraordinary ignominy, who will paint his nose red, who will allow people to kick him about, who will have the most disastrous falls, if only he can make people laugh.

This is a curious psychological thing. It has prevented me from being a really great author. I have unfortunately this desperate temptation that suddenly comes on me, just when I am really rising to the height of my power, that I may become really tragic and great: some absurd joke occurs, and the anti-climax is irresistible. . . . I cannot deny that I have got the tragedian and I have got the clown in me; and the clown trips me up in the most dreadful way.[7] . . . But the object of the mental procedure is plain enough. It is to select from the unmeaning mass of events which you can record by cinematographing a crowded city street—a spectacle which leaves you as ignorant and bewildered as it has left many a bootblack who has seen it day after day for years—a set of imaginary but possible persons and a series of imaginary but possible actions which make life intelligible and suggest some interpretation of it. When the great dramatists are driven by their evolutionary appetite to do this, and have invented the theatre and the art of acting, and the dramatic form in literature to communicate their lesson to the world, then smaller men in the theatre work for smaller ends to raise a laugh, to tell naughty stories in dramatic form, to tomfool or sentimentalise according to their taste and depth and that of the paying public; but the root of the business is our desire for larger and clearer consciousness of the nature and purpose of that wonderful mystery Life, of which we find ourselves the tormented and erratic, but still aspiring vehicles.

All my plays are masterpieces except the last one. They always were. The donkey, no matter how fast he scampers, never overtakes the carrot. There is, in fact, a force in nature which impels all born leaders in the arts continually to extend the scope of their works beyond the established and familiar form and content of such things. And, what is less often recognised, this same force impels audiences to come and endure this pioneering until they first discover that their old favorites have become stale and unbearable, and then that the new ones are not half bad when you get the hang of them.

14

Saint Joan

WHEN I WAS A VESTRYMAN I had to check the accounts of the Public Health Committee. It was a simple process: I examined one in every ten or so of the receipted accounts and passed it whilst my fellow members did the same; and so enough of the accounts got checked to make their falsification too risky.

As it happened, one which I examined was for sulphur candles to disinfect houses in which cases of fever had occurred. I knew that experiments had proved that the fumes of burning sulphur had no such effect. Pathogenic bacilli like them and multiply on them.

I put the case to the Medical Officer of Health, and asked why the money of the ratepayers should be spent on a useless fumigant. He replied that the sulphur was not useless: it was necessary. But, I urged, the houses are not being disinfected at all.

"Oh yes they are," he said.

"How?" I persisted.

"Soap and water and sunshine," he explained.

"Then why sulphur?"

"Because the strippers and cleaners will not venture into an infected house unless we make a horrible stink in it with burning sulphur."

I passed the account. It was precisely equivalent to liquefying the blood of Saint Januarius.

Some twenty years later I wrote a play called Saint Joan in which I made an archbishop explain that a miracle is an event that creates faith, even if it is faked for that end. Had I not been a vulgar vestryman as well as a famous playwright I should not have thought of that.

All playwrights should know that had I not suspended my artistic activity to write political treatises and work on political committees long enough to have written twenty plays, the Shavian idiosyncrasy which fascinates some of them (or used to) and disgusts the Art for Art's Sake faction, would have missed half its value, such as it is.

Until I began Saint Joan, Methuselah *was* my last play. Every play I write is my last play until I begin another. But the play in which the playwright reaches his farthest point is really his last play, even though he may write others that are later in the calendar. . . . I wrote it in 1923. During that year I was at Glengarriff from the 18th July to the 15th August, and at Parknasilla from the 15th August to the 18th September, working at the play all the time. . . . But the play was neither begun nor finished in Eire. A good deal of it was written in rapidly moving trains between King's Cross and Hatfield on the London, Midland and Scottish Railway: and to locate this part of it is a problem in Cartesian geometry. . . .

Not long before the war I was returning from Germany through the Vosges, not tied to time in any way, and pleasing myself as to my route. I took Domremy on my way for the sake of St Joan of Arc, and Rheims for the sake of its datelessly unique French sculpture, especially a Virgin whom I intended some day to put into a play. I spent an evening in a French garrison town, and reflected, not for the first time (for my tour had taken me through Toul and its warlike frontier region at its outset), on the impression of hardbeaten efficiency, sudden readiness and dangerousness, and an extraordinary recklessness of everything else, including appearances, made by the French army rehearsing. They never brushed their clothes: they never cleaned their horses or their wagons or their guns. They said that a Frenchman is never clean and always ready, implying unmistakably that an Englishman is always clean and never ready. I compared them with the endless column of German soldiers I had seen not long before one morning in Trier (Treves) flowing down the street to a sentimental German tune in a march that was almost a dance. . . .

At Rheims it occurred to me that I had never seen Ypres, and that I had a Belgian triptych in my pocket. So instead of making straight for Boulogne I turned north, through Ham, Bapaume, Arras, Lille, and Ypres, little knowing that it was my last chance of seeing them as they were. I found Arras a Spanish town, dating from the day of Alva, with a Little Square that made me wonder how big the Great Square could be if this was indeed the little one. Its facades, made up of rows of ornamental gable-ends, were unlike anything else in France that I had seen; and though its cathedral was pseudo-classical in the late Renascence manner, which is a trifle better than the eighteenth century or Dublin manner, there was a mediaeval town hall.

Ypres was altogether charming. As I emerged from the Vlamertinge road and saw the Cloth Hall, it was noon of a fine and pleasant day, and the Carillon was ringing out a shower of tunes that would have delighted Couperin, Flemish in their gaiety and French in their brilliancy of tone and elegance of execution. I stopped the car and listened, quite enchanted, until it was over. Then I went to the Hotel de la Chêtellenie, in the Great Square at the east end of the Cloth Hall, and had my *déjeuner,* followed by the usual argument with the hostess, who supposed that I was a vegetarian for the sake of economy, and had reduced her *table d'hôte* price accordingly. When I had convinced her that I was a millionaire giving extra trouble and prepared to pay on that basis, we parted in high good humor; and, after seeing the cathedral, I made my way round by Furnes, Dunkirk, and Calais, to Boulogne, wiling the last evening stretch of the journey by inventing a play on the Rodin theme[1] of The Burgesses of Calais. . . .

The Six of Calais is an acting piece and nothing else. As it happened, it was so well acted[2] that in the eighteenth century all the talk would have been about [Mrs] Siddons as Philippa. But the company got no thanks except from the audience: the critics were prostrated with shock. . . . The most amusing thing about the first performance of this little play was the exposure it elicited of the quaint illiteracy of our modern London journalists. Their only notion of a king was a pleasant and highly respectable gentleman in a bowler hat and Victorian beard, shaking hands affably with a blushing football team. To them a queen was a dignified lady, also Victorian as to her coiffure, graciously receiving bouquets from excessively washed children in beautiful new clothes. Such were their mental pictures of Great Edward's grandson and his queen Philippa. They were hurt, shocked, scandalised at the spectacle of a mediaeval soldier-monarch publicly raging and cursing, crying and laughing, asserting his authority with thrasonic ferocity and the next moment blubbering like a child in his wife's lap or snarling like a savage dog at a dauntless and defiant tradesman: in short, behaving himself like an unrestrained human being in a very trying situation instead of like a modern constitutional monarch on parade keeping up an elaborate fiction of living in a political vacuum and moving only when his ministers pull his strings. Edward Plantagenet the Third had to pull everybody else's strings and pull them pretty hard, his father having been miserably killed for taking his job too lightly. But the journalist critics knew nothing of this. A King Edward who did not behave like the son of King Edward the Seventh seemed unnatural and indecent to them, and they rent their garments accordingly.

They were perhaps puzzled by the fact that the play has no moral whatever. Every year or so I hurl at them a long play full of insidious propaganda, with a moral in every line. They never discover what I am driving at: it is always too plainly and domestically stated to be grasped by their subtle and far flung minds; but they feel that I am driving at something: probably something they had better not agree with if they value their livelihoods.

I . . . had to improve considerably on the story as told by that absurd old snob Froissart,[3] who believed that "to rob and pill was a good life" if the robber was at least a baron. He made a very poor job of it in opinion. . . . He told the story, but got it all wrong; for though he was the most voluminous of chroniclers, and the father of all tuft-hunters, he understood women so little that the only lady he ever loved pulled his hair and would have nothing to do with him. Auguste Rodin contributed the character of Peter Hardmouth; but his manner of creation was that of a sculptor and not that of a playwright. Nothing remained for me to do but to correct Froissart's follies and translate Rodin into words.

Joan is a first-class dramatic subject ready made. You have a heroic character, caught between "the fell incenséd points" of the Catholic Church and the Holy Roman Empire, between Feudalism and Nationalism, between Protestantism and Ecclesiasticism, and driven by her virtues and her innocence of the world to a tragic death which has secured her immortality. What more do you want for a tragedy as great as that of Prometheus? All the forces that bring about the catastrophe are on the grandest scale; and the individual soul on which they press is of the most indomitable force and temper. The amazing thing is that the chance has never been jumped at by any dramatic poet of the requisite calibre. . . .

Job himself would have burned the real Joan. . . . The pseudo-Shakespearean Joan ends in mere Jingo scurrility. Voltaire's mock-Homeric epic is an uproarious joke. Schiller's play is romantic flapdoodle. All the modern attempts known to me are second-rate opera books. I felt personally called on by Joan to do her dramatic justice; and I dont think I have botched the job.

I was impressed in my Irish Protestant infancy with the belief that every Catholic, including especially the Pope, must go to hell as a matter of divine routine. When I was seven years old, Pope Pius IX ruled that I, though a little Protestant, might to go heaven, in spite of my invincible ignorance regarding the Catholic religion, if I behaved myself properly.[4] But I made no reciprocal concessions at the time; and . . . . I hope this service of mine to the Church may be accepted as a small set-off against the abominable bigotry of my Irish Protestant childhood, which I renounced so vigorously when I grew up to some sort of discretion and decency that I emptied the baby out with the bath, and left myself for a while with no religion at all.

St Joan did not claim toleration: she was so far from believing in it that she wanted to lead a crusade of extermination against the Husites, though she was burnt for sharing their heresy. That is how all the martyrs have missed the point of their defence. They all claimed to possess absolute truth as against the error of their persecutors, and would have considered it their duty to persecute for its sake if they had had the power. Real toleration: the toleration of error and falsehood, never occurred to them as a principle possible for any sane government. And so they have left us no model defence. And there is no modern treatise known to me which quite supplies this need. Stuart Mill's Essay on Liberty satisfied the nineteenth century, and was my own first textbook on the subject; but its conclusion that selfregarding actions should not be interfered with by the authorities carries very little weight. . . . In a complex modern civilization there are no purely selfregarding actions in the controversial sphere. . . . All great art and literature is propaganda. Most certainly the heresies of Galileo were not selfregarding actions: his feat of setting the earth rolling was as startling as Joshua's feat of making the sun stand still. The Church's mistake was not in interfering with his liberty, but in imagining that the secret of the earth's motion could be kept, and fearing that religion could not stand the shock of its disclosure, or a thousand such. It was idiotic to try to adapt Nature to the Church instead of continually adapting the Church to Nature. . . . The Church may, and perhaps some day will, canonize Galileo without compromising such infallibility as it claims for the Pope, if not without compromising the infallibility claimed for the Book of Joshua by simple souls whose rational faith in more important things has become bound up with a quite irrational faith in the chronicles of Joshua's campaigns as a treatise on physics. Therefore the Church will probably not canonize Galileo yet awhile, though it might do worse. But it has been able to canonize Joan without any compromise at all. She never doubted that the sun went round the earth: she had seen it do so too often.

Galileo is a favored subject with our scientists; but they miss the point because they think that the question at issue at his trial was whether the earth went round the sun or was the stationary centre round which the sun circled. Now that was not the issue. Taken by itself it was a mere question of physical fact without any moral significance, and therefore no concern of the Church. As Galileo was not burnt and certainly not abhorred, it is quite credible that both his immediate judges and the Pope believed with at least half their minds that he was right about the earth and the sun. But what they had to consider was whether the Christian religion, on which to the best of their belief not only the civilization of the world but its salvation depended, and which had accepted the Hebrew scriptures and the Greek testament as inspired revelations, could stand the shock of the discovery that many of its tales, from the tactics of Joshua in the battle of Gideon to the Ascension, must have been written by somebody who did not know what the physical universe was really like. I am quite familiar with the pre-Galileo universe of the Bible and St Augustine. As a child I thought of the earth as being an immense ground floor with a star studded ceiling which was the floor of heaven, and a basement which was hell. That Jesus should be taken up into the clouds as the shortest way to heaven seemed as natural to me as that, at the Opera, Mephistopheles should come up from hell through a trap in the floor. But if instead of telling me that Jesus was taken up into the clouds and that the disciples saw him no more, which still makes me feel quite holy, you tell me that he went up like a balloon into the stratosphere, I do not feel holy: I laugh obstreperously. The exalting vision has suddenly become a ribald joke. That is what the Church feared; and that is what has actually happened. Is it any wonder that the Pope told Galileo that he really must keep his discoveries to himself, and that Galileo consented to deny them? Possibly it was the Pope who, to console him, whispered, *"E pur se muove."*

. . . Since the report of the legal case against Joan and her rehabilitation by Quicherat,[5] there has been no room for opinion: the facts are too simple. All controversies raised with regard to the subject are nothing but attempts to obscure the facts in order to satisfy one opinion or another, whether party or not. Much fiction has been added with the intention of rendering the operation easier and more plausible. Anti-feminist opinion has refused to accept Joan as a political and military genius, in spite of her campaign on the Loire and of her policy which brought about the coronation, which would have confirmed the reputation of any adventurer of the male sex. Anti-clericals and Protestants have refused to believe that the proceedings against her were honest and her execution inevitable. Psychologists have attempted to prove that she was insane. Romanticists insisted on the fact that she was a heroine . . . of striking beauty. . . . A straightforward attempt to tell the truth is usually misunderstood. The French people are indignant in their belief that I have belittled their national heroine. Roman Catholics protest that I have written Saint Joan as an attack on their Church. Neither was intended or achieved. I have merely written a play based upon the facts as they exist. . . . The Frenchman, while abundantly recognizing the talent of his country, cannot admit French genius. Joan was a Frenchwoman of genius, just as Rodin was a Frenchman of genius, and . . . obliged to go to London in order to find recognition. I am quite aware, of course, that Joan is widely celebrated in France as a saint, and that a number of equestrian statues have been set up in her honor, but the real woman in her is still as unpopular in her own country as she was when the Burgundians sold her to the English and the latter delivered her to the French Church and the Inquisition to be burned.

. . . Joan was the first great Protestant, and France has never shown herself friendly to Protestantism, although a great part of her population adhered to it with ardor. She was a great nationalist. And less than 45 per cent of the citizens of the French Republic are French. Joan was also a masterful woman, a capable woman, and, as France is the land of masterful women par excellence, the French groan under the tyranny of their wives and their mothers, and they cannot stand the thought that Joan, even at the age of eighteen, possessed more mastery than most women of brains possess at fifty; in fact, this is why the French and the English so thoroughly agreed upon burning her. . . .

. . . Although the burning of Joan was an inexcusable thing, because it was a uselessly cruel thing, the question arises whether she was not a dangerous woman. That question arises with almost every person of distinguished or extraordinary ability. Let us take an example from our own times. After the [1914] war the late Marshal Foch was asked by somebody, "How would Napoleon have fought this war?"

Foch answered, "Oh! he would have fought it magnificently, superbly. But . . . what on earth would we have done with him afterwards?" Now that question arose in Joan's case. I want to bring it close to the present day. . . .

If you want to have an example from your own time, if you want to find [out] what women can feel when they suddenly find the whole power of society marshaled against them and they have to fight it . . . , read a very interesting book . . . by Miss Sylvia Pankhurst describing what women did in the early part of this century in order to get the parliamentary vote.[6] Miss Pankhurst, like so many other women in that movement, was tortured. In fact, except for burning, she suffered actual physical torture which Joan was spared. Other women suffered in that way with her. She describes from her own experience what those women felt, and how they did it. They were none of them exactly like St Joan, but I believe every one of them did regard herself as, in a measure, repeating the experiences of St Joan. . . .

For the story of Joan I refer the reader to the play. . . . It contains all that need be known about her; but as it is for stage use I have had to condense into three and a half hours a series of events which in their historical happening were spread over four times as many months; for the theatre imposes unities of time and place from which Nature in her boundless wastefulness is free. Therefore the reader must not suppose that Joan really put Robert de Baudricourt in her pocket in fifteen minutes, nor that her excommunication, recantation, relapse, and death at the stake were a matter of half an hour or so. Neither do I claim more for my dramatizations of Joan's contemporaries than that some of them are probably slightly more like the originals than those imaginary portraits of all the Popes from Saint Peter onward through the Dark Ages which are still gravely exhibited in the Uffizi in Florence (or were when I was there last). My Dunois would do equally well for the Duc d'Alencon. Both left descriptions of Joan so similar that, as a man always describes himself unconsciously whenever he describes anyone else, I have inferred that these goodnatured young men were very like one another in mind; so I have lumped the twain into a single figure, thereby saving the theatre manager a salary and a suit of armor. Dunois' face, still on record at Châteaudun, is a suggestive help. But I really know no more about these men and their circle than Shakespear knew about Falconbridge and the Duke of Austria, or about Macbeth and Macduff. In view of things they did in history, and have to do again in the play, I can only invent appropriate characters for them in Shakespear's manner.

I have, however, one advantage over the Elizabethans. I write in full view of the Middle Ages, which may be said to have been rediscovered in the middle of the nineteenth century after an eclipse of about four hundred and fifty years. The Renascence of antique literature and art in the sixteenth century, and the lusty growth of Capitalism, between them buried the Middle Ages; and their resurrection is a second Renascence. Now there is not a breath of mediaeval atmosphere in Shakespear's histories. His John of Gaunt is like a study of the old age of Drake. Although he was a Catholic by family tradition, his figures are all intensely Protestant, individualist, sceptical, self-centered in everything but their love affairs, and completely personal and selfish even in them. His kings are not statesmen: his cardinals have no religion: a novice can read his plays from one end to the other without learning that the world is finally governed by forces expressing themselves in religions and laws which make epochs rather than by vulgarly ambitious individuals who make rows. The divinity which shapes our ends, rough hew them how we will, is mentioned fatalistically only to be forgotten immediately like a passing vague apprehension.

. . . It is the business of the stage to make its figures more intelligible to themselves than they would be in real life; for by no other means can they be made intelligible to the audience. And in this case Cauchon and Lemaître have to make intelligible not only themselves but the Church and the Inquisition, just as Warwick has to make the feudal system intelligible, the three between them having thus to make a twentieth-century audience conscious of an epoch fundamentally different from its own. Obviously the real Cauchon, Lemaître, and Warwick could not have done this: they were part of the Middle Ages themselves, and therefore as unconscious of its peculiarities as of the atomic formula of the air they breathed. But the play would be unintelligible if I had not endowed them with enough of this consciousness to enable them to explain their attitude to the twentieth century. All I claim is that by this inevitable sacrifice of verisimilitude I have secured in the only possible way sufficient veracity to justify me in claiming that as far as I can gather from the available documentation, and from such powers of divination as I possess, the things I represent these three exponents of the drama as saying are the things they actually would have said if they had known what they were really doing. And beyond this neither drama nor history can go in my hands.

The protagonists of my play, although they appear on the stage as soldiers and feudal noblemen, are in reality the Church, the Inquisition, and the Holy Roman Empire. All united irresistibly to destroy a warrior saint. I have not belittled Joan, as would have been the case if I had turned her story into a melodrama about a wicked Bishop and a virtuous virgin. I have carried the tragedy completely beyond the taste of lovers of such melodrama and probably beyond their comprehension. . . . They like duels and divorce cases, and cannot conceive a human being taking interest in the Middle Ages or in the Church or the Empire. The inquisitor, in my play a very amiable gentleman, delivers a speech of six minutes without making a single allusion to any of the subjects forming the theatrical fare of all the public markets of the boulevards. The New York critics declared that the public would never stand such lengths, and that if the play was to be saved, all long speeches, all references to the Church, and the epilogue dealing with the history of Joan after her torture, must be cut without pity. Not a word was cut. Nevertheless, the play had an enormous success and had to be transferred to a larger theatre, able to hold the crowds desirous for the sake of Joan of Arc to listen for three and a half hours to a dialogue dealing with religion and with the politics of the Middle Ages. They were only too glad to escape from the divorce cases and scenes of adultery and prostitution which appear to be the Alpha and Omega of drama in the eyes of the boulevardiers.

. . . In London the critics are reinforced by a considerable body of persons who go to the theatre as many others go to church, to display their best clothes and compare them with other people's; to be in the fashion, and have something to talk about at dinner parties; to adore a pet performer; to pass the evening anywhere rather than at home: in short, for any or every reason except interest in dramatic art as such. In fashionable centres the number of irreligious people who go to church, of unmusical people who go to concerts and operas, and of undramatic people who go to the theatre, is so prodigious that sermons have been cut down to ten minutes and plays to two hours; and, even at that, congregations sit longing for the benediction and audiences for the final curtain, so that they may get away to the lunch or supper they really crave for, after arriving as late as (or later than) the hour of beginning can possibly be made for them.

Thus from the stalls and in the Press an atmosphere of hypocrisy spreads. Nobody says straight out that genuine drama is a tedious nuisance, and that to ask people to endure more than two hours of it (with two long intervals of relief) is an intolerable imposition. Nobody says, "I hate classical tragedy and comedy as I hate sermons and symphonies; but I like police news and divorce news and any kind of dancing or decoration that has an aphrodisiac effect on me or on my wife or husband. And whatever superior people may pretend, I cannot associate pleasure with any sort of intellectual activity; and I dont believe anyone else can either." Such things are not said; yet nine tenths of what is offered as criticism of the drama in the metropolitan Press of Europe and America is nothing but a muddled paraphrase of it. If it does not mean that, it means nothing.

I do not complain of this, though it complains very unreasonably of me. But I can take no more notice of it than Einstein [did] of the people who are incapable of mathematics. I write in the classical manner for those who pay for admission to a theatre because they like classical comedy or tragedy for its own sake, and like it so much when it is good of its kind and well done that they tear themselves away from it with reluctance to catch the very latest train or omnibus that will take them home.

As a playwright I have had countless letters from young women for whom St Joan has set up a standard which uplifted them beyond vulgarity and meanness. The schoolboy who, having seen my play, told his headmaster that he could pray to St Joan but not to Jesus Christ, justified the theatre as one of the most vital of public institutions. Without such uplift the playwright may be a pander or a buffoon, an actor only a mountebank or a common clown. It is this alone which can raise a theatre to the dignity and national value of a church. Wherever "two or three are gathered together" to see great acting, both actor and playwright can claim equality with lords temporal and spiritual.

15

Fabian Politics

IF I, a playwright and philosopher by profession and predilection, . . . found it not only possible but interesting to spend my afternoons for six years [1898–1904] in the committee rooms of a Suburban Vestry and Borough Council[1] . . . , the most romantic of my literary customers may very well endure to hear me draw the moral of my experience. . . . I knew, and everybody who had ever served on a public body knew, that the first hour spent on a committee would knock out of the new representatives most of the nonsense they had been talking at their election meetings. . . . In London the issue was . . . confused with the usual political party considerations.

What, then, should the municipalities do for their constituents? What should they charge for it? How much revenue should be spent in wages and how much sacrificed to cheapening services? Should consumers be overcharged for them or undercharged at the expense of the whole body of ratepayers? Such questions cannot be understood, much less answered, by councillors without the special knowledge and capacity needed for intelligent dealing with them. I was expected to answer them in council and a collection of local shopkeepers, licensed victuallers (publicans), builders, auctioneers, and the like, with an occasional doctor or two and a Methodist minister, I being a playwright. Our ablest leaders were a greengrocer and a bootmaker, both of them much more capable than most members of parliament; for it needs considerable character and ability to succeed as a shopkeeper, especially as a publican, whereas persons with unearned money enough can easily get into parliament without having ever succeeded in anything. I found them excellent company, and liked and respected them for their personal qualities. In the hands of a town clerk or mayor who happened to be a Richelieu they could have achieved notable feats of municipal enterprise, and had in fact proved this in the past. But Richelieus occur seldom and are not immortal. And without a Richelieu we were absurdly unequal to the magnitude of our task of making the best of the local government of a quarter million people. Such training and education as we had was for private and personal profiteering, not for public welfare work. Not only could we not solve our problems; we did not know they existed. Of those that circumstances forced on us we knew only one side. I, a Fabian permeator, knew the questions and had doctrinaire answers ready for some of them; and my friend the Methodist minister (. . . Ensor Walters) was a spiritual force that always acted in the right direction; but in the effective lump we were as ignorantly helpless politically as the mob of ratepayers who elected us, and who would never have elected me had they had the faintest suspicion of my ultimate political views.

In such conditions corruption was unconscious and automatic. It was practised with the best intentions in perfect honesty. The situation was often saved by the famous English intuitive wisdom so accurately observed and described by my friend Keyserling in his book on Europe. . . .[2] We "muddled through." Keyserling, by the way, . . . a Baltic baron . . . , set up a university of wisdom in Darmstadt which was badly needed in St Pancras (my constituency). Now I know very well that the rational practice and training which my colleagues lacked, and which they mistrusted and even hated when they came up against it, sometimes leads to grave error when intuitive wisdom jumps instantly to the right conclusion. I have sufficient intellectual faculty and practice to laugh at the Jacobin delusion that reason is infallible. Intellect can blunder disastrously; but so can intuition when it is ignorant. Neither of them can reach sound conclusions without authentic facts; and if the known facts are too few, or, being imaginary, are not facts at all, the inferences and guesses will be alike unsound. Besides, facts do not always lead to reasoned inferences. They may provoke vindictive resentments, sentimental leniencies, hopes and fears, prejudices and cupidities, leading to explosions of emotion that sweep reason from minds that have not had stern judicial training and natural judicial consciences. Competent municipal councillors must be taught and trained as well as born.

All municipal corruption, however, is not innocent, though it is mostly too childish to matter much. And it is—at least within my experience—never straightforward, being usually expected and accepted as a customary perquisite rather than as a bribe. . . .

But it is not among councillors that corruption is rife. It is the employees who have to be watched. Everywhere the ordinary citizen, politically uneducated and undisciplined as he is, regards public service, not as a responsible job which it is his duty and his point of personal honor to make the best of without respect of persons (including his own), but as a sinecure in which his official dignity obliges him to be insolent to the public. Any disappointment of his expectation of having nothing to do disposes him to exact additional payment from the citizens for whom he has to do it. How this view percolates down from the haughtiest jobbers to the humblest municipal employees came to my notice early in my career as a propagandist of municipal Socialism.

One Sunday morning I walked in a public park in a provincial capital, and was pleased to see that the municipality had provided a dressing-room for the footballers and cricketers who played there. I went into this dressing-room to inspect it, and found myself witnessing a lively altercation between the municipal custodian of the room and a footballer who had not tipped him. The custodian made no secret of his expectations. He demanded loudly in the hearing of all present whether the player thought he could come there and use the place "without leaving something." And the only defence the player made was that he could not leave anything because he had nothing to leave. Thereupon he was told roundly that if he had no money he had no right to use the dressing-room. And this seemed to be the general opinion, including that of the supposed delinquent, who evidently did not know that he had only to complain to the municipality to have the custodian sacked for demanding bribes. This was the remarkable part of the business. Nobody present except myself had any conception of communal institutions. No doubt some of the footballers who had tipped or were going to tip the custodian, though they were poor enough themselves, were quite willing to pay a trifle for the exclusion of the absolutely penniless; but neither they nor the custodian himself saw anything dishonest or antisocial in the transaction. No doubt if a police constable had refused to allow them to walk through a main street of their city unless they tipped him, they would have been scandalised, because they were unused to such demands and thought of a street, however well lighted, paved, swept, and policed, as a gratuity of nature, like sunlight or rain water; but they had always paid someone for a dressing-room, and therefore regarded the grafter-custodian as quite in order.

That this limitation is by no means confined to the masses who have had no secondary education was shewn by a ridiculous incident which occurred during the premiership of . . . Ramsay MacDonald. He had recommended a friend of his, on quite good grounds, for a baronetcy, which was accordingly conferred. Somebody then discovered that MacDonald's friend had once made him a present of a motor car. There was a tremendous fuss about it, rightly enough; for a Prime Minister should not accept costly presents from anyone who could conceivably have interested motives. Poor Ramsay, who had not thought of this aspect of the affair and was quite innocent of any corrupt intention, had to get rid of his car.[3] But the fuss was not about the valid point. What agitated the newspapers and the public was whether a Socialist (Ramsay professed himself a Socialist) could consistently with his principles own a motor car. A Socialist, they believed, was a sort of Franciscan who stripped off his gentlemanly clothes, sold all that he had, and threw the price into the street to be scrambled for by the poor. Apparently, if MacDonald had not professed himself a Socialist, he might have owned a dozen motor cars, all presented to him by prominent figures in the honors list, without being blamed in the least.

The Fabian vogue was shortlived. The Liberal Party, having come into power on Webb's programme, dropped it and went on exactly as before, and were in fact so unconscious of it in the Cabinet that it was amazed and outraged when the Fabian Society suddenly attacked it with all the Fabian guns in action. Webb and I drafted and launched a magazine article headed "To your tents, O Israel"; and the Progressives were swept from their moment of power by the Imperialism roused by the South African war. The Fabian conquest of the London County Council lasted only twenty years. Then the capitalists woke up and plastered the walls with a picture of a very ugly stage villain glaring at the ratepayers and growling, "It's your money we want." The Fabians had no funds to combat this expensive weapon; and the Progressive Party was defeated, and, for the moment, annihilated.

Following these clashes came dissension for the first time within the Society. The South African war was an Imperialist war; and anti-Imperialism was so strong a habit in all the democratic vanguards that a section of them broke off as "pro-Boers" led by the Liberal Lloyd George, the Socialist Ramsay MacDonald, and the Distributive free lance and insurgent genius Gilbert Chesterton.

I managed to pull the Fabian Society through this convulsion with the loss of less than two dozen members by drafting a tract called Fabianism and the Empire. Ibsen gave the pro-Boers a timely shock by asking whether they were seriously on the side of Boer Theocracy as against international Democracy. Finally Edward VII insisted on peace for his coronation; and the war collapsed in a nominally British victory which was a surrender, not to the Transvaal, but to South Africa led by Smuts, Christian de Wet, and the rest of its ablest generals. And so the rift was closed.

But another opened. The Conservative Government passed a much needed Education Act by which the Church schools were subsidised as well as the State schools. Immediately a furious anti-clerical agitation broke out; and a prominent Free Church leader and member of the Society, Dr Clifford, refused to pay his rates and had his furniture distrained year after year. A blameless clerical member of the Fabian executive committee lost his seat.

The Society had to stem this stampede. Half the children in the country were in Church schools, which very urgently needed the State inspection and control their endowment involved. The Fabian Society's leaders had to support the Bill and point out that Dr Clifford had paid his taxes without protest for the endowment of the Roman Catholic Church in Malta and for making the sale of Bibles a punishable offence in the Sudan.

The Act passed; and soon nothing remained of the agitation against it but the yearly sale of Dr Clifford's umbrella stand to pay his rates until his death. But, like the pro-Boer split, it had proved that the Socialist movement was confused and divided by the Radical superstition that Progressives must always vote against the Government, against the Church, and in fact against all collective as opposed to individualist legislation except such as had been demanded by the Trade Unions and opposed up to the last moment by the Conservatives. The Fabian policy was to support and take advantage of every legislative step towards Collectivism no matter what quarter it came from, nor how little its promoters dreamt that they were advocating an instalment of Socialism. On the platform and in the Press . . . it is assumed that we have to choose between "totalitarian" regimentation or totalitarian individual liberty, totalitarian Communism or Capitalism, totalitarian Socialism or Fascism, totalitarian soot or whitewash. That is all baby talk. Modern civilization could not exist for a week without a broad basis of Communism (roads and bridges, water supply, street lighting, police, civil and military services, etc.) and a superstructure of Socialism (posts, telegraphs, wireless), Fascism (State-financed Capitalism), and Cobdenism, all making what is called private enterprise possible. Only through using them all can we achieve the utmost practicable release from the slavery imposed on us, not by governments, but by Nature.

In 1911 the survivors of the Fabian essayists, after twenty-seven years service, resigned their official leadership to make room for younger men. The Society immediately replaced them by middle-aged and elderly old friends who sat comfortably doing comparatively nothing until the return to the Society of G. D. H. Cole,[4] who had begun as a Guild Socialist with an apology for calling the essayists fools on the ground that he should have called them bloody fools, but ended in his succession to Fabian leadership with the co-operation of a "Fabian Nursery." St John Ervine was conspicuous among its figureheads.[5]

Meanwhile, however, the Society did not come fully to life . . . as a constituent of the new Labour Party, whilst the essayists had by this time reached positions in which the Society was too small and too poor for their activities. Graham Wallas was the first to secede: he found his place as a member of the old London School Board, a University Extension lecturer, and finally as a favourite speaker in America and an independent author. Olivier, in the Colonial Office, became successively Governor of Jamaica, Auditor General at home, Secretary of State for India, and ended in the peerage. Annie Besant, a great orator, found herself a fifth wheel to the Fabian coach, and left it to succeed Helena Petrovna Blavatsky in India as queen of the Theosophites plus educator and moderniser of native Indian policy. William Clarke, rising rapidly as a journalist and a speaker, died prematurely. Hubert Bland found a rostrum in a weekly column in the provincial Press that gave him a freedom and independence unattainable by him in the Fabian Society, where, though the only founder of it among the essayists, he had always played the difficult part of a suburban Conservative converted to Socialism, and representing single-handed that point of view against a phalanx of former Liberals.

Webb and myself were left; but we also had achieved positions and publicity that took us far beyond the limits of the Society. When its pennilessness was momentarily relieved by a bequest from the Town Clerk of Derby, who wisely made it personal to Webb, he, who by that time had married and left the Colonial Office to become a supremely efficient chairman of the Technical Education Committee of the London County Council, hired a modest office in the Adelphi; installed a Director; and called it the London School of Economics. This, by sheer diplomacy, he developed into the present opulent school of London University in palatial quarters. He founded The New Statesman, now the leading political weekly and actually flourishing financially. His gifted wife and collaborator Beatrice took up the work begun by Dickens's Oliver Twist, and abolished the old Poor Law by imposing a crushing Minority Report on a Royal Commission. Meanwhile the pair poured out their world-standard series of volumes on Trade Unionism, Industrial Democracy, Local Government, the decay of Capitalism, and finally on Russian Fabianism as a new civilization.

These feats were entirely beyond the resources of the Fabian Society with its handful of 2000 most elderly members, and its chronic impecuniosity. Already it had suffered a sensational loss in the resignation of its most famous recruit H. G. Wells, who, on having his costly proposals sorrowfully rejected as far beyond the Society's means or credit, shook its dust from his feet, and pursued his far-reaching vision of a Socialist world-State as a free lance. . . . He literally cost me personally over a thousand pounds hard cash by wasting my time; for it fell to my lot to undo the mischief he did daily. At last he demanded: first, that the order of public meeting should be abolished, and he himself made both chairman and speaker when he addressed the public; and, second, that the Fabian Society should pass a vote, not merely of censure, but of contempt, on its executive committee, in order that its old leaders should be compelled to resign and leave him sole Fabian Emperor. At this point any other man would have been hurled out of the Society by bodily violence and heated objurgation. Wells was humbly requested to withdraw his demand, as it was not convenient just then to serve him up Sidney Webb's head on a charger.

As a reward for his condescension in complying he was elected to the executive committee nearly at the top of the poll. . . .[6]

I forced myself on the committee as its spokesman to save him from being slaughtered by sterner hands. That I easily and utterly defeated him was nothing; it was like boxing with a novice who knocked himself out in every exchange; but the Society, though it did not give him a single vote, reproached me for my forensic ruthlessness and gave all its sympathy to H. G. If he had been the most tactful and self-controlled of mortals he would not have been half so well beloved. . . . He repaid these acts of faith by refusing to attend committees or do any routine work whatever, and presently resigned, writing a letter for publication at the same time to explain that he had done so because we were a parcel of sweeps. . . .[7]

He was the most completely spoilt child I have ever known, not excepting even Lord Alfred Douglas, who, having been flogged at Eton, had had to bear criticism at least once, though indeed neither of them could bear it at all. This puzzled people who regarded Wells's youth as one of genius chastened by poverty and obscurity. As a matter of fact it was one of early promotion from the foot of the ladder to the top without a single failure or check. He never missed a meal, never wandered through the streets without a penny in his pocket, never had to wear seedy clothes, never was unemployed, and was always indulged as more or less of an infant prodigy. When he reproached me for being a snob and a ready-made gentleman, I had to tell him that he knew nothing at first hand of the horrors of chronic impecuniosity in the progeny of the younger sons of the feudal class who had the pretensions and obligations of gentility without the means of supporting them. Editors had jumped at his stories and publishers at his novels at the first glance: I wrote five massive novels and had to endure nine years of unrelieved failure, before any considerable publisher would venture on mine. It hardened me until my shell was like iron: H. G. was pampered into the most sensitive plant in the literary greenhouse.[8] His readers imagined that this man who understood everything could pardon everything. In fact the faintest shadow of disapproval threw him into transports of vituperative fury in which he could not spare his most devoted friends.

But do not infer from all this that H. G. was an intolerably unamiable person who made enemies of all his friends. One remembers the saying of Whistler's wife: "If I die, in twelve months Jimmy will not have a friend left in the world." Douglas could not live in the same house with his wife, though they lived and died on affectionate terms. Yet H. G. had not an enemy on earth. He was so amiable that, though he raged against all of us none of us resented it. There was no malice in his attacks: they were soothed and petted like the screams and tears of a hurt child. He warned his friends that he went on like that sometimes and they must not mind it. When Beatrice Webb, whom he consulted as to his filling some public position, told him frankly but authoritatively that he had not the manners for it, which was true, he caricatured, abused, vilified, and lampooned her again and again; but I never heard her speak unkindly of him; and they ended as the best of friends. He filled a couple of columns of the Daily Chronicle on one occasion with abuse of me in terms that would have justified me in punching his head; but when we met next day at a subcommittee of the Society of Authors our intercourse was as cordial as before; it never occurred to me that it could be otherwise, though he entered with obvious misgivings as to his reception, which at once gave way to our normally jolly friendliness.

Nothing could abate his likeableness. . . . H. G. was honest, sober, and industrious: qualifications not always associated with genius. He loved to assemble young people and invent new games for them, or referee the old ones, whistle in hand, as became the son of his father. In an age of masters of the art of conversation like Chesterton, Belloc, and Oscar Wilde, the Prince of Talkers, he was first-rate company without the least air of giving a performance. Nobody was ever sorry to see him. . . . To Fabian Socialist doctrine he could add little; for he was born ten years too late to be in at its birth pangs: the work had been done by the Old Gang of the Society as well as it could be done. Finding himself only a fifth wheel in the Fabian coach he cleared out, but not before he had exposed very effectively the obsolescence and absurdity of our old parish and county divisions as boundaries of local government areas.

As for me, I still served the Society as its pamphleteer, its economist, and its star speaker until I had to superannuate myself. But I, too, found my work far wider than the Society's. I was an author, a playwright, a philosopher, and a neo-biologist; and the Fabians were hopelessly Philistine . . . and, in the lump, classed metaphysics as pedantic nonsense and science as having abolished religion and substituted an agnosticism which relieved them from going to church. I could not operate within such limits, and fought for my own hand in my own way through the theatre, the Press, and the platform. In this way the Fabian essayists ceased to be known as Fabians or to work through the Society. They became celebrities with personal reputations. I myself had several reputations, and was for many years taken very seriously by proletarian audiences long before I was discussed half jocularly, half angrily, in literary circles.

I remained the star speaker of the Fabian Society's public lecturers to the end of my platform career. But in fact I was associated in these courses with other very able and enlightened lecturers. Between us we dealt with all the political and social problems with a thoroughness that reduced all the current Parliamentary Party oratory to irrelevant platitude and twaddle. Yet whilst the twaddlers were always reported in the newspapers as if their empty verbosities were of the first importance, I never saw a report of a Fabian lecture in any of our dailies. . . . My speeches were never reported, and my letters and articles inserted only when I could combine what I believed and wanted to say with something that the paper wanted to have said, or when I could disguise it as an attractively readable . . . criticism, the queer result being that my reputation was made in Conservative papers whilst the Liberal, Radical, and Socialist editors dared not mention my name except in disparagement and repudiation. I owe more of my publicity to The Times than to any other daily newspaper. The same is true of my Fabian colleagues. The Webbs, now in Westminster Abbey,[9] never could get into the British daily newspapers. . . . British Freedom of the Press was a favourite topic of the windbags; but as a matter of fact no censorship on earth could be more complete than the simple practice of the British Press in private hands. In the earliest days of the movement I was present on one occasion when the late H. H. Champion delivered a blamelessly reasoned and documented lecture to a crowded audience. Suddenly he declared that if the entire capitalist class had only one throat, he would cut it without a moment's hesitation. Whilst we were gasping at this outburst he rushed to the edge of the platform, and, pointing down at the Press table, shouted, "Look: they are all scribbling as hard as they can, though they have not put pen to paper while I was talking sensibly."

. . . During my greatest activities in that department there were no loud speakers except human ones: my utmost art could not make me audible or intelligible to more than five thousand people; and it was only on exceptional occasions that my audiences reached that number or the room could hold it. If I had been a political careerist, in the Cabinet or at least on the Front Bench, my speeches would have been seriously reported by qualified persons on the staffs of the leading newspapers. As I was only a man of letters, and an Intellectual at that, the Press table was abandoned to desperate free lances, hoping against hope to extract from the evening's proceedings something silly enough to be accepted by a sub-editor to fill up a vacant corner of his space. . . .

My career as a public speaker was not only futile politically: it was sometimes disgraceful and degrading. For I was in some request at election meetings, and could not always refuse. I had my platform triumphs, and was vociferously acclaimed a jolly good fellow in town halls crowded with enthusiastic partisans, after which my candidate friends would be duly defeated by opponents who had not a word to say that would have imposed on the giddiest rabbit. . . . I was specially proud of a speech in the Usher Hall in Edinburgh, where 8640 pennies were collected at the end. . . . But whether my candidate was returned or not I suffered agonies of disgust at the whole business and shame for my part in it. . . .

This state of things is still largely prevalent not only as to avowedly Socialist doctrine and criticism, but as to art, science, religion, and all subjects seriously treated. The invention of broadcasting has made it much more mischievous. If I were beginning my career as a propagandist preacher now, I would never set my foot on a platform. I would take the field as a newsreel and television artist. The essayists included some of the best public speakers and debaters in the country; but they all found that lecturing to the Fabian Society was, as far as Press publicity was concerned, waste of breath.

So much for *fin de siècle* Fabianism, now an old wives' tale. After the dropping of the Newcastle Programme[10] by the Liberal Party in power, and the extinction for the moment of the Progressive Party in municipal London by the unlimited expenditure of the so-called Municipal Reformers on pure calumny, we published A Plan of Campaign for Labour, advocating the entry of the proletariat into parliament as an Independent Party. It was taken up by Keir Hardie.

At the initial meeting in Bradford he was rather at a loss for a programme. I settled one with him in two minutes' conversation as we crossed one another on the stairs.

At the General Election of 1906 the reaction from the South African war, combined with the countenance given by the Conservative leaders to proposals to introduce Chinese labour, produced a wild Liberal-Labour landslide in which almost anybody could get into parliament by heaping abuse on the khaki Government. Nothing like it occurred again until 1945, when, however, the quality of the Labour candidates was enormously higher.

With the entry of Labour into parliament as an independent party our money difficulties vanished. There were then only a million and a half trade unionists in the electorate; but a million and a half pennies are enough to finance a political party. In 1927, the Conservatives woke and passed an Act excluding the Trade Unions from political action and making compulsory levies for it illegal. It was repealed chock-a-block by the victorious Labour Government in 1946.

Nobody noticed that this was a very questionable step. It had always been an unwritten tradition in our parliament that though successive Governments might amend previous legislative Acts, they would not simply wipe them off the statute book. Otherwise Parliamentary Party Government would be reduced to futile absurdity by wholesale repeals of new legislation at every swing of the political pendulum. The Labour Party, drunk with power, betrayed its inexperience and lack of historic sense by repealing the 1927 Act instead of amending it. . . . Meanwhile the handful of *bourgeois* Fabians meeting in each other's drawing rooms, without a fixed subscription or a banking account, successfully explored the path of Socialism on constitutional lines; made it respectable. . . .

Trade Union money removed many difficulties from the Fabian path. But I well remember that when Edward Pease, then our honorary secretary, told me triumphantly that the opulent Miners' Federation had joined the new party, my comment, not at all triumphant, was that as the Trade Unions would pay the piper, they, and no longer the Fabians, would call the tune.

Fabianism . . . was meant for the workers and offered to the workers when the Fabians planned the Labour Party in the tract, drafted by Webb and myself, entitled A Plan of Campaign for Labour.[11] But we could not publish it for the workers without publishing it for the capitalists as well. And the capitalists, cleverer than the workers, seized it and turned it to their own account by combining the enormous productiveness, power, and scope of State financed enterprise with their private property. . . . The Labour Party, dominated by the power of the Trade Union purse, simply missed the bus. . . . British Trade Unionism, though Fabianized into calling itself Socialist and adopting parliamentary methods as well as direct action by strikes, is not socialistic: its aim is to exploit the capitalist system so as to secure the lion's share of its product for the proletarian Trade Unionists instead of for the landlords and capitalists. . . .

The Fabians, preoccupied with industrial problems and their solutions, had said not a word on foreign policy, but assumed throughout that the British Parliamentary Party system, with everybody voting for anybody, however incompetent and illiterate, was democratic, and that the socialization of all the vital industries and the nationalization of the rents of land, capital, and ability, in short, of the "Surplus Value" of Marx, would by themselves attract the electorate and solve all the social problems.

This was pure assumption; and the facts soon contradicted it. . . . Though I am one of Marx's converts I have no use for the Marxist dialectic; my mind does not work in Hegelian grooves, though I had no more difficulty than William Morris had in understanding that private property produces a government of "damned thieves," who cannot help themselves, and must, willy nilly, live by robbing the poor. Fabian Essays, which I edited . . . , does not mention Marx, nor contain any chain of reasoning on Hegelian lines. It is British from beginning to end, though an Irishman edited it.[12] Later on I had to show that Marx's theory of value was a blunder, and that, like Ruskin, he did not understand the Ricardian law of rent, a grasp of which is fundamental in Socialism.

I had awakened to this omission before my resignation from the executive committee. Also I had on my own responsibility and without any consultation of the Society announced that our domestic problem is a distributive one, and its final aim the equalization of income. The Fabians, like the rest of the Intelligentsia, regarded this as one of the infantile crudities of the man in the street, and were taken aback when it was put into the shop window by an arch-Fabian. Nobody knew better than they that human character and talent and political capacity varied from supreme genius to complete incompetence; and they could not at once rid themselves of the notion that a clever person should be paid more than a stupid one. But the case for equality of income as indispensable in a stable civilization was overwhelming on the grounds set forth in my Intelligent Woman's Guide to Socialism.

The book in its first edition [1928] . . . endeared [itself] to collectors by several errors, one of which was a mistake in the number of one of the Articles of the Church of England. It passed entirely unnoticed in this country, but was detected and very kindly pointed out to me by a well-known French atheist. Of the general reception of the book I cannot speak, because I have no means of knowing what its readers felt. . . . The reviews mean little, because reviewers are not paid enough to read more than the chapter headings of a long book: that is why I made the chapter headings so complete, having been a reviewer myself once. A reviewer has to think of his wife and family as well as of the authors he reviews; and when I read criticisms clumsily refuting fallacies which my book refutes with sound science and some elegance, or patronisingly calling my attention to considerations which I have insisted on in chapter after chapter, I bear no malice, but, as an old hand, estimate the price of the review and the burdens of the reviewer, and muttering, "Two guineas: three children," or "Fifteen shillings: several children: husband an unappreciated artist" (for all these tragedies are wrapped up in our newspapers and oppress the conscience of an incorrigible economist like myself), I drop the press cutting into the waste paper basket. . . . My aims and proposals go so much further than any of my hostile critics are yet capable of conceiving that I am only too thankful to be mistaken for a mere harmless Utopian instead of being hanged without benefit of clergy. When the spirit drives me to tell the truth, and the flesh reminds me of the police and of the fate of those who have yielded to that temptation in the past, I screw my courage up by reflecting on the extreme improbability of anybody seeing anything in my treatise but a paradoxical joke. . . .

Nowadays the word Socialism means no more than the word Christianity. Even in the last century Sir William Harcourt[13] said, "We are all Socialists now," just as every military recruit who describes himself as having no religion is at once catalogued as Church of England. . . . When Ibsen was invited to assume a Party label he replied that he had both the Left and the Right in him, and was glad to have his ideas adopted by any Party. I find myself very much in the same position, and am sometimes surprised and amused, as I go farther and farther to the Left, to find that the world is round. . . . I could expatiate for many columns on this theme; for I foresee that [as] Socialist politics develop, our stalwarts will be crying in all directions though not in the original French, that "The more things change the more they remain the same," or worse, for there will be no new world: we must still put up with the old one, and make the best of it. And that process will be full of surprises, most of which to the best of our Utopian stalwarts will present themselves as bitter disappointments. And I, who will not be surprised by the surprises, and will work for half a loaf as better than no bread, will be described, as Sir Harold Webbe . . . described me, as "that fine old Tory, Mister Bernard Shaw."

16

The Apple Cart

THE FIRST PERFORMANCES of [The Apple Cart] at home and abroad[1] provoked several confident anticipations that it would be published with an elaborate prefatory treatise on Democracy to explain why I, formerly a notorious democrat, . . . apparently veered round to the opposite quarter and became a devoted Royalist. In Dresden the performance was actually prohibited as a blasphemy against Democracy.

What was all this pother about? I had written a comedy in which a King defeats an attempt by his popularly elected Prime Minister to deprive him of the right to influence public opinion through the press and the platform: in short, to reduce him to a cipher. The King's reply is that rather than be a cipher he will abandon his throne and take his obviously very rosy chance of becoming a popularly elected Prime Minister himself. To those who believe that our system of votes for everybody produces parliaments which represent the people it should seem that this solution of the difficulty is completely democratic, and that the Prime Minister must at once accept it joyfully as such. He knows better. The change would rally the anti-democratic royalist vote against him, and impose on him a rival in the person of the only public man whose ability he has to fear. The comedic paradox of the situation is that the King wins, not by exercising his royal authority, but by threatening to resign it and go to the democratic poll.

That so many critics who believe themselves to be ardent democrats should take the entirely personal triumph of the hereditary king over the elected minister to be a triumph of autocracy over democracy, and its dramatization an act of political apostasy on the part of the author, convinces me that our professed devotion to political principles is only a mask for our idolatry of eminent persons. The Apple Cart exposes the unreality of both democracy and royalty as our idealists conceive them. Our Liberal democrats believe in a figment called a constitutional monarch, a sort of Punch puppet who cannot move until his Prime Minister's fingers are in his sleeves. They believe in another figment called a responsible minister, who moves only when similarly actuated by the million fingers of the electorate. But the most superficial inspection of any two such figures shews that they are not puppets but living men, and that the supposed control of one by the other and of both by the electorate amounts to no more than a not very deterrent fear of uncertain and under ordinary circumstances quite remote consequences. The nearest thing to a puppet in our political system is a Cabinet minister at the head of a great public office. Unless he possesses a very exceptional share of dominating ability and relevant knowledge he is helpless in the hands of his officials. He must sign whatever documents they present to him, and repeat whatever words they put into his mouth when answering questions in parliament, with a docility which cannot be imposed on a king who works at his job; for the king works continuously whilst his ministers are in office for spells only, the spells being few and brief, and often occurring for the first time to men of advanced age with little or no training for and experience of supreme responsibility. George the Third and Queen Victoria were not, like Queen Elizabeth, the natural superiors of their ministers in political genius and general capacity; but they were for many purposes of State necessarily superior to them in experience, in cunning, in exact knowledge of the limits of their responsibility and consequently of the limits of their irresponsibility: in short, in the authority and practical power that these superiorities produce. Very clever men who have come into contact with monarchs have been so impressed that they have attributed to them extraordinary natural qualifications which they, as now visible to us in historical perspective, clearly did not possess. In conflicts between monarchs and popularly elected ministers the monarchs win every time when personal ability and good sense are at all equally divided. . . .

Besides, the conflict is not really between royalty and democracy. It is between both and plutocracy, which, having destroyed the royal power by frank force under democratic pretexts, has bought and swallowed democracy. Money talks: money prints: money broadcasts:

money reigns; and kings and labor leaders alike have to register its decrees, and even, by a staggering paradox, to finance its enterprises and guarantee its profits. Democracy is no longer bought: it is bilked. Ministers who are Socialists to the backbone are as helpless in the grip of Breakages, Limited, as its acknowledged henchmen: from the moment when they attain to what is with unintentional irony called power (meaning the drudgery of carrying on for the plutocrats) they no longer dare even to talk of nationalising any industry, however socially vital, that has a farthing of profit for plutocracy still left in it, or that can be made to yield a farthing for it by subsidies.

King Magnus' little tactical victory, which bulks so largely in the playhouse, leaves him in a worse plight than his defeated opponent, who can always plead that he is only the instrument of the people's will. . . . A Prime Minister cannot help himself within the limits of the Constitution. Power is to the powerful. King Magnus outwitted his ministers at the party game, but was left entirely helpless in the face of Big Business. . . .

The Apple Cart has also a topical air. In it a British king brings about the catastrophe by a threat to abdicate. And now a British king, very astonishingly, has abdicated. And note well . . . how natural and reasonable and probable the play is, and how improbable, fantastic, and outrageous the actual event was. There was not a single circumstance of it which I should have dared to invent. If you could raise Macaulay or Disraeli from the dead . . . to see The Apple Cart just to ask him "Could this thing actually happen?" he would have replied "Oh, quite possibly. Queen Elizabeth threatened to abdicate; and Queen Victoria used to hint at it once a week or so." But if you had told him the story of the Duke of Windsor, he would have said, "If you put a tale like that into a play you will spend the rest of your days in a lunatic asylum."

So much for holding the mirror up to nature! Yet there was enough to tempt any playwright in the comedy of the utter helplessness of Earl Baldwin and the British Parliament while the affair was settled over their supposedly omnipotent heads by the Royal Family. . . . I never dreamt of using . . . any . . . living person as a model, though every living ruler in the world will find a melancholy resemblance between his predicament and that of King Magnus. . . .

And now a word about Breakages, Limited. Like all Socialists who know their business I have an exasperated sense of the mischief done by our system of private Capitalism in setting up huge vested interests in destruction, waste, and disease. The armament firms thrive on war; the glaziers gain by broken windows; the operating surgeons depend on cancer for their children's bread; the distillers and brewers build cathedrals to sanctify the profits of drunkenness; and the prosperity of Dives costs the privation of a hundred Lazaruses.

The title Breakages, Limited, was suggested to me by the fate of that remarkable genius, . . . Alfred Warwick Gattie, with whom I was personally acquainted. I knew him first as the author of a play.[2] He was a disturbing man, afflicted—or, as it turned out, gifted—with chronic hyperaesthesia, feeling everything violently and expressing his feelings vehemently and on occasion volcanically. I concluded that he was not sufficiently cold-blooded to do much as a playwright; so that when, having lost sight of him for some years, I was told that he had made an invention of first-rate importance, I was incredulous, and concluded that thc invention was only a Utopian project. Our friend Henry Murray was so provoked by my attitude that to appease him I consented to investigate the alleged great invention in person on Gattie's promising to behave like a reasonable being during the process, a promise which he redeemed with the greatest dignity, remaining silent whilst an engineer explained his miracles to me, and contenting himself with the reading of a brief statement shewing that the adoption of his plan would release from industry enough men to utterly overwhelm the Central Empires with whom we were then at war.

I approached the investigation very sceptically. Our friend spoke of "the works." I could not believe that Gattie had any works, except in his fervid imagination. He mentioned "the company." That was more credible: anyone may form a company; but that it had any resources seemed to me doubtful. However, I suffered myself to be taken to Battersea; and there, sure enough, I found a workshop, duly labelled as the premises of The New Transport Company, Limited, and spacious enough to accommodate a double railway line with a platform. The affair was unquestionably real, so far. The platform was not provided with a station: its sole equipment was a table with a row of buttons on it for making electrical contacts. Each line of railway had on it a truck with a steel lid. The practical part of the proceedings began by placing an armchair on the lid of one of the trucks and seating me in it. A brimming glass of water was then set at my feet. I could not imagine what I was expected to do with the water or what was going to happen; and there was a suggestion of electrocution about the chair which made me nervous. Gattie then sat down majestically at the table on the platform with his hand hovering over the buttons. Intimating that the miracle would take place when my truck passed the other truck, he asked me to choose whether it should occur at the first passage or later, and to dictate the order in which it should be repeated. I was by that time incapable of choosing; so I said the sooner the better; and the two trucks started. When the other truck had passed mine I found myself magically sitting on it, chair and all, with the glass of water unspilled at my feet.

The rest of the story is a tragi-comedy. When I said to Gattie apologetically (I felt deeply guilty of having underrated him) that I had never known that he was an engineer, and had taken him to be the usual amateur inventor with no professional training, he told me that this was exactly what he was: just like Sir Christopher Wren. He had been concerned in an electric lighting business, and had been revolted by the prodigious number of breakages of glass bulbs involved by the handling of the crates in which they were packed for transport by rail and road. What was needed was a method of transferring the crates from truck to truck, and from truck to road lorry, and from road lorry to warehouse lift without shock, friction, or handling. Gattie, being, I suppose, by natural genius an inventor though by mistaken vocation a playwright, solved the mechanical problem without apparent difficulty, and offered his nation the means of effecting an enormous saving of labor and smash. But instead of being received with open arms as a social benefactor he found himself up against Breakages, Limited. The glass blowers whose employment was threatened, the exploiters of the great industry of repairing our railway trucks (every time a goods train is stopped a series of 150 violent collisions is propagated from end to end of the train, as those who live within earshot know to their cost), and the railway porters who dump the crates from truck to platform and then hurl them into other trucks, shattering bulbs, battering cans, and too often rupturing themselves in the process, saw in Gattie an enemy of the human race, a wrecker of homes and a starver of innocent babes. He fought them undauntedly; but they were too strong for him; and in due time his patents expired and he died almost unrecognised, whilst Unknown

Soldiers were being canonized throughout the world. So far, The Apple Cart is his only shrine; and as it does not even bear his name, I have written it here pending its tardy appearance in the roll of fame.

I must not leave my readers to assume that Gattie was an easy man to deal with, or that he handled the opposition in a conciliatory manner with due allowance for the inertia of a somewhat unimaginative officialdom which had not, like myself, sat on his trucks, and probably set him down as a Utopian (a species much dreaded in Government departments) and thus missed the real point, which was that he was an inventor. Like many men of genius he could not understand why things obvious to him should not be so at once to other people, and found it easier to believe that they were corrupt than that they could be so stupid. Once, after I had urged him to be more diplomatic, he brought me, with some pride, a letter to the Board of Trade which he considered a masterpiece of tact and good temper. It contained not a word descriptive of his invention; and it began somewhat in this fashion: "Sir: If you are an honest man you cannot deny that among the worst abuses of this corrupt age is the acceptance of City directorships by retired members of the Board of Trade." Clearly it was not easy for the Board of Trade to deal with an inventor who wished to interest them, not in his new machines, but in the desirability of its abolishing itself as infamous.

The last time I saw him he called on me to unfold a new scheme of much greater importance, as he declared, than his trucks. He was very interesting on that occasion. He began by giving me a vivid account of the pirates who used to infest the Thames below London Bridge before the docks were built. He described how the docks had come into existence not as wharves for loading and unloading but as strongholds in which ships and their cargoes could be secure from piracy. They are now, he declared, a waste of fabulously valuable ground; and their work should be done in quite another way. He then produced plans of a pier to be built in the middle of the river, communicating directly by rail and road with the shore and the great main lines. The ships would come alongside the pier; and by a simple system of hoists the contents of their holds would be lifted out and transferred (like myself in the armchair) to railway trucks or motor lorries without being touched by a human hand and therefore without risk or breakage. It was all so masterly, so simple in its complexity, so convincing as to its practicability, and so prodigiously valuable socially, that I, taking it very seriously, proceeded to discuss what could be done to interest the proper people in it.

To my amazement Gattie began to shew unmistakable signs of disappointment and indignation. "You do not seem to understand me," he said. "I have shewn you all this mechanical stuff merely by way of illustration. What I have come to consult you about is a great melodrama I am going to write, the scene of which will be the Pool of London in the seventeenth century among the pirates!"

What could I or anyone do with a man like that? He was naively surprised when I laughed; and he went away only half persuaded that his scheme for turning the docks into building land; expediting the Thames traffic; saving much dangerous and demoralizingly casual labor; and transfiguring the underpaid stevedore into a full-fed electrician, was stupendously more important than any ridiculous melodrama. He admitted that there was of course all that in it; but I could see that his heart was in the melodrama.

As it was evident that officialdom, writhing under his insults and shocked by his utter lack of veneration for bigwigs, besides being hampered as all our Government departments are by the vested interests of Breakages, Limited, would do nothing for him, I induced some less embarrassed public persons to take a ride in the trucks and be convinced that they really existed and worked. But here again the parallel between Gattie and his fellow amateur Sir Christopher Wren came in. Wren was not content to redesign and rebuild St Paul's: he wanted to redesign London as well. He was quite right: what we have lost by not letting him do it is incalculable. Similarly, Gattie was not content to improve the luggage arrangements of our railways: he would not listen to you if your mind was not large enough to grasp the immediate necessity for a new central clearing house in Farringdon Market, connected with the existing railways by a system of new tubes. He was of course right; and we have already lost by sticking to our old ways more than the gigantic sum his scheme would have cost. But neither the money nor the enterprise was available just then, with the war on our hands.[3] The Clearing House, like the Thames pier, remains on paper; and Gattie is in his grave. But I still hold that there must have been something great in a man who, having not only imagined them but invented their machinery, could, far from being crushed by their rejection, exclaim, "Perish all my mechanical trash if only it provides material for one bad play!"

This little history will explain how it actually did provide material for Breakages, Limited, and for the bitter cry of the Powermistress General.[4] Not until Breakages is itself broken will it cease to have a message for us.

17

Touring in Russia

WHEN LENIN came into power . . . I was . . . offered a very handsome commission by Mr William Randolph Hearst to go out to Russia and describe what there was to see there; but I refused because I knew only too well that what I should see was Capitalism in ruins and not Communism *in excelsis*. Not until 1931 did I visit the U.S.S.R.; and by that time the tide had returned.

For ten days I lived and travelled in perfect comfort[1] . . . and found no such horrors as I could have found in the distressed areas and slums of the Capitalist west, though the Soviet government was still finding out its mistakes. September and October are, they tell me, the best months. I went in July; but that is the hottest time, when the theatres are closed and the Opera suspended. . . . Your friends implore you to do nothing so rash and hazardous. You will be starved, they tell you. You will be eaten by lice. You will be seized by the Cheka and bumped off, or as the Russians put it, "liquidated." All the females in your party will be nationalised. You will see nothing except what the Soviet wishes you to see,[2] and that will be like the Russia that Patiomkin staged for Catherine II, a theatrical imposture. You go all the same, to be able to say that you have done something adventurous that nobody else dare do.

. . . I went . . . by Brussels, Berlin, Warsaw to Moscow. . . . I went by rail, and slept three nights in the train. On the Russian section I paid double fare to secure a compartment all to myself; for the sleeping cars, though sumptuous and more comfortable for a man of my inches because of the broad gauge (you cannot invade Russia in the western narrow-gauge train) are double berthed.

At the frontier you pass under an arch inscribed, "Communism will do away with frontiers." No doubt it will; but for the present you must take the arch as a reminder to have your passport ready. Then you are in Russia, prepared for the worst.

It is not very dreadful. The clock has jumped forward two hours from English summertime, which has held good all across Europe so far. You are not hurried or fussed: the Moscow train will not start for ever so long. You clear your luggage through the customs. You declare how much foreign cash you have about you, and receive a certificate. You must not have more than $150 or £30. (You can exchange it for roubles at not quite ten roubles to the pound or two to the dollar.) You stroll off through the great hall which is being added to the station, and discover that its walls are being covered by religious paintings like the Scuola di San Rocco in Venice. The religion, of course, is Marxism, not Christianity. If you are an Englishman you recall with a twinge that when G. F. Watts, the greatest of the Victorian idealist painters, offered to adorn the London terminus of the London and North Western Railway in this fashion for nothing, his offer was contemptuously refused as more likely to attract loiterers than business. The Soviet knows better, and actually pays artists to do this kind of thing.

As we had plenty of time to spare we took a walk through the village. A Russian village is so horrid that the Communists very properly burn it the moment they have persuaded its inhabitants to come into a collective farm and live decently. English people, accustomed to the beauty of their native rural villages, would hardly wait so long. Imagine a Brobdingnagian dog kennel of unpainted ugly brown wood. That is a Russian peasant's house. Inside is a frowsy cupboard without a door, which is the family bed, and a kiln, politely called a stove, on the top of which you can sleep if you are chilly. The rest of the space is kept as free from furniture as possible for the accommodation of the live stock of the strip of land which the peasant cultivates. If you are a well-dressed person the proprietor bows low to you, repeatedly and effusively. If you deign to converse with him, he seizes your hand and buries it in his big beard whilst he kisses it and overwhelms you with expressions of endearment. You may think him a more lovable person than the clean-shaven agricultural mechanic of the collective farm; but that the Soviet, in "liquidating" him and burning his kennel as soon as possible, is acting in the interests of civilization, is obvious at the first glance.

These kennels are dotted at wide intervals on both sides of the broad dirt road. There are no rows of houses, no village shops, no variety, nothing to distinguish one kennel from another except a number and a little plaque with a rude picture of an axe or a bucket, signifying that the owner is prepared to devote that implement to the extinction of any fire which may break out in the neighbourhood.

We strolled back towards the station, passing a few rather careworn, scantily dressed women carrying heavyish sacks, and evidently no happier than the human beasts of burden one sees all over Europe in similar remote countrysides. Close to the station we found something new. A bevy of girls were seated in two rows, one above the other, on some agricultural contraption that lent itself to this theatrically effective arrangement. They were armed with long-handled spades. There was neither stocking, sock, nor shoe among them; and their athletic freedom of limb and fearless air, which marked even the youthfully shy ones, had such a pleasant effect that we at once crowded round them and began talking to them as a matter of course. A natural leader at once asserted herself and did most of the talking. It did not come to much except by way of information; for our western pleasantries only puzzled them by their silliness. They were doing railway work as holiday volunteers, and the spades were for unloading the freight trains.

Whilst we were talking and chaffing, a freight train came in. Instantly these girls sprang to their feet and bounded to the train with a rhythmic grace and vigour that would have delighted Diaghileff. It was the only Russian ballet we saw in Russia. Its occurrence was a piece of luck for Communism, as it made us very sceptical about the stock assurances of the enemies of the Soviet that volunteer holiday labour is always really reluctant and compulsory. The contrast between these girls as they dashed at the freight cars with their spades and the old style women with their burdens was irresistible.

Presently a Russian broad-gauge train took us to Moscow. It was a twelve-hour journey, involving a Russian dinner, a Russian breakfast, and a night in a Russian sleeping car. . . . In spite of the Kremlin and the imposing grandeur of the churches . . . Moscow . . . is a domestic sort of city. Even its temporary shabbiness (fresh paint had to come last in the Five Year Plan) is homely. It is frightfully overcrowded and under-trammed: a car constructed to carry twenty-four people carries, at a rough guess, fifty. The palaces of the extinct millionaires contain in each room as many beds as will fit along the walls; and the less interesting of the temples, now as empty as the churches in London city because the people no longer believe in the priests, and, as in the west, will not attend the old services, are being demolished to make room for piles of offices and flats. Privacy is as impossible in Moscow as it is in a British or American barrack, battleship, slum, or working-class quarter. . . . You can look down on the poor wretches who in London and Chicago, to say nothing of meaner cities, have to pay a quarter of their scanty and precarious wage for damp cellars to sleep in; but the fact remains that I saw a man tried by a magistrate for the heinous crime of wrangling a room all to himself. That luxury can be snatched in rare cases if you are one of the intellectual proletariat. . . .

However, all this did not affect me. My suite at the Hotel Metropole consisted of a spacious salon, a bedroom, a bathroom with all sanitary accessories, and an entrance hall for my hats and overcoats. An even more grand-ducal apartment awaited me in Leningrad at the Hotel de l'Europe. . . . At the State Bank my letter of credit was waived aside with the assurance that my cheque would be honoured to any amount.

Not a band, not a flag, not a red scarf, not a street cheer from one end of the trip to the other,[3] though I was certainly treated as if I were Karl Marx in person, and given a grand reception (a queer mixture of public meeting, snack bar banquet, and concert), . . . where they celebrated my seventy-fifth birthday, . . . in the Hall of Nobles, which holds four thousand people and was crammed. The speeches were short. One of the concert performers wore evening dress, which seemed an absurd anachronism. One of the orators was in shirt and trousers, which seemed natural enough . . . ; and the chairman was picturesque in a heavy black leather coat and cap. . . . Lunacharsky[4] spoke. He and Litvinoff[5] went about with me a good deal because, as I soon discovered, they wanted to see the wonders of Sovietism, which they had never had time to see before. Every possible civility and facility was heaped on me without any ceremony; and the absence of ceremony and platform bunk made it extraordinarily pleasant.

The climax of the tour was an interview with Stalin. The sentry at the Kremlin who asked who we were was the only soldier I saw in

Russia. Stalin played his part to perfection, receiving us as old friends, and letting us talk ourselves dry before he modestly took the floor. Our party was Lord and Lady Astor, Phil Kerr (the late Marquess of Lothian),[6] and myself. Litvinoff and a few other Russians were present. On our way in we passed through three or four offices. In each of them sat an official at a writing table. We guessed a revolver handy in the drawer.

The proceedings opened with a violent attack by Lady Astor, who told Stalin that the Bolshevists did not know how to treat children. Stalin, for a moment taken aback, said contemptuously with a gesture, "In England you BEAT children."

Lady Astor promptly told him (in effect) not to be a damned fool, and to send some sensible woman to London to be instructed at Margaret McMillan's camp in Deptford in how children of five should be handled and dressed and taught.[7] Stalin immediately made a note of her address. We thought this mere politeness. But hardly had we got home when the sensible woman arrived with half a dozen others hungry for instruction. They were duly taken to Deptford, on which much Astor money has been lavished. . . .

Lord Astor strove to impress on Stalin that there was plenty of good feeling towards the Soviet in England, and nothing to prevent the friendliest understanding in the future. In fact he went so far that I had to warn Stalin that Lloyd George, implacably hostile to Bolshevism, was not wholly unrepresentative in that respect. I asked Stalin whether he had ever heard of Oliver Cromwell and his precept, preserved in the refrain of a song well known in Ireland,

> Put your trust in God, my boys,
> And keep your powder dry.

When he had taken this in he intimated that he would certainly keep his powder dry. He left God out of the question. I then asked what about inviting Mr Churchill to Russia. His geniality became, I thought, slightly sardonic as he replied that he would be delighted to see Mr Churchill in Moscow.

. . . The other thing which I did say quite freely to . . . [Stalin's] intense and great amusement is that it is a definitely religious system. Russia is a religious country. They could not imagine that we were serious when we said that the Third International is a Church, distinctly and unmistakably, but it is perfectly true. But I say it is Fabian Socialism, and its inspiration is a religious one all through. . . .

When we left (after midnight) we thought we had been a little over half an hour in the presence. Our watches scored two hours and thirty-five minutes.

Tourists who are bent on the usual routine of tramping through picture galleries and prowling through churches, to which I am myself greatly addicted, will be happy in Leningrad and Moscow. Incredible as it may seem in the west, the Russian revolution, though a fairly sanguinary one, was effected without vandalism or looting. When I went through the endless picture galleries and treasure chambers that begin with the Hermitage, and found that all the masterpieces of art had been held sacred where human lives were not worth a penny a dozen, I turned scornfully on my guides and said, "You call yourselves revolutionists, and you let all that priceless loot go! In the glorious west it would have been looted or smashed to the last ounce of gold and the last dab of paint. You ought to be ashamed of yourselves."

I compared, too, the undamaged churches with the defaced and mutilated remains of our English cathedrals, which would not have one stone left on another were it not that most of the stones are out of the reach of men no taller than six feet at most. But then our cathedral wreckers were fanatically religious, whereas the Communists hold what we call religion in utter contempt.

But the churches are a difficulty for the Soviet. The three fascinating churches in the Kremlin, and a few outside it, are kept for tourists and for their own artistic sake; but the others are like the city churches in London and several at the West End which are now shops and garages: nobody goes to them; and there is no popular sentiment in their favour like that which prevents the attempts of the Church of England to sell the city churches as the West-End ones have been sold, for the sake of their huge site values. One gigantic but uninteresting modern church in Moscow, with a metalled dome of considerable value (they said it was gold, but I could not believe it) is marked out for demolition and replacement by a State building. Close to it is a quaint little William and Mary church (as we should call it) in which I found a priest officiating. The congregation was a very devout one:

their worship was so fervently demonstrative as they knelt and smote the ground with their foreheads, punctuating the priest's intonations with moans of intense faith, that in Westminster Abbey they would have been handed over to the police and charged with "brawling"; but there were very few of them, not more than fifteen at the outside, including myself. However, as I have peeped into an English church and fled from the spectacle of a rector reading the service to his clerk and one pious lady, I thought the fifteen enough to justify the Soviet in sparing the William and Mary church; and I was interested, besides, in seeing for myself that public worship is as lawful in Russia as it is anywhere else, though Russia's rulers do not pretend to believe things that persons qualified to rule modern States could not possibly believe, nor will they allow children to be proselytized, even by their parents, until they are old enough to think for themselves in such matters. Besides, churches must pay rent to the State like other buildings; and if the priests cannot collect it from the congregation, out they go, and the State takes possession.

There are even so-called anti-religious museums which would delight the soul of Martin Luther and all sturdy Protestants from Belfast to Philadelphia. They are really historical museums to warn the people against the abuses of priestcraft and the horrors of religious persecution. The exhibits include one or two natural mummies, like the undecayed bodies in certain churches in Bremen and Dublin, to shew that such preservation is not miraculous, but may happen to you or me as easily as to St Clare at Assisi. Any Russian boy will tell you that there is no God; but as you find, on ascertaining what he means by that statement, that he is only reaffirming the first article of the Church of England, your fears for his salvation are quickly allayed.

The moment a revolution becomes a government it necessarily sets to work to exterminate revolutionists. Quite the most ridiculous exhibition I saw in Soviet Russia was the revolutionary museum in Moscow, devoted to the glorification of the heroes and martyrs who suffered and often perished in the struggle between Socialism and Capitalist Imperialism that lasted for seventy years before the triumph of the proletariat in Russia in 1917. . . . Many of them had been personally known to me. Most of them, in their frock coats and long beards, seemed strangely and solemnly respectable, and, compared with Russian commissars, enormously futile. They had talked and written and got themselves into trouble and been beaten every time by the *bour-*

geois police. The women, more practical, had killed a petty tyrant or two who had gone too far. Spiridonova,[8] for instance. I forget the name of the intolerable scoundrel she shot when it became quite plain that his death was as necessary as that of a cobra let loose in a nursery, and no man would take on the job. She was beaten to a jelly for it and otherwise horribly maltreated: I suppose because killing her would have been too merciful. But what a woman! A gentle, slight, delicate, and devoted district visitor, dressed as for a British rectory breakfast on Sunday morning. What must she, who lived to become the heroine of the revolution, have thought of its ruthless suppression of revolutionists? We know what Kropotkin,[9] the gentle, the noble, the Christ-like Kropotkin (how he would have repudiated the comparison!) felt about it. I know what Tolstoy's daughter felt about it: she told me herself; for she had seen a smiling countryside . . . where she had been born and brought up, . . . where good farming had brought to everybody such prosperity as was possible for them in the days of Tsardom, blasted into ruin and desolation, squalor and misery, by the Soviet expropriation and persecution of the Kulaks. . . . It was hard for her to forgive the Bolsheviks for that; and she was quite right; for the expulsion of the Kulaks, like the confiscation of the shops, before the Government was ready to carry on, was a stupid anti-Fabian blunder. . . . I visited Krupskaya, Lenin's widow, the most fascinating widow in the world, a woman to be adored by children and courted by savants; and the story went that she had given the Soviet a piece of her mind so roundly that Stalin had threatened that if she did it again he would appoint another widow for Lenin. Gorki, too, the sensitive, the hater of cruelty and injustice, the discoverer of touching virtues in the most impossible people: to him the revolution has not brought the millennium, though he can forgive it as he can forgive worse things. . . .

The persecution of the Intelligentsia in Russia did not last very long. It was, I think, justified at the time when it was not yet perceived to be impracticable. I have often said myself that if I were a revolutionary dictator my first care would be to see that persons with a university education, or with the acquired mentality which universities inculcate and stereotype, should be ruthlessly excluded from all direction of affairs, all contact with education especially with their own children, and, if not violently exterminated, at least encouraged to die out as soon as possible. Lenin shared my views and attempted to carry them into action. If Napoleon was able to find the very competent generals whom he made famous as his Marshals in the French stable yards and attorneys' offices, and snap his fingers at his former aristocratic comrades, why should not Lenin do likewise? But it was no use. . . . Trotsky's new army, like Cromwell's New Model, needed thirty thousand officers. The new communal industries required countless bosses; for Communism does not alter the natural division of modern mankind into 95 per cent who have their work cut out for them and 5 per cent who can cut it out. The proletarian supply ran short: the *bourgeois* supply was indispensable. The notice "no *bourgeois* need apply" was not formally taken down, nor was the ban lifted from the persecuted intelligentsia; but a new classification . . . was set up. . . .

I had great misgivings about the persecution of the Intelligentsia by putting them on smaller rations (like Karl Marx's *villicus*) and giving them the last chances of secondary education instead of the first. Why, I thought, should authors, artists, men of science, and mental workers generally be thus despised and stinted? But when representatives of these groups met me on my arrival, and, instead of begging me to give them a cake of soap or a pair of old shoes, seemed much better off and jollier than their fellows in London, I was nonplussed. "You authors," I explained, "are you not Intelligentsia?"

"Certainly not," they replied disdainfully.

"Well," I said, "of course I knew that; but I did not think the Russian Government knew it. Pray if you are not Intelligentsia, in heaven's name what are you?"

"We are the intellectual proletariat," they said. . . . As far as I could make out none of them had more than £500 a year and a two room flat to escape overcrowding in, nor any hope of greater luxury for many years to come. This may seem miserable poverty when you have forsytic[10] ideas and standards, and are in commercial competition, and your wife and daughter in social competition. . . .

There is so much to be said that I can only take odd bits and scraps to illustrate. . . . I remember going through a big electrical factory in Moscow. . . . A young man, with an air of conscious virtue, was presented to me. He had an Order of some sort pinned to his coat, and he was the young man who had set the pace in that factory in the carrying out of the Five Year Plan. He had done more than any other, and I said to him, "Young man, if you were in England, and you set up about double the pace of your fellow workers, you would not be a popular character, you would be called a 'slogger'—at least, that was the oldfashioned word, I dont know what it may be now—and you would run the risk of a brick being dropped on your head in a dark lane. If you are going on in this way, my friend, you stay in Russia." Certainly there the young man was popular. He led for efficiency.

I saw nothing of the hideous aftermath of the war: the hordes of deserted or orphaned child bandits, diseased, derelict, taking refuge at night from the terrible winter cold in the cooling asphalt containers of the street menders, following the weather from region to region as the seasons changed, dividing their little commonwealths spontaneously into scrupulous and timid, into little children who would not or dare not steal but who would spy out the land and locate the booty for the bolder and stronger who did the actual stealing, and, most amazing of all to our forsytes, their equal division of the spoils between big and little, bold and cowardly, strong and weak. There were millions of such children in Russia (and elsewhere) after the war. . . .

In the country I saw the domesticated children of the uncommunized peasant proprietors; and they certainly were dirty little savages; but they were living with their parents in the English agricultural fashion. In striking contrast to them were the children on the collective farm, who were so appallingly civilized that my first impulse was to denounce them as a parcel of insufferable little Marxian prigs. They were much too clean and well behaved and prettily dressed—as far as they were dressed at all. When a small and very prettily got up little girl sang a Sunday School song about how happy and glorious it was to work for the commune, I pinched myself to assure myself that I was awake and that this was indeed Russia and not Canterbury, and this child a genuine little Bolshevik and not the Dean's youngest daughter. I console myself with the hope that what I saw was the company manners of the children dressed up to receive distinguished visitors, and that the moment our backs were turned they behaved, as our nurses used to reproach us for behaving, "like wild Indians," as small children ought to behave.

However, I went to a prison for young delinquents, and saw there a batch of new arrivals who looked just as unpleasant as a batch of boy criminals in any of our big industrial towns. They were a bad lot, sulky, slouchy, furtively on their guard against the police or an assault from one of themselves. They were, I think, all the more suspicious because in Russia "stone walls do not a prison make"; and this prison was not a villainous house of torment spotted all over with half black, half opaque windows like an English jail, but a place rather like Battersea Park, bound by split wood palings which any moderately enterprising boy could climb over. Several of the lads had just come in; and the only conclusion they could draw from this absence of such prison arrangements as they could understand was that new, unforeseen, and frightful forms of torture were in store for them. Was not the genial commissar already beginning to improve their minds as he talked, ostensibly to us, but really over our heads at them? So they slouched at us and stared at us slantwise, and were afraid to pick our pockets lest their unexpected freedom to crowd up to us should be a trap. To get on terms with them we assured them, through the commissar, that though we were persons of the greatest eminence, whose success in life had exceeded the utmost that our most respectable parents could ever have hoped for us, yet the sole reason why we had not fallen into the hands of the police in our youth was that we were not found out. This broke the ice so effectively, and produced such a volley of questions as to what we had done, that we hastily moved on to avoid the dilemma of having either to disappoint them bitterly or else accuse ourselves of all the assassinations and burglaries they were thirsting for.

When we came to the old hands in the workshops we discovered that the cardinal difference between an English and a Russian prison is that in England a delinquent enters as an ordinary man and comes out as a "criminal type," whereas in Russia he enters, like those boys, as a criminal type and would come out an ordinary man but for the difficulty of inducing him to come out at all. As far as I could make out they could stay as long as they liked. In a competitive Capitalist state if prisoners are set to do or make anything useful there is a wild clamor from all the private traders that the prisons are taking their business away from them. I can remember when the extensive trade now done in photographs, picture postcards, and all sorts of fine art reproductions at the stalls in our public museums and art galleries, had to be conducted secretly and guiltily lest all the stationers in the neighborhood should terrify the Government with their protests. As to criminals in prisons their right to do anything useful that could possibly be done by a private contractor at a profit is still fiercely contested. But in Russia a prison (if prison it can be called) may be, and indeed is expected to be, as vigorously productive as a farm or factory, and therefore becomes a farm or factory or both. The only sign I saw of anything painful in the place was in the heavy industry shops, where strong lumps of women were operating big machinery whose handling was no child's play, in buildings which had some rather ugly holes and corners. The machines kept them at work intensely; and it may have been their preoccupation with it that gave them a sullen air and gave me a feeling that they objected to being exhibited to *bourgeois* tourists. Anyhow I cleared out as fast as might be.

Except for this I saw no sign of the way of the transgressor being made unnecessarily hard; and none of these women would have been any better off as innocent persons earning their living in an English factory. As for the men, mostly skilled woodworkers (wood is a congenial material to the Russian), they were turning out skis and tennis racquets at a tremendous rate and seemed to be enjoying it. One jolly young expert, obviously not mentally defective or congenitally criminal in any way, told me that he was able to send his old father a substantial allowance out of the pocket money he earned at his ski making. I forebore to ask what he had done to bring him there; but there was certainly not a trace about him, or any of the men working with him, of the criminal type which our prisons produce. . . .

I went one day into a big building which turned out to be a police court. It was many other things as well. But at last I found a room in it in which people were sitting about on forms before a raised table on which a busy and evidently capable woman was discussing something with a couple of men on the nearest form. I asked who she was, and was told that she was the magistrate. I asked what the man sitting at the table on her left, and the woman on her right, were doing here, and learnt that they were there on behalf of the public to see fair play. There were no police in sight. I gathered that one of the parties to the discussion had wanted a room all to himself, being entitled to a bed only. Of his fate I know nothing for when the magistrate presently left the court with the two public assessors to consider her decision I also left that court and went to another.

Here the magistrate—she too was a woman—had already retired; and though I was told it was a serious case of an abortionist who had been convicted before for the same offence, there were no police and nothing to distinguish the accused from anyone else in the room. I was surprised at the nature of the charge; for much virtuous indignation has been exercised in England, where to abort a pregnancy is a very serious crime, over the wickedness of its toleration in Russia. We believe that our institutions and criminal codes are divine and universal, and have no suspicion that such toleration is by no means peculiar to Russia, or that some British and American surgeons make a good deal of money by performing abortions on very thin pretexts. I was informed that if a woman not more than two months pregnant can give satisfactory reasons for abortion she can be licensed to undergo it, and the surgeon licensed to perform it. The case in court was that of a woman who had performed it without these formalities, as a private speculation.

The magistrate soon came back with the assessors and read a reasoned sentence of a year's imprisonment. And now, I thought, I shall see this malefactress seized by warders and hauled off to undergo her sentence. But not a bit of it. A woman who was sitting against the wall at the end of one of the benches rose up with a burst of tears and fury, and (as I guessed, for I do not know more than five words of Russian) calling on the heavens to witness that there is no justice on earth, that the magistrate was a monster of cruelty; and that she would never speak to her again, walked indignantly out of the room.

"Is nobody going to take her to prison?" I demanded amazedly.

"Oh no," was the reply. "She is going back to work."

Apparently her punishment was to be compelled to work in a factory for a year on rather short commons; not allowed to go to the opera and lodged under lock and key at night.

Nothing happens in Russia in the sense put on it in Britain and America.

18

Burning the Candle at Both Ends

The central error of the time[1] was an impatient disposition to flout all theory, and consequently all principle, in politics, industry, and finance. It produced also an extravagant reaction against any sort of rule in private relations. A license in sexual intercourse, in the use of drugs and alcohol, in dress and undress, accompanied by a mania for dancing, did both good and harm; but both ways it was anarchic, myopic, and defiant of every plea for a constructive policy. It was pleasant to see bright young things having a good time; but it was not pleasant to see how very soon they ceased to be either bright or young. They looked battered and thirty-five when they should have looked still beautiful and twenty-five, all through unrestrained thoughtlessness and ignorance of how to live.

The dull old things in the political world were just as disastrous. They, too, would not hear of anything so painful as thinking. During the war they had met every appeal to their minds with the formula, "Remember: we are at war"; and when the Armistice called even more urgently for mental exercise they said, in effect, "We went through the war without thinking; and we won. Why should we not get through the peace without it?"

. . . When wars were waged by professional armies, the reversal of morality which they involved was kept in a conscience-tight compartment: a civilian population might talk wickedly enough in its patriotic fervor; but it did not know what it was talking about: the actual slaughter and sack and rapine was only a story in the newspapers, not a real experience. But a war like that of 1914–18, in which the whole male population of military age was forced to serve, hosts of women volunteered for work under fire, and the new feature of aerial bombardment brought the bloody part of the business crash into the civilians' bedrooms, was quite another matter. The shock to common morals was enormously greater and more general. So was the strain on the nerves. . . . What the bright young things after the war tried to do, and what their wretched survivors are still trying to do, is to get the reaction without the terror, to go on eating cocaine and drinking cocktails as if they had only a few hours' expectation of life instead of forty years.

In my play the ex-war nurse and the ex-airman-ace persuade a respectable young lady, too respectable to have ever had a good time, to come with them and enjoy the sort of good time they had in the nightmare of 1914–18. . . . The demonstration is rather funny at first; but . . . somehow my play, Too True To Be Good, . . . in performance excited an animosity and an enthusiasm which will hardly be accounted for by the printed text. Some of the spectators felt that they had had a divine revelation, and overlooked the fact that the eloquent gentleman through whose extremely active mouth they had received it was the most hopeless sort of scoundrel: that is, one whose scoundrelism consists in the absence of conscience rather than in any positive vices, and is masked by good looks and agreeable manners. The less intellectual journalist critics sulked as they always do when their poverty but not their will consents to their witnessing a play of mine; but over and above the resultant querulousness to which I have long been accustomed I thought I detected an unusual intensity of resentment, as if I had hit them in some new and unbearable sore spot.

I remember a soldier of the old never-do-well type drifting into a little Socialist Society which I happened to be addressing more than fifty years ago. As he had evidently blundered into the wrong shop and was half drunk, some of the comrades began to chaff him, and finally held me up to him as an example of the advantages of teetotalism. With the most complete conviction he denounced me a hypocrite and a liar, affirming it to be a well-known and inexorable law of nature that no man with money in his pocket could pass a public house without going in for a drink.

I have never forgotten that soldier, because his delusion, in less crude forms, and his conception of happiness, seem to afflict everybody in

England more or less. When I say less crude forms I do not mean truer forms; for the soldier, being half drunk, was probably happier than he would have been if quite sober, whereas the plutocrat who has spent a hundred pounds in a day in the search for pleasure is not happier than if he had spent only five shillings. . . .

Where, then, was the offence that so exceedingly disgruntled these unhappy persons? I think it must have been the main gist and moral of the play, which is not, as usual, that our social system is unjust to the poor, but that it is cruel to the rich. Our revolutionary writers have dwelt on the horrors of poverty. Our conventional and romantic writers have ignored those horrors, dwelling pleasantly on the elegances of an existence free from pecuniary care. The poor have been pitied for miseries which do not, unfortunately, make them unbearably miserable. But who has pitied the idle rich or really believed that they have a worse time of it than those who have to live on ten shillings a day or less, and earn it? My play is a story of three reckless young people who come into possession of, for the moment, unlimited riches, and set out to have a thoroughly good time with all the modern machinery of pleasure to aid them. The result is that they get nothing for their money but a multitude of worries and a maddening dissatisfaction. . . . The despair of the shell-shocked young gentleman-burglar-clergyman who made such a pitiful attempt to be happy by spending a lump of unearned money, is not my despair, though I share his opinion of the utter unsatisfactoriness of that popular receipt for a good life. I made him a good preacher to warn the world against mere fluency. . . .

Long ago I suggested that we should all be obliged to appear before a Board (virtually an inquisition) every five years, and justify our existence to its satisfaction on pain of liquidation. . . . I wrote a play called The Simpleton of the Unexpected Isles, ending with the Day of Judgment, which turned out to be a prosaic inquiry, on a fine summer morning without any apocalyptic terrors, into the questions of whether we were pulling our weight in the social boat, followed by the mysterious disappearance of those who were not.

The increasing bewilderment of my journalist critics as to why I should write such plays as The Simpleton culminated in New York in February 1935, when I was described as a dignified old monkey throwing cocoanuts at the public in pure senile devilment. This is an amusing and graphic description of the effect I produce on the newspapers; but as a scientific criticism it is open to the matter-of-fact objection that a play is not a cocoanut nor I a monkey. Yet there is an analogy. A cocoanut is impossible without a suitable climate; and a play is impossible without a suitable civilization. If author and journalist are both placid Panglossians, convinced that their civilization is the best of all possible civilizations, and their countrymen the greatest race on earth: in short, if they have had a university education, there is no trouble: the Press notices are laudatory if the play is entertaining. Even if the two are pessimists who agree with Jeremiah that the heart of man is deceitful above all things and desperately wicked, and with Shakespear that political authority only transforms its wielders into angry apes, there is still no misunderstanding; for that dismal view, or a familiar acquaintance with it, is quite common.

Such perfect understanding covers much more than nine hundred and ninety cases out of every thousand new plays. But it does not cover the cases in which the author and the journalist are not writing against the same background. . . .

What I miss . . . is a proper respect for the Apocalypse. As a child I was taught to fear the Day of Judgment, which was presented to my young imagination in so clear a fashion that once when I dreamt of it, I thought I had stepped into our garden in the middle of the night and seen above the gloom of the garden wall a great silver radiance in the sky, and in the middle of it a black equestrian statue like that of King William in College Green, Dublin, whom I immediately identified with God, come to judge the world. I did not call on the mountains to hide me; but I slipped back very quickly into the house and fastened the door noiselessly before the all-seeing eye lighted on me; for you cannot get it out of the head of a Christian child, or a Christian adult either, that God cannot be dodged and cheated like an earthly father.

That vision of judgment of mine was not more unlike any conceivable possible event than the great fresco by Michael Angelo in the Sistine Chapel in Rome, or that other one by Tintoretto in the ducal palace in Venice, or than the more compact painting by Albrecht Dürer. Such visions and pictures do not impose on the children in this age of science; and I should as soon think of dramatising Jack and the Beanstalk as Michael Angelo's picture. But in rejecting all this imagery, we are apt to make the usual blunder of emptying the baby out with the bath. By all means dismiss the scenes painted by Tintoretto, Albrecht Dürer, and the rest as having no more reality than a red lion on a signboard. Cancel the authority of the Book of Revelation as the hallucinations of a drug addict which should never have been included in the canon. But do not think you have got rid of the idea of a judgment to which all human lives must finally come, and without which life has no meaning. On the contrary, the burning up of the old stage scenery and the exorcism of the old spectres only brings into clearer reality the need for justifying one's existence as well as merely enjoying or suffering it. The question, "What good are you?" cannot be disposed of by the simple retort, "Mind your own business!" Even if it were not everybody's business in a civilized society, it is a question which people with properly trained social consciences cannot help asking themselves. . . . This terrifying judgment is the theme of The Simpleton. . . . But you need not fear: you can depend on me to get plenty of fun out of the most dismal subjects[2] and to improve your mind into the bargain.

How many people have heard of the Intellectual Co-operation Committee? It will probably be dismissed by the critics as an overstrained fiction. It is nothing of the sort. The League of Nations had not been long in existence when a Frenchman, perceiving that without intellectual co-operation the League could do nothing but practise the old diplomacy, founded the Committee in Paris. Everyone was delighted; and the most eminent intellects in the world gave their names as intellectual co-operators. The Frenchman gave a million francs to endow the Committee; but as the French franc had dropped to twopence (having been largely borrowed at tenpence) the Committee was stony-broke at the end of a month. It still survived in a little office somewhere (I have invented one in Geneva for it in the play) and even did . . . some clerical work in listing universities, learned societies, and the like; but intellectually it sank into a profound catalepsy.

When Romain Rolland, with . . . Henri Barbusse and their friends tried from time to time to organize some international movement on the extreme Left, and invited me, as they always did, to join them, I asked them why they did not operate through the I.C. Committee of the League, which was sleeping ready to their hands. The suggestion struck them dumb.

At last the Committee, which occasionally woke up in the person of Gilbert Murray, asked me to correspond with the League. This very nearly struck me dumb; for what on earth was I to correspond about? . . . And so it came about that I found it growing on me that there was some fun to be got on the stage out of the Committee.

That was how the play began.

Geneva is a title that speaks for itself. The critics . . . complain that I have not solved all the burning political problems of the present and future in it. . . . They always do. I am flattered by the implied attribution to me of omniscience and omnipotence; but I am also infuriated by the unreasonableness of the demand. I am neither omniscient nor omnipotent; and the utmost I or any other playwright can do is to extract comedy and tragedy from the existing situation and wait to see what will become of it.[3]

In providing a historical play for the Malvern Festival of 1939 I departed from the established practice sufficiently to require a word of explanation. The "histories" of Shakespear are chronicles dramatized; and my own chief historical plays, Caesar and Cleopatra and St Joan, are fully documented chronicle plays of this type. Familiarity with them would get a student safely through examination papers on their periods. . . . I became a historian myself. I wrote a play entitled In Good King Charles's Golden Days. For the actual occurrence of the incidents in it I cannot produce a scrap of evidence, being quite convinced that they never occurred; yet anyone reading this play or witnessing a performance of it will not only be pleasantly amused, but will come out with a knowledge of the dynamics of Charles's reign—that is, of the political and personal forces at work in it—that ten years of digging up mere facts in the British Museum or the Record Office could not give. And whereas most of us leave school resolved never to open a schoolbook again or even think of these instruments of torture, I should starve if the effects of my books and plays were not to make the sort of people I write for buy another of them and yet another until there are no more to read.

A much commoner theatrical product is the historical romance, mostly fiction with historical names attached to the stock characters of the stage. Many of these plays have introduced their heroines as Nell Gwynn, and Nell's principal lover as Charles II. As Nell was a lively and lovable actress, it was easy to reproduce her by casting a lively and lovable actress for the part; but the stage Charles, though his costume and wig were always unmistakable, never had any other resemblance to the real Charles, nor to anything else on earth except what he was not: a stage walking gentleman with nothing particular to say for himself.

Now the facts of Charles's reign have been chronicled so often by modern historians of all parties, from the Whig Macaulay to the Jacobite Hilaire Belloc, that there is no novelty left for the chronicler to put on the stage. As to the romance, it is intolerably stale: the spectacle of a Charles sitting with his arm round Nell Gwynn's waist, or with Moll Davis seated on his knee, with the voluptuous termagant Castlemaine raging in the background, has no interest for me, if it ever had for any grown-up person.

But when we turn from the sordid facts of Charles's reign, and from his Solomonic polygamy, to what might have happened to him but did not, the situation becomes interesting and fresh. For instance, Charles might have met that human prodigy Isaac Newton. And Newton might have met that prodigy of another sort, George Fox, the founder of the morally mighty Society of Friends, vulgarly called the Quakers. Better again, all three might have met. Now anyone who considers a 150th edition of Sweet Nell of Old Drury[4] more attractive than Isaac Newton had better avoid my plays: they are not meant for such. And anyone who is more interested in Lady Castlemaine's hips than in Fox's foundation of the great Cult of Friendship should keep away from theatres and frequent worse places. Still, though the interest of my play lies mainly in the clash of Charles, George, and Isaac, there is some fun in the clash between all three and Nelly, Castlemaine, and the Frenchwoman Louise de Kéroualle, whom we called Madame Carwell. So I bring the three on the stage to relieve the intellectual tension.

There is another clash which is important and topical in view of the hold that professional science has gained on popular credulity since the middle of the nineteenth century. I mean the eternal clash between the artist and the physicist. I have therefore invented a collision between Newton and a personage whom I should like to have called Hogarth; for it was Hogarth who said, "The line of beauty is a curve," and Newton whose first dogma it was that the universe is in principle rectilinear. He called straight lines right lines; and they were still so called in my school Euclid eighty years ago. But Hogarth could not by any magic be fitted into the year 1680, my chosen date; so I had to fall back on Godfrey Kneller.[5] Kneller had not Hogarth's brains; but I have had to endow him with them to provide Newton with a victorious antagonist. In point of date Kneller just fitted in.

But I must make an exception to this general invitation. If by any chance you are a great mathematician or astronomer you had perhaps better stay away. I have made Newton aware of something wrong with the perihelion of Mercury. Not since Shakespear made Hector of Troy quote Aristotle has the stage perpetrated a more staggering anachronism. But I find the perihelion of Mercury so irresistible as a laugh catcher (like Weston-Super-Mare) that I cannot bring myself to sacrifice it. I am actually prepared to defend it as a possibility. Newton was not only a lightning calculator with a monstrous memory: he was also a most ingenious and dexterous maker of apparatus. He made his own telescope; and when he wanted to look at Mercury without being dazzled by the sun he was quite clever enough to produce an artificial eclipse by putting an obturator into the telescope, though nobody else hit on that simple device until long after. My ignorance in these matters is stupendous. . . . The most gifted genius cannot study everything. I am a competent playwright; but nothing would make a competent mathematician of me. I can manipulate a calculating machine, and I daresay I could be taught to use a table of logarithms just as I use a ready reckoner. But my time is better employed in writing plays and books. Everything else I must leave undone or get somebody else to do it for me, or, if I do it myself, do it by rule of thumb, using the method without pretending to understand it. In literature and drama, I am a celebrity: in an aeroplane factory I should be a mental defective. When I contemplate what I know and have done (not that I ever do) I have a high opinion of myself. When I contemplate what I dont know and cannot do (which I am often forced to do) I feel as a worm might if it knew how big the world is. . . . But I refuse to believe that Newton's system did not enable him to locate Mercury theoretically at its nearest point to the sun, and then to find out with his telescope that it was apparently somewhere else.

For the flash of prevision in which Newton foresees Einstein's curvilinear universe I make no apology. Newton's first law of motion is pure dogma. So is Hogarth's first law of design. The modern astronomers have proved, so far, that Hogarth was right and Newton wrong. But as the march of science during my long lifetime has played skittles with all the theories in turn I dare not say how the case will stand by the time this play of mine reaches its thousandth performance (if it ever does). Meanwhile let me admit that Newton in my play is a stage astronomer: that is, an astronomer not for an age but for all time. Newton as a man was the queerest of the prodigies; and I have chapter and verse for all his contradictions.

I recall a summer evening many years ago, when [I was] a very young man, standing on the pier at Broadstairs [in Kent] at midnight. There was a beautiful moon. Not being a romantic person—I was enjoying the air and the landscape, but I was not sentimental. and I was alone—except for the presence of a gentleman, whom I did not know then, who was a member of the Royal [Astronomical] Society, and who, I think, was a hundred and two years of age.[6] But this gentleman, seeing me looking at the moon for a long time, stepped up to me, and said to me very politely, "You are looking at the moon very attentively, sir."

I said, "Yes, it is a fine night."

He said, "May I ask how far off you would say the moon was?"

Well, I looked at the moon, and I said perfectly sincerely and frankly—I have no scientific professions; I gave an honest answer—I said, "I should think about forty miles."

I will confess I had expected to shock this gentleman a little, and I perceived I had interested him in quite a notable way. "That," he said, "is a very interesting answer. May I ask how you arrived at that figure?"

I said, "I am judging by the look of the thing."

"Ah!" he said, "well, you are a very good judge, because . . . the exact distance, leaving out fractions of miles, is thirty-seven miles."

Well then, I began to perceive that, whereas I had not altogether been innocent of an intention to get a slight rise out of the old gentleman, the old gentleman had, as a matter of fact, got a rise out of me. I said, "I have no doubt you are quite right, but I think it is somewhat less than the usual calculation," and he said, "That is so." Then he gave me a very elaborate and, to me, entirely convincing—because I did not understand it—demonstration. The only thing I can remember now about it,[7] and it is possible some mathematician or astronomer in the audience may understand it—the only thing I can remember of what he said was, if astronomers, instead of using the

P

method of parallax and calculating the distance of a star in that way, would trace the actual orbit of the star by using a geometric chuck on a lathe, they would arrive at correct conclusions. I am shortening the explanation very considerably. I have a slight knowledge of what a lathe is, but not the slightest of what a geometric chuck is. The only association one has of a chuck is perhaps with the pier at midnight, and the moon, and so on, but it is not a geometric chuck. That gentleman, at intervals until he died—which I think occurred about ten years later—used to send me elaborate documents, which I read with great interest, and this demonstration that the astronomers were all wrong seemed to me to be just as convincing as the demonstrations by the astronomers themselves, which I occasionally come across, that they are all right.

. . . Please do not infer that being a hopeless duffer mathematically and mechanically I cannot comprehend mathematics and physics in all their immense democratic importance. Lightning calculators and great inventors may have no such comprehension. Newton was so great a mathematician that when he invented infinitesimal calculus he kept it secret as an unprofessional dodge until Leibniz invented it also and was highly praised for it. Yet Newton was as credulous as a child in the nursery in his elaborate study of historical chronology. It is by confusing the practitioner with the comprehensionist that we have come to believe in England that metaphysicans and philosophers are fools, and practical men safe guides. Certainly the practical men know where they are, but not always whither we are going, whereas the thinkers who know whither we are going do not always know where we are.

As to Charles, he adolesced as a princely cosmopolitan vagabond of curiously mixed blood, and ended as the first king in England whose kingship was purely symbolic, and who was clever enough to know that the work of the regicides could not be undone, and that he had to reign by his wits and not by the little real power they had left him. Unfortunately the vulgarity of his reputation as a Solomonic polygamist has not only obscured his political ability, but eclipsed the fact that he was the best of husbands. Catherine of Braganza, his wife, has been made to appear a nobody, and Castlemaine, his concubine, almost a great historical figure. When you have seen my play[8] you will not make that mistake, and may therefore congratulate yourself on assisting at an act of historical justice. . . .

The . . . mistresses could make him do nothing that his good nature did not dispose him to do, whether it was building Greenwich Hospital or making dukes of his bastards. As a husband he took his marriage very seriously, and his sex adventures as calls of nature on an entirely different footing. In this he was in the line of evolution, which leads to an increasing separation of the unique and intensely personal and permanent marriage relation from the carnal intercourse described in Shakespear's sonnet. This, being a response to the biological decree that the world must be peopled, may arise irresistibly between persons who could not live together endurably for a week but can produce excellent children. Historians who confuse Charles's feelings for his wife with his appetite for Barbara Villiers do not know chalk from cheese biologically.

WITHDRAWN

19

Ending as a Sage

WHEN I WAS . . . young . . . the world seemed to me to be unchangeable, and a year seemed a long time. . . . I remember using tallow candles which needed trimming with a scissors called a snuffers to light me to bed, and smelly oil burners to read by in the evenings. I have had a tooth cavity scraped out with a spike. I have lived to have my teeth (when I had any) drilled by electricity, my hair cut by electricity, my rooms not only lighted but swept and dusted by electricity turned on from a tap in the wall. . . . When I had lived for fifty-eight years free from the fear that war could come to my doorstep, the thing occurred. And when the war to end war had come to a glorious victory, it occurred again, worse than ever. I have . . . lived through two "world wars" without missing a meal or a night's sleep in my bed, though they have come near enough to shatter my windows, break in my door, and wreck my grandfather clock, keeping me for nine years of my life subject to a continual apprehension of a direct hit next time blowing me and my household to bits.

I cannot pretend that this troubled me much: people build houses and live on the slopes of Etna and Vesuvius and at the foot of Stromboli as cheerfully as on Primrose Hill. I was too old to be conscribed for military service; and the mathematical probabilities were enormously against a bomb coming my way; for at the worst of the bombardments only from ten to fifteen inhabitants of these islands were killed by air raids every day; and a dozen or so out of forty-five millions is not very terrifying even when each of us knows that he or she is as likely as not to be one of the dozen. The risk of being run over by a motor bus, which townsmen run daily, is greater.

It was this improbability which made pre-atomic air raiding futile as a means of intimidating a nation, and enabled the government of the raided nation to prevent the news of the damage reaching beyond its immediate neighborhood. One night early in the resumed war I saw, from a distance of thirty miles, London burning for three hours. Next morning I read in the newspapers that a bomb had fallen on the windowsill of a city office, and been extinguished before it exploded. Returning to London later on I found that half the ancient city had been levelled to the ground, leaving only St Paul's and a few church towers standing. The wireless news never went beyond "some damage and a few casualties in Southern England" when in fact leading cities and seaports had been extensively wrecked. All threatening news was mentioned only in secret sessions of parliament, hidden under heavy penalties until after the victory. In 1941, after the Dunkirk rout, our position was described by the Prime Minister to the House of Commons in secret session as so desperate that if the enemy had taken advantage of it we should have been helplessly defeated; and it is now the fashion to descant dithyrambically on the steadfast heroism with which the nation faced this terrible emergency. As a matter of fact the nation knew nothing about it. Had we been told, the Germans would have overheard and rushed the threatened invasion they were bluffed into abandoning. Far from realizing our deadly peril, we were exulting in the triumph of our Air Force in "the Battle of Britain" and in an incident in South America in which three British warships drove one German one into the River Plate. Rather than be interned with his crew the German captain put to sea again against hopeless odds; scuttled his ship; and committed suicide.[1] The British newspapers raved about this for weeks as a naval victory greater than Salamis, Lepanto, and Trafalgar rolled into one.

Later on our flight from Tobruk to the border of Egypt did not disturb us at home: it was reported as a trifling setback, whilst trumpery captures of lorries or motor bicycles by British patrols figured as victories. After major engagements German losses were given in figures: Allies' losses were not given at all, the impression left being that the Allies had killed or taken prisoner tens of thousands of Axis troops without suffering any casualties worth mentioning. Only by listening to the German broadcasts, similarly cooked, could the real facts and fortunes of the war be estimated. Of course the truth leaked out months later; but it produced only a fresh orgy of bragging about our heroic fortitude in the face of the deadly peril we knew nothing of.

All this was necessary and inevitable. It was dangerous to tell the truth about anything, even about the weather. The signposts on the roads had to be taken down and hidden lest they should help an invader to find his way. It was a crime to give an address with a date, or to scatter a few crumbs for the birds. And it was an act of heroic patriotism to drop a bomb weighing ten thousand pounds on dwellings full of women and children, or on crowded railway trains. Our bombing of foreign cities not only in Germany but in countries which we claimed to be "liberating" became so frightful that at last the word had to be given to two of our best broadcasters of war reports to excuse them on the ground that by shortening the war they were saving the lives of thousands of British soldiers.

Meanwhile nobody noticed how completely war, as an institution, had reduced itself to absurdity. . . . But the resources of decivilization were not exhausted. When we were exulting in our demolition of cities like Cologne and Hamburg we were very considerably frightened by the descent on London of new projectiles, unmanned yet aimed and guided, which demolished not only streets but districts. And when we and our allies "liberated" German-occupied territory (blowing its cities to smithereens largely in the process) we discovered that the manufacture of these new horrors had been planned for on such a scale that but for their capture in time the tables might have been turned on us with a vengeance.

But we had another card up our sleeve: this time a trump so diabolical that when we played it the war, which still lingered in Japan, was brought to an abrupt stop by an Anglo-American contrivance which may conceivably transform the globe into a cloud of flaming gas in which no form of life known to us could survive for a moment. . . . Though the victory was not a triumph of Christianity it was a triumph of Science. American and British scientists, given *carte blanche* in the matter of expense, had concentrated on a romantic and desperate search for a means of harnessing the mysterious forces that mould and hold atoms into metals, minerals, and finally into such miracles as human geniuses, taking some grains of metal and a few salts purchasable at the nearest oil-shop and fashioning with them the head of Shakespear, to say nothing of my own.

. . . The experiment was tried on two Japanese cities. . . .

I am in the condition of Macbeth in his last Act: "I have supped full with horrors: direness, familiar to my slaughterous thoughts, cannot once start me."

I commit this to print within a few weeks of completing my ninety-second year. At such an age I should apologize for perpetrating another play or presuming to pontificate in any fashion. I can hardly walk through my garden without a tumble or two; and it seems out of all reason to believe that a man who cannot do a simple thing like that can practise the craft of Shakespear. Is it not a serious sign of dotage to talk about oneself, which is precisely what I am now doing? Should it not warn me that my bolt is shot, and my place silent in the chimney corner?

Well, I grant all this; yet I cannot hold my tongue nor my pen. As long as I live I must write. If I stopped writing I should die for want of something to do. . . .

When I take my pen or sit down to my typewriter, I am as much a medium as Browning's Mr Sludge or Dunglas Home,[2] or as Job or John of Patmos. When I write a play I do not foresee nor intend a page of it from one end to the other: the play writes itself. I may reason out every sentence until I have made it say exactly what it comes to me to say; but whence and how and why it comes to me, or why I persisted, through nine years of unrelieved market failure, in writing instead of in stockbroking or turf bookmaking or peddling, I do not know. You may say it was because I had a talent that way. So I had; but that fact remains inexplicable. What less could Mr Sludge say? or John Hus, who let himself be burnt rather than recant his "I dont know. Instruct me"?

When I was a small boy I saw a professional writing medium, pencil in hand, slash down page after page with astonishing speed without lifting his pencil from the blank paper we fed on to his desk. The fact that he was later transported for forgery did not make his performance and his choice of mediumship as his profession less unaccountable. When I was an elderly man, my mother amused herself with a planchette and a ouija, which under her hands produced what are called spirit writings abundantly. It is true that these screeds might have been called wishful writings (like wishful thinkings) so clearly were they as much her own story-telling inventions as the Waverley novels were Scott's. But why did she choose and practice this senseless activity? Why was I doing essentially the same as a playwright? I do not know. We both got some satisfaction from it or we would not have done it.

This satisfaction, this pleasure, this appetite, is as yet far from being as intense as the sexual orgasm or the ecstasy of a saint, though future cortical evolution may leave them far behind. Yet there are the moments of inexplicable happiness. . . . To me they have come only in dreams not oftener than once every fifteen years or so. I do not know how common they are; for I never heard anyone . . . mention them. They have an exalted chronic happiness, as of earth become heaven, proving that such states are possible for us even as we now are.

. . . My powers are waning; but so much the better for those who found me unbearably brilliant when I was in my prime. It is my hope that a hundred apter and more elegant parables by younger hands will soon leave mine as far behind as the religious pictures of the fifteenth century left behind the first attempts of the early Christians at iconography. . . . Shakespear, with all his flashes and divinations, never understood . . . how any man who was not a fool could, like Bunyan's hero, look back from the brink of the river of death over the strife and labor of his pilgrimage, and say, "Yet do I not repent me"; or, with the panache of a millionaire, bequeath "my sword to him that shall succeed me in my pilgrimage, and my courage and skill to him that can get it." This is the true joy in life, the being used for a purpose recognized by yourself as a mighty one; the being thoroughly worn out before you are thrown on the scrap heap; the being a force of Nature instead of a feverish selfish little clod of ailments and grievances complaining that the world will not devote itself to making you happy. And also the only real tragedy in life is the being used by personally minded men for purposes which you recognize to be base. All the rest is at worst mere misfortune or mortality: this alone is misery, slavery, hell on earth; and the revolt against it is the only force that offers a man's work to the poor artist, whom our personally minded rich people would so willingly employ as pandar, buffoon, beauty monger, sentimentalizer, and the like.

I am myself much idolized. I receive almost daily letters from devout Shavians who believe that my income is unlimited, my knowledge and wisdom infinite, my name a guarantee of success for any enterprise, my age that of Jesus at his death, and the entire Press at my command, especially The Times, of which I am assumed to be the proprietor.

If this is not idolatry the word has no meaning. The fact that I am ascertainably, and indeed conspicuously, only a superannuated (not supernatural) journalist and playwright does not shake the faith of my idolaters in the least. . . . And the ordinary citizen, knowing that an author who is well spoken of by a respectable newspaper must be all right, reads me, as he reads Micah, with undisturbed edification from his own point of view. It is narrated that in the eighteen-seventies an old lady, a very devout Methodist, moved from Colchester to a house in the neighborhood of the City Road, in London, where, mistaking the Hall of Science for a chapel, she sat at the feet of Charles Bradlaugh for many years, entranced by his eloquence, without questioning his orthodoxy or moulting a feather of her faith. I fear I shall be defrauded of my just martyrdom in the same way.

However, I am digressing, as a man with a grievance always does. And after all, the main thing in determining the artistic quality of a book is not the opinions it propagates, but the fact that the writer has opinions. The old lady from Colchester was right to sun her simple soul in the energetic radiance of Bradlaugh's genuine beliefs and disbeliefs. . . .

I am not at all dashed by the fact that my preachings and prophetisings, like those of the many sages who have said the same things before me, seem to have produced no political change—that . . . the world has been going from bad to worse since I gave tongue and pen. . . . The England of Pecksniffs and Podsnaps has not become an England of Ruskins and Bernard Shaws.

. . . My experience as an enlightener, which is considerable, is that what is wrong with the average citizen is not altogether deficient political capacity. It is largely ignorance of facts, creating a vacuum into which all sorts of romantic antiquarian junk and cast-off primitive religion rushes. I have to enlighten sects describing themselves as Conservatives, Socialists, Protestants, Catholics, Communists, Fascists, Fabians, Friends (Quakers), Ritualists, all bearing labels which none of them can define, and which indicate tenets which none of them accept as practical rules of life and many of them repudiate with abhorrence when they are presented without their labels. . . . They group themselves in political parties and clubs in which none of them knows what he or she is talking about. Some of them have Utopian aspirations, and have read the prophets and sages, from Moses to Marx, and from Plato to Ruskin and Inge; but a question as to a point of existing law or the function of a County Council strikes them dumb. They are more dangerous than simpletons and illiterates because on the strength of their irrelevant schooling they believe themselves politically educated, and are accepted as authorities on political subjects accordingly.

Now this political ignorance and delusion is curable by simple instruction as to the facts without any increase of political capacity. I am ending as a sage with a very scrappy and partial knowledge of the world. I do not see why I should not have begun with it if I had been told it all to begin with: I was more capable of it then than I am now in my dotage. When I am not writing plays as a more or less inspired artist I write political schoolbooks in which I say nothing of the principles of Socialism or any other Ism (I disposed of all that long ago), and try to open my readers' eyes to the political facts under which they live. I cannot change their minds; but I can increase their knowledge. A little knowledge is a dangerous thing; but we must take that risk because a little is as much as our biggest heads can hold; and a citizen who knows that the earth is round and older than six thousand years is less dangerous than one of equal capacity who believes it is a flat ground floor between a first floor heaven and a basement hell.

I know now that I am mortal, which, in my Saturday Review-ing days, I had come to doubt. My will contains directions for my funeral, which will be followed, not by mourning coaches, but by herds of oxen, sheep, swine, flocks of poultry, and a small travelling aquarium of live fish, all wearing white scarves in honour to the man who perished rather than eat his fellow-creatures. It will be, with the single exception of Noah's Ark, the most remarkable thing of the kind yet seen.

Of these reminiscences and memoranda I must now make an end, as there must be an end to everything. I have tried, as I promised, not to plague my readers with details common to myself and ninetynine and a half per cent of the human race; but I have included matter that, though not peculiar to myself, may be instructive to beginners in my various professions or to historians of my period. . . . Whether the result is readable or not I am in doubt; for at my age . . . I cannot be sure that my sayings and writings are not the senile drivellings of a garrulous and too old man.

However, enough of it was written years ago to embolden me to let it take its chance, such as it is. I will not even say Hail and Farewell. . . .

APPENDIX I

Last Will and Testament

This is the last Will and Testament of me George Bernard Shaw of 4 Whitehall Court in the County of London and of Ayot Saint Lawrence in the County of Herts Author.

1.

I revoke all Wills and testamentary dispositions heretofore made by me.

2.

I appoint the Public Trustee as the sole Executor and Trustee of this my Will who is hereinafter referred to as "my Trustee."

3.

I desire that my dead body shall be cremated and its ashes inseparably mixed with those of my late wife now in the custody of the Golders Green Crematorium and in this condition inurned or scattered in the garden of the house in Ayot Saint Lawrence where we lived together for thirty five years unless some other disposal of them should be in the opinion of my Trustee more eligible. Personally I prefer the garden to the cloister.[1]

4.

As my religious convictions and scientific views cannot at present be more specifically defined than as those of a believer in Creative Evolution I desire that no public monument or work of art or inscription or sermon or ritual service commemorating me shall suggest that I accepted the tenets peculiar to any established church or denomination nor take the form of a cross or any other instrument of torture or symbol of blood sacrifice.

5.

I bequeath my copyrights performing rights filming rights television rights and all cognate rights now in existence or hereafter to be created with the manuscripts typescripts and other documents in which I have such rights to my Trustee Upon trust to apply the proceeds resulting from the exploitation of such rights or the sale or other lucrative use of such documents as income of my estate.[2]

6.

I bequeath all papers and documents in my possession in which I have no copyright and which belong to me as material objects only to my Trustee to be examined as soon as conveniently after my death and divided as nearly as may be into sections as follows:

SECTION A. Papers (if any) concerning my late wife's family or affairs.

SECTION B. Old Diaries account books Bank passbooks paid cheques and their counterfoils expired agreements box office returns and other records of my business operations and personal and domestic expenditure capable of being used by economic or legal historians or by biographers seeking documentary evidence as to prices and practices during the period covered by my lifetime.

SECTION C. Such letters and documents as might be worth preserving in a public collection such as that of the British Museum.

SECTION D. All documents needed for the administration of my estate and the carrying out of the provisions of this my Will.

SECTION E. Uninteresting documents of no use except as waste paper.

I bequeath the contents of these sections to my Trustee with the suggestion that the contents of Section A (if any) be presented to my late wife's niece Mrs Cecily Charlotte Colthurst or should she predecease me to such surviving relative of hers as my Trustee may select; that the contents of Section B be offered to the British Library of Political Science in Clare Market London for the purpose indicated and those of Section C to the British Museum or failing acceptance to any other suitable public collection whilst the contents of Sections D and E can be retained or destroyed by my Trustee as may be expedient. And I declare that if any doubt or disputes should arise as to which papers shall be thus dealt with the question shall be settled by my Trustee whose decision shall be final Provided always that my Trustee shall retain all or any of the aforesaid papers and documents for such period as shall in his opinion be desirable.

7.

I declare that my Trustee shall manage and deal with my author's rights with all the powers in that behalf of an absolute owner (subject as hereinafter provided) for so long as may prove necessary or expedient during a period ending at the expiration of twenty years from the day of the death of the last survivor of all the lineal descendants of His late Majesty King George the Fifth who shall be living at the time of my death (hereinafter called "the Special period") bearing in mind that the licensing of theatrical performances and especially of cinematographic exhibitions and the like with the collection of royalties thereon will be a principal source of revenue besides continuing my practice in England of manufacturing my literary works at the cost of my estate and causing copies thereof to be sold on commission by a Publisher and shall make such other arrangements with Publishers and others as my Trustee shall think fit Provided always that my Trustee shall not sell assign or alienate such copyrights and other rights or any of them and shall not grant any licence or enter into any agreement or other arrangement in respect of the said copyrights and other rights or any of them which shall irrevocably bind or affect the same for a period exceeding five years (unless with power of revocation) at any one time calculated from the date of the execution of such licence agreement or arrangement but with power to renew or re-grant the same for any period not exceeding the aforesaid period and so on from time to time And I further declare that my Trustee shall not in dealing with any such rights be bound by commercial considerations exclusively it being my desire that he shall give due weight to artistic and public and human considerations to the best of his judgment and counsel.

8.

I desire that my Trustee shall do all things and make out of my estate all payments necessary to preserve my aforesaid copyrights or any of them and to procure any renewal of the same that can be obtained And I authorise him to make such payments accordingly And for the guidance of my Trustee I record that with regard to my copyrights in the United States of America (which are of considerable value) the same do not continue automatically for a period of fifty years from the author's death (as in England and other countries) but continue for a period of twenty eight years only from the date of first publication with a right of renewal for a further period of twenty eight years upon application being made and registered within one year prior to the expiration of the first term.

9.

I direct my Trustee without charging any payment to authorise Mrs Stella Mervyn Beech now residing at 122 Sussex Gardens in the County of London W.2 daughter of the late eminent actress professionally known as Mrs Patrick Campbell to print and publish after my death all or any of the letters written by me to the said eminent actress and in the event of Mrs Beech's death before publication to give such authority (which is a permission and not an assignment of copyright) to Mrs Patrick Campbell's grandson Patrick Beech and without imposing any trust I desire that the proceeds of such publication should be reserved as far as possible by Mrs Beech or Patrick Beech for the secondary education of Mrs Campbell's grandchildren and their children (such being her own wish) and any legacy duty payable by reason of such authority being given shall be paid out of my estate.[3]

10.

Whereas I possess a bust of myself in white marble by the eminent Hungarian sculptor Sigismund Strobl and now in the custody of the London County Council I bequeath it to the as yet unbuilt Shakespear Memorial National Theatre in London and I direct my Trustee to leave the said bust in the said custody until the opening of the said National Theatre.

11.

Whereas certain portraits of myself in painting or sculpture are at present in public galleries or institutions as for example the marble bust by Rodin in the Dublin Municipal Gallery a painting by Augustus John in the Fitzwilliam Museum in Cambridge a bust in bronze by Paul Troubetskoy in the National Gallery of British Art at Millbank in London (known also as The Tate Gallery) and an earlier bronze by the same sculptor in the Foyer of the Theatre Guild at 245 West 52nd Street in New York City I bequeath all of them and any others that may be in the like circumstances at my death to the several institutions in whose custody they stand save that in the case of the said Theatre Guild which is not in its nature a permanent institution I direct that on the Guild's dissolution or the winding up of its business from any cause during the special period the bust shall pass to the Metropolitan Museum in New York City or failing its acceptance for immediate or future exhibition in that institution to the next most eligible (in my Trustee's opinion) American public collection willing to accept it.

12.

I bequeath absolutely the Crayon drawing of the late Harley Granville-Barker by John Singer Sargent to the Trustees for the time being of the National Portrait Gallery in London in whose custody it now is.

13.

I bequeath to the National Trust all that is mine of the furniture cars and other contents except my cars and their appurtenances of the house garage and garden and grounds in the village of Ayot Saint Lawrence ordinance mapped as "Shaw's Corner" now the property of the said National Trust to be preserved as objects of memorial or artistic interest or disposed of or held in reserve for the benefit of the said premises or the said village as to the said Trust may in its judgment seem advisable.[4]

14.

Whereas it has been my custom to allow the Actor's Orphanage to receive and retain fees collected by the Collection Bureau of the Incorporated Society of Authors Playwrights and Composers for performance in the United Kingdom of my play entitled "Passion Poison and Petrification" and I desire that such arrangement shall be continued Now I hereby direct my Trustee to continue such arrangement accordingly and to permit and authorise the performance (but without expense to my estate) of my aforesaid play at any time on the request of the Secretary of the aforesaid Society or of the aforesaid Orphanage and for the benefit thereof and to allow the aforesaid Society to continue to collect all fees in respect of the aforesaid play and pay the same to the aforesaid Orphanage for the benefit thereof and if any such fees as aforesaid shall come to the hands of my Trustee then my Trustee shall hold the same Upon trust for such Orphanage absolutely And I declare that the receipt of the Secretary Treasurer or other officer of the aforesaid Society or of the aforesaid shall be a sufficient discharge for the same and that any legacy duty payable in respect of the same shall be borne by the said Orphanage.

15.

I authorise the Fabian Society of London so long as it shall remain an avowedly Socialistic Society and after it shall have ceased so to be if and whilst such avowal shall be contrary to law to print and publish for the benefit of such Society and its Cause all writing of mine which are or shall be at the time of my death included or with my consent about to be included amongst its publications And I direct my Trustee if necessary to grant to such Society such license as will give effect completely or as far as possible to the provisions of this clause which however must not be construed as giving the said Society any sole or exclusive property in the copyrights concerned and any legacy duty payable by reason of such license being given shall be borne by the said Society.

16.

I empower my Trustee to procure all necessary assistance and expert advice legal artistic literary or other for the discharge of his relevant functions and to pay its cost out of my estate.

17.

Provided always And I declare that as my fashion of literary composition often obliges me to make my first draft without full and final regard to temperance of expression generosity or justice to individuals accuracy of history or public propriety generally and to remedy this imperfection by later corrections it is my wish and I charge my Trustee and all others under whose eyes any of my literary works and documents may pass not to publish or quote or suffer to be published or quoted any edition or extracts from my works in which any earlier text shall be substituted either wholly or partly for the text as contained in the printed volumes finally passed by me for press except in the case of texts which I may be prevented by death or disablement from so passing And further that in any critical or biographical notes that may from good reasons make public any passages written by me but subsequently altered or discarded heed be taken both to the credit and the feelings of any surviving person alluded to therein but no suppressions need be made for the purpose of whitewashing my own character or conduct.

18.

I bequeath to every indoor and outdoor servant or labourer including charwoman chauffeur and gardener (hereinafter respectively referred to as such servant) of mine (other than any such as may be entitled to an annuity or pension under the provisions of the following clauses of this my Will) who shall be in the exclusive employ or in the case of my residing in a service flat the daily service of me at the time of my death and shall then have been in such employ for a continuous or virtually continuous period (that is to say only interrupted by illness or the like or military service and not by a formal discharge) of not less than seven years a sum equal to one year's wages or periodical gratuity of such servant and to every such servant of mine (other than as aforesaid) who shall be in the exclusive employ of me at the time of my death and shall then have been in my employ for a period of less than seven years but for a continuous or virtually continuous period of not less than three years a sum equal to six months' wages or periodical gratuity of such servant and to every such servant of mine (other than as aforesaid) who shall be in the exclusive employ of me at the time of my death and shall then have been in such employ for a period of less than three years a sum equal to three months' wages or periodical gratuity of such servant all such bequests as aforesaid to be in addition to any wages that may be or become legally due to any such servant as aforesaid Provided always And I further declare that whether the foregoing bequests shall become operative or not my Trustee shall have absolute power to act reasonably and generously in the case of any servant of mine or of my late wife who in the opinion of my Trustee is not sufficiently dealt with under the provisions hereinbefore made and accordingly to make to any such servant any such payment or additional payment out of my Estate as my Trustee shall in his discretion think desirable but without imposing any obligation upon him to make any such payment.

19.

I declare that every annuity hereinafter or by any Codicil hereto bequeathed is bequeathed subject to the provisions relating to annuities hereinafter contained.

20.

I declare that if at the time of my death any person or persons who shall not then be in my employ but shall have formerly been in the employ of me or of my late wife and who shall not otherwise become entitled to any benefit under this my Will and shall be in receipt of a pension or allowance from me then I bequeath to such person or persons an annuity equal in amount to the amount of such pension or allowance of which such former servant shall be then in receipt.

21.

I bequeath to my retired gardener Harry Batchelor Higgs an annuity of One hundred and fifty six pounds and I direct my Trustee to see to it that the monument I have erected in Windlesham Cemetery to him and his late wife shall on his death at the cost of my estate have its inscription completed and thereafter be cared for by the Cemetery authorities in consideration of an appropriate capital sum.

22.

I bequeath to Emma Hodgman formerly in my service as Housemaid and now or lately resident at 130 Windmill Road in Gillingham Kent an annuity of Fifty two pounds.

23.

I bequeath to Mrs Margaret Bilton now or lately residing at 48 Wilmer Road Tunbridge Wells and formerly in my service as housekeeper an annuity of One hundred and fifty six pounds to be continued after her death to her daughter Alice Bilton if surviving and on the respective deaths of the said Margaret Bilton and the said Alice Bilton I direct my Trustee to pay or apply for the benefit of the survivor of them or to such other person or persons and in such manner as he shall in his discretion think fit a sum of Twenty five pounds out of the capital of my Residuary Estate for or towards the funeral expenses incurred consequent on their respective deaths.

24.

Whereas the annuities hereby bequeathed to Harry Batchelor

Higgs Frederick William Day and Margaret Day Mrs Margaret Bilton and Alice Bilton and Emma Hodgman are provided for as from my death by the Will of my late wife Charlotte Frances Shaw my bequests to them herein shall be subject to such reductions and increases as may bring their benefits to the same level as if only one Will and that the most favorable to them shall come into force at my decease.

25.

I bequeath to Mrs Georgina Musters the daughter of my mother's half sister Arabella Gillmore an annuity of Three hundred and sixty five pounds.

26.

I bequeath to Eames Bagenal Rogers now or lately residing at 1249 Yale Street Santa Monica California the son of my mother's late half sister Charlotte Rogers and to his wife after his death if she shall survive him an annuity of Fifty two pounds.

27.

I bequeath to Georgina Meredith now residing at 34 Barron Street in the City of Dublin daughter of my mother's late half sister Charlotte Rogers an annuity of Fifty two pounds.

28.

I bequeath to Ethel Gordon Walters at present residing at 34 Queens Gardens in the County of London W. 1. daughter of my first cousin the late James Cockaigne Shaw an annuity of Two hundred and thirty four pounds.

29.

I bequeath to my former housemaid Mrs Ronald Smith (born Margaret Cashin) a deferred annuity of Fifty two pounds a year should she survive or be separated from her husband Ronald Smith or a later husband if any.

30.

I bequeath to my chauffeur and gardener Frederick William Day and his wife Margaret Day jointly an annuity of One hundred and fifty six pounds to be continued in full to the survivor of them.

31.

I bequeath to Eva Maria Schneider now residing at 196 Rivermead Court Hurlingham London S. W. 6. an annuity of One hundred and twenty pounds in remembrance of her devoted services to my late sister Lucy.

32.

I bequeath to my Secretary Blanche Patch Spinster an annuity of Five hundred pounds.

33.

The following provisions shall apply to all annuities hereby or by any Codicil hereto bequeathed-

(1) The bequest of an annuity shall become operative only if the named annuitant shall not at my death have done or suffered anything whereby the bequeathed annuity or any part of it would become vested in or payable to some other person or persons and shall continue only until the annuitant shall become bankrupt or assign or change the said annuity or any part thereof or do or suffer anything whereby the said annuity or any part thereof would become vested in or payable to any other person and in the event of any annuity not becoming or ceasing to become payable by the effect of this sub clause my Trustee may at his absolute discretion during the rest of the life of the annuitant apply out of the income of my residuary trust funds hereinafter defined any sums not exceeding in any year the amount of the relevant annuity for the benefit of the annuitant and for the purposes of sub clause (3) of this clause any sums which my Trustee decides to apply as aforesaid in any year shall be treated as if the aggregate of the same was an annuity.

(2) Every annuity shall be payable by equal quarterly pay-

ments payable in advance the first payment to become payable as at my death and to be paid as soon thereafter as my Trustee is in a position to pay the same.

(3) Every annuity shall unless and until a sum shall have been appropriated to provide for the same as hereinafter authorised or until the expiration of twenty one years from my death or the previous cesser whether partial or complete of the trust of the balance of the income of my Residuary Trust Funds hereinafter contained be payable only out of the income of my Residuary Trust Funds in each year from my death available for the payment thereof and if the income of my Residuary Trust Funds shall be insufficient to pay the said annuities in full the annuitant shall be entitled to be paid any capital sum in satisfaction of his or her annuity as a legacy but the said annuity shall abate pro rata for such period and to such an extent as shall be necessary having regard to the insufficiency of such income as aforesaid but if at the end of any year from my death there should be income available (after paying the full amounts of the said annuities for the time being payable for that year) to pay the amounts or part of the amounts by which the annuities then still payable had previously abated my Trustee shall out of such income pay the said amounts or such parts of the said amounts and rateably in proportion to such last mentioned annuities as such income shall be sufficient to satisfy. Upon the expiration of twenty one years from my death or the cesser whether partial or complete of the said trust of the balance of the said income the annuities then subsisting if not then provided for under sub-clause (4) hereof and any amounts by which such annuities had previously abated if not made good shall be a charge on the capital of my Residuary Trust Funds.

(4) My Trustee may in his discretion at any time provide for the payment of the annuities for the time being subsisting by appropriating and retaining out of my Residuary Trust Funds and investing in the name of my Trustee in any of the investments hereinafter authorised (with power for my Trustee to vary or transpose such investments for others hereby authorised) such a sum as when so invested shall at the time of investment be sufficient by means of the income thereof to pay the said annuities And I declare that such appropriation as aforesaid shall be com-

plete provision for such annuities and that in case the income of the appropriated fund shall at any time prove insufficient for payment in full of such annuities resort may be had to the capital thereof from time to time to make good such deficiency and the surplus (if any) of the income of the said fund from time to time remaining after payment of such annuities shall form part of the income of my Residuary Trust Funds And I declare that as and when any annuity provided for by means of the appropriated fund as aforesaid shall cease to be payable so much of the appropriated fund as my Trustee shall not think it necessary to retain to answer any remaining annuities shall revert to the capital of my Residuary Trust Funds.

(5) My Trustee shall have power if in his absolute discretion he thinks fit during the lives or life of any of the annuitants out of the income of my Residuary Trust Funds in any year not required for payment of such of the annuities as shall for the time being be payable or if he thinks fit out of the capital of my Residuary Trust Funds to make such additional payment to the annuitants for the time being living as in his opinion may be required to make good to such annuitants any decrease in the values of their annuities which shall be due to any decrease in the purchasing power of the £ sterling after the date of this my Will.

34.

I declare that all legacies (whether pecuniary or specific) and annuities bequeathed by this my Will or any Codicil shall be paid without deduction of legacy duty or any other duties payable in respect of the same and that the said duties including any duty chargeable by reason of an annuity arising on or being increased by the death of any annuitant shall be paid out of my real personal estate hereinafter devised and bequeathed by way of residue.

35.

I devise and bequeath all my real and personal estate not otherwise specifically disposed of by this my Will or any Codicil hereto and all property over which I have general power of appointment unto my Trustee Upon trust that my Trustee shall (subject to the power of postponing the sale and conversion thereof hereinafter contained) sell my real estate and sell call in or otherwise convert into money as much as may be needed of my personal estate (other than any copyrights which as provided by Clause 7 of this my Will are not to be sold) to increase the ready monies of which I may be possessed at my death to an amount sufficient to pay my funeral and testamentary expenses and debts estate duty legacy duty and all the duties payable on my death in respect of my estate or the bequests hereby made free of duty (other than testamentary expenses) and the legacies bequeathed by this my Will or any Codicil hereto or to make such other payments or investments or change of investments as in his opinion shall be advisable in the interest of my estate and shall invest the residue of such monies in manner hereinafter authorized And shall stand possessed of the said residuary trust moneys and the investments for the time being representing the same and all other investments for the time being forming part of my residuary estate (herein called my Residuary Trust Funds) and the annual income thereof Upon the trusts hereby declared of and concerning the same

(1) To institute and finance a series of inquiries to ascertain or estimate as far as possible the following statistics (a) the number of extant persons who speak the English language and write it by the established and official alphabet of 26 letters (hereinafter called Dr. Johnson's Alphabet) (b) how much time could be saved per individual scribe by the substitution for the said Alphabet of an Alphabet containing at least 40 letters (hereinafter called the Proposed British Alphabet) enabling the said language to be written without indicating single sounds by groups of letters or by diacritical marks instead of by one symbol for each sound (c) how many of these persons are engaged in writing or printing English at any and every moment in the world; (d) on these factors to estimate the time and labour wasted by our lack of at least 14 unequivocal single symbols; (e) to add where possible to the estimates of time lost or saved by the difference be-

tween Dr. Johnson's Alphabet and the Proposed British Alphabet estimates of the loss of income in British and American currency. The enquiry must be confined strictly to the statistical and mathematical problems to be solved without regard to the views of professional and amateur phoneticians, etymologists, Spelling Reformers, patentees of universal languages, inventors of shorthand codes for verbatim reporting or rival alphabets, teachers of the established orthography, disputants about pronunciation, or any of the irreconcilables whose wranglings have overlooked and confused the single issue of labour saving and made change impossible during the last hundred years. The inquiry must not imply any approval or disapproval of the Proposed British Alphabet by the inquirers or by my Trustee.

(2) To employ a phonetic expert to transliterate my play entitled Androcles & The Lion in the Proposed British Alphabet[5] assuming the pronunciation to resemble that recorded by His Majesty our late King George V and sometimes described as Northern English.

(3) To employ an artist-calligrapher to fair-copy the transliteration for reproduction by lithography photography or any other method that may serve in the absence of printers' types.

(4) To advertise and publish the transliteration with the original Dr Johnson's lettering opposite the transliteration page by page and a glossary of the two alphabets at the end and to present copies to public libraries in the British Isles, the British Commonwealth, the American States North and South and to national libraries everywhere in that order.

36.

I desire my Trustee to bear in mind that the Proposed British Alphabet does not pretend to be exhaustive as it contains only sixteen vowels whereas by infinitesimal movements of the tongue countless different vowels can be produced all of them in use among speakers of English who utter the same vowels no oftener than they make the same finger prints. Nevertheless they can understand one another's speech and writing sufficiently to converse and correspond: for instance, a graduate of Trinity College Dublin has no difficulty in understanding a graduate of Oxford University when one says that "the sun rohze," and the other "the san raheoze" nor are either of them puzzled when a peasant calls his childhood his "chawldid." For a university graduate calls my native country Awlind.

37.

It is possible that the ministry of Education may institute the inquiry and adopt the Proposed British Alphabet to be taught in the schools it controls in which event subsection 1 of Clause 35 foregoing and its relevant sequels will be contra-indicated as superfluous and Clause 40 come into operation accordingly but the adoption must be exact and no account taken of the numerous alternative spelling Reforms now advocated or hereafter proposed.

38.

I hereby devise and bequeath the balance of the income of my Residuary Trust Funds not required during the period of twenty one years after my death to pay the annuities hereby or by any Codicil hereto bequeathed or for any other purpose upon which income of my Residuary Trust Funds may under the trusts hereinbefore contained be applicable Upon trust during the special period but subject to cesser as hereinafter provided To apply the same as follows:-

(A) To remunerate the services and defray the expenses incidental to these proceedings and generally to the launching advertising and propaganda of the said British Alphabet.

(B) To acquire by employment purchase or otherwise the copyright and patents (if any) created by or involved in the designing and manufacture of the said Alphabet or the publication of the works printed in it without exploiting the said rights or for commercial profit.

(C) To wind-up the enterprise when the aforesaid steps have been taken or if and when its official adoption or general vogue shall make further recourse to my estate and action on the part of my Trustee in respect of this charitable Trust superfluous.

39.

Pending the operation of the foregoing clause I direct that my Trustee shall for the said period of twenty one years from my death accumulate the said balance of the income of my Residuary Trust Funds in the way of compound interest by investing the same and the resulting income thereof from time to time in any investment in which my Residuary Trust Funds are authorised to be invested.

40.

Subject to the trusts hereinbefore declared of my Residuary Trust Funds and the income thereof or if and so far as such trusts shall fail through judicial decision or any other cause beyond my Trustee's control my Trustee shall stand possessed of my Residuary Trust Funds and the income thereof but subject to a charge on the capital as well as the income thereof for payment of such of the annuities hereby bequeathed as shall be subsisting Upon trust as to one third thereof for the Trustees of the British Museum in acknowledgment of the incalculable value to me of my daily resort to the Reading Room of that Institution at the beginning of my career as to one third of the same Upon trust for the National Gallery of Ireland and as to the remaining one third of the same Upon trust for the Royal Academy of Dramatic Art at 61 Gower Street in the County of London and should any of these three institutions be permanently closed at the date when the trust to accumulate the said balance of income of my Residuary Trust Fund shall cease the others or other shall succeed to its share and if more than one equally.[6]

41.

I authorise my Trustee to postpone for such period as he shall in his discretion think fit the sale and conversion of all or any part of my real and personal estate hereinbefore devised and bequeathed in trust for sale and conversion notwithstanding the same may be of a perishable or wearing out nature (but if any part of my estate shall be of a reversionary nature the same shall not be sold or converted into money until it falls into possession unless my Trustee shall think it probable that a loss will arise to my estate by postponing the sale and conversion thereof) and to retain any stocks shares or securities of which I may be possessed at my death whether fully paid up or not (but my real estate shall be impressed with the quality of personal estate from the time of my death) And I declare that the net income arising from any part of my real or personal estate previous to the sale or conversion thereof shall as well during the first year after my death as afterwards be applied in the same manner as if the same were income arising from such investments as are by this my Will authorized but that no reversionary or other property forming part of my estate not actually producing income shall be treated as producing income.

42.

Should my Trustee have occasion to realize any of my investments in the shares and loan stocks of Friendly Societies not quoted on the Stock Exchange and therefore often sold by Executors and others at less than their value I direct my Trustee not to dispose of them without first offering them to the Directors of the said Societies they being commonly ready to liquidate such stocks at their face value.

43.

I declare that my Trustee shall be at liberty to grant time or other indulgence to any debtor in respect of any unsecured personal loans made by me and (in particular when the loan has not in his judgment been a matter of business) to forego payment of and absolutely release all or any part of the amount of any such debts or loan without being answerable for any loss which may thereby arise and with regard to any such debts owing to me or claims I may have against any person or persons I express it to be my wish that my Trustee shall in the exercise of the aforesaid power deal kindly or leniently with all such debtors or other person or persons where a strict observation of the law would involve manifest injustice hardship or meanness (but no distinction in this respect is to be made in favour of my relatives as distinguished from other persons) And I also declare that certain bequests I have made in former Wills in favour of various persons I have now omitted to make not on account of any change of feeling on my part towards them but because deaths marriages and change of circumstances have rendered such bequests unnecessary and I also record my regret that my means are not sufficient to provide for material pledges of my regard for the many friends who as colleagues in the Socialistic movement or as artists co-operating with me in the performance of my plays or otherwise have not only made my career possible but hallowed it with kindly human relations.

44.

I declare that all monies liable to be invested under my Will may be invested in any investment or securities for the time being authorised by law for the investment of trust funds.

45.

I authorise my Trustee to apportion as my Trustee shall think fit among the trust premises any charges deductions or outgoings whatsoever and to determine whether any money shall for the purpose of this my Will be considered annual income or not and the power of appropriation conferred by the administration of Estates Act 1925 shall be exercisable by my Trustee whether acting as personal representative or trustee and without any of the consents made requisite by that Act.

46.

I declare that the Executor and Trustee for the time being of this my Will may instead of acting personally employ and pay a Solicitor Accountant Agent Literary Executor Bibliographer or any other person or persons to transact any business or do any act required to be done in connection with the administration of my estate or the trusts hereby declared including the receipt and payment of money and the keeping and preparation of books and accounts And I express it to be my wish (but without imposing any obligations) that my present English Solicitors the firm of J.N. Mason & Co. of 41-44 Temple Chambers in the City of London my American Attorneys the firm of Stern & Reubens of 1 East 45th Street in New York City my Accountant Walter Smee now practising at 22 Shaftesbury Avenue West Central London, my British Publishers Messrs. Constable & Co. of 10 Orange Street in the County of London my Printers Messrs. R & R Clark of Brandon Street Edinburgh, my present Secretary Blanche Patch, my Bibliographer Fritz Erwin Loewenstein[7] Doctor of Philosophy and Founder of the London Shaw Society (now residing at Torca Cottage in Saint Albans) whose knowledge of my literary affairs and interest in my reputation qualify him exceptionally for such employment shall be consulted and employed by my Executor and Trustee whenever their assistance may be desirable and available and that the Incorporated Society of Authors Playwrights and Composers shall continue to be employed as my Theatrical Agents on the special conditions now established between us. To this I add that my country Solicitor Ivo L. Currall of 2 Gordon Chambers 1 Upper George Street Luton in the County of Bedford is also familiar with my local affairs.

47.

Having been born a British subject in Ireland in 1856 subsequently registered as a citizen of Eire and finally privileged to remain a British subject by the Home Secretary's letter dated the twenty seventh day of June One thousand nine hundred and forty nine

I declare that my domicile of choice is English and desire that my Will be construed and take effect according to English law. In witness whereof I have hereunto set my hand to this and the thirteen preceding sheets of paper this twelfth day of June One thousand nine hundred and fifty.

Signed and acknowledged by the said George Bernard Shaw the Testator as and for his last Will and Testament in the presence of us who in his presence at his request and in the presence of each other all being present at the same time have hereunto subscribed our names as witnesses

G. BERNARD SHAW

E. Marjorie White Married woman
22 Compton Avenue, Luton, Beds.
Harold O. White Master Printer
22 Compton Avenue, Luton, Beds.[8]

APPENDIX II

How Frank Ought to Have Done It

The late Frank Harris was a distinguished figure in literary London in the last decade of the nineteenth century. As editor of The Fortnightly Review and subsequently and especially of The Saturday Review he surrounded himself with a galaxy of brilliant writers chosen with uncommon judgment and courage, myself among them. His own works included short stories of the kind then made fashionable by De Maupassant, a biography of Oscar Wilde, a book on Shakespear, a scandalously candid autobiography (later on), and a series of notably trenchant and pungent Contemporary Portraits.

In one of these, purporting to be a portrait of me, he was neither trenchant nor pungent; for in writing it he had been embarrassed and disabled by a sense of obligation to me because I had remained loyal to our old connection through a period in which he was neither popular nor prosperous, and had to take a refuge finally in exile. The result was a piously grateful eulogy which made me laugh; so I took up my pen and sent him the following example of how he ought to have portrayed me.

Harris published it in his last volume of Contemporary Portraits; but I cannot believe he ever read it. He knew next to nothing of my career after The Saturday Review episode. When he was dying an American publisher commissioned him to write a biography of me; and his needs obliged him to make a desperate attempt to fulfil this task. But his inventions and conjectures were so wide of the mark, that to enable them to be published after his death I had to rewrite his book myself on matters of fact, thus doing seriously what in the following lines I had done as a jeu d'esprit.[1]

I have taken this opportunity to add some sentences which could only have been written by Harris's ghost, as they mention circumstances which occurred after his death.

Dramatizing myself from an objective point of view (the method natural to me) enabled me to say things I could not gracefully have said from my own subjective angle: but it obliges me to add Errors and Self-Delusions Excepted.

BEFORE attempting to add Bernard Shaw to my collection of Contemporary Portraits, I find it necessary to secure myself in advance by the fullest admission of his extraordinary virtues. Without any cavilling over trifles I declare at once that Shaw is the just man made perfect. I admit that in all his controversies, with me or anyone else, Shaw is, always has been, and always will be, right. I perceive that the common habit of abusing him is an ignorant and silly habit, and that the pretence of not taking him seriously is the ridiculous cover for an ignominious retreat from an encounter with him. If there is any other admission I can make, any other testimonial I can give, I am ready to give it and apologize for having omitted it. If it will help matters to say that Shaw is the greatest man that ever lived, I shall not hesitate for a moment. All the cases against him break down when they are probed to the bottom. All his prophecies come true. All his fantastic creations come to life within a generation. I have an uneasy sense that even now I am not doing him justice: that I am ungrateful, disloyal, disparaging. I can only repeat that if there is anything I have left out, all that is necessary is to call my attention to the oversight and it shall be remedied. If I cannot say that Shaw touches nothing that he does not adorn, I can at least testify that he touches nothing that he does not dust and polish and put back in its place much more carefully than the last man who handled it.

I will tell some anecdotes of Shaw. Oscar Wilde said of him, "He has not an enemy in the world; and none of his friends like him."

Once, at a public dinner given by the Stage Society, Shaw had to propose the health of the dramatic critics; and Max Beerbohm had to reply. Before the speaking began Max came to Shaw and said "You are going to say, aren't you, that you are a critic yourself?"

"I don't know what I am going to say," said Shaw; "but I daresay I could bring that in."

"Promise me that you will," said Max: "I want to make a point about it."

"Anything to oblige you," said Shaw; and he did.

Max began his speech thus: "I was once at a school where the master used always to say, 'Remember, boys, I am one of yourselves.'" A roar of laughter saved Max the trouble of pointing the moral.

Robert Lynd said of Shaw's Common Sense About the War that though nobody could take any reasonable exception to it, yet, from the moment it appeared, the war was spoken of and written about as a war between the Allies on the one hand, and, on the other, Germany, Austria, Turkey, and Bernard Shaw.

When Shaw contested a seat at the London County Council election as a Progressive, after six years' hard Progressive drudgery on a Borough Council, with the advantage of being one of the inventors of municipal Progressivism, not only was he defeated by the defection of all but the irreducible minimum of Liberals and temperance reformers (Shaw is a teetotaller), but the leading Progressive papers openly exulted in his defeat as a most blessed deliverance. The only other people who voted for him were those who had never voted before. This was proved by an increase in the poll at the next election, when the adored actor George Alexander was the victorious candidate.

These are the things that happen to him in his most popular moments, when he is in no way breasting and opposing the current of public opinion. When, as often happens, he has to take his chance of being lynched for telling some unpalatable truth, numbers of persons who have never before dared to betray any hostility to him believe that they have him "on the run" at last, and vent on him a bitterness and violence which must have been rankling in them for years.

The result is that hardly anyone who has not met Shaw thinks of him otherwise than as a man of disagreeable appearance, harsh manners, and insufferable personality. He knows this, and says, "I always astonish strangers by my amiability, because, as no human being could possibly be so disagreeable as they expect me to be, I have only to be commonly civil to seem quite charming."

No truthful contemporary portrait can ignore either this extraordinary power of exciting furious hostility, or the entire absence of any obvious ground for it. It has been said that Shaw irritates people by always standing on his head, and calling black white and white black. But only simpletons either offer or accept this account. Men do not win a reputation like Shaw's by perversity and tomfoolery. What is really puzzling is that Shaw irritates us intensely by standing on his feet and telling us that black is black and white white whilst we please ourselves by professing what everyone knows to be false.

There is something maddening in being forced to agree with a man against whom your whole soul protests. It is not that he expresses your own view more accurately than you yourself could. But you cannot bear your inmost convictions to be shared by a man whose nature you hold to be monstrous and subversive. It is as if a man had offered to walk a bit of the way with you because you were going in the direction of his home, and you knew that home to be the bottomless pit.

As a matter of fact there is nothing in Shaw's political and social program, not even his insistence on basic equality of income and its dissociation from every kind of personal industry or virtue, at which a thinker of adequate modern equipment need turn a hair. He is a perfectly safe man on a committee of any sort: a man of tact and circumspection who kept the Fabian Society, of which he was a leader for twenty-seven years, free from the quarrels that broke up all the other Socialist organizations.

Yet the monstrosity is there; for Shaw works at politics in the spirit of one helping a lame dog over a stile which he believes to be insurmountable. "Every man over forty is a scoundrel!" he proclaimed when he was himself over forty. He makes no secret of his conviction that the problems raised by modern multitudinous civilization are beyond our political capacity and may never be solved by us. He attaches little value to mere experience, holding that it is expectation of life and not recollection of it that determines conduct. He reminds us repeatedly that as Evolution is still creative Man may have to be scrapped as a Yahoo,[2] and replaced by some new and higher creation, just as man himself was created to supply the deficiencies of the lower animals.

It is impossible to take offence at this, because Shaw is as merciless to himself as to us. He does not kick us overboard and remain proudly on the quarter deck himself. With the utmost good-humor he clasps us affectionately round the waist and jumps overboard with us, and that too, not into a majestic Atlantic where we might perish tragically, but into a sea of ridicule amid shrieks of derisive laughter. And this intolerable trick is played on us at the most unexpected and inopportune moments. "No man" said Sir Henry Norman "knows how to butter a moral slide better than Shaw." Shaw's championship thus becomes more dreaded than the most spiteful attacks of others. During the first Ibsen boom in London he proposed to help an American actress in an Ibsen enterprise by interviewing her. To his atonishment the lady[3] told him with passionate earnestness that if he wrote a word about her she would shoot him. "You may not believe here in England that such things are possible," she said; "but in America we think differently; and I will do it: I have the pistol ready."

"General Gabler's pistol," was Shaw's unruffled comment; but he saw how intensely the lady shrank from being handled by him in print; and the interview was not written. Some of his best friends confess that until they were used to him quite friendly letters from him would sometimes move them to furious outbursts of profanity at his expense. He tells a story of a phrenologist with whom he got into conversation at a vegetarian restaurant in his early days. This man presently accused Shaw of being "a septic," meaning a sceptic. "Why?" said Shaw. "Have I no bump of veneration?"

"Bump!" shouted the phrenologist: "It's a hole." If Shaw's manners were offensive one could at least punch his head; but his pity for your inadequacy and his own is so kindly, so covered by an unexceptionable observance of the perfect republican respect to which you are entitled, that you are utterly helpless: there is nothing to complain of, nothing to lay hold of, no excuse for snatching up the carving knife and driving it into his vitals.

I, Frank Harris, was editing The Fortnightly Review when I first met Shaw about an article. He had an engaging air of being more interested in me than in the article. Not to be mock modest, I suppose I *was* more interesting than the article; and I was naturally not disposed to quarrel with Shaw for thinking so, and shewing it. He has the art of getting on intimate and easy terms very quickly; and at the end of five minutes I found myself explaining to him how I had upset my health by boyishly allowing myself to be spurred into a burst of speed on the river in an outrigger, and overstraining myself. He gave his mind to my misfortune as sympathetically as my doctor, and asked me some questions as to how much care I was taking of myself. One of the questions was, "Do you drink?" I was equal to the occasion, and did not turn a hair as I assured him that a diagnosis of delirium tremens could not be sustained; but I could not help becoming suddenly conscious that I expected from men an assumption that I am not a drunkard, and that I was face to face with a man who made no such assumption. His question was too like one of those asked in Butler's Erewhon to be entirely agreeable to human frailty. In Shaw's play Captain Brassbound's Conversion, the captain introduces his lieutenant with the words (or to this effect), "This is the greatest scoundrel, liar, thief, and rapscallion on the west coast."

On which the lieutenant says "Look here, Captain: if you want to be modest, be modest on your own account, not on mine." The fact that Shaw *is* modest on his own account, and gives himself away much more freely than his good manners allow him to give away his friends, does not really make the transaction any more agreeable to its victims: it only robs them of their revenge, and compels them to pay tribute to his amiability when they are furiously annoyed with him.

It is difficult to class a man who gives himself away even to the point of making himself ridiculous as vain. But all Shaw's friends agree that he is laughably vain. Yet here again he confuses our judgment by playing up to it with the most hyperbolical swank about his intellect. He declares that he does so because people like it. He says, quite truly, that they love Cyrano, and hate "the modest cough of the minor poet." Those who praise his books to his face are dumbfounded by the enthusiasm with which he joins in his own praise, and need all their presence of mind to avoid being provoked into withdrawing some seventy-five per cent or so of their eulogies. Such play acting makes it difficult to say how much real vanity or modesty underlies it all. He himself denies that he is conceited. "No man can be" he says, "if, like me, he has spent his life trying to play the piano accurately, and never succeeded for a single bar." I ask him to give me a list of his virtues, his excellences, his achievements, so that I may not do him the injustice of omitting any. He replies, "It is unnecessary: they are all in the shop window."

Shaw plays the part of the modest man only in his relations with the arts which are the great rivals of literature. He has never claimed to be "better than Shakespear," though he does claim to be his successor. The much quoted heading to one of his prefaces[4] has a note of interrogation after it; and the question is dismissed by himself with the remark that as Shakespear in drama, like Mozart in opera, and Michael Angelo in fresco, reached the summit of his art, nobody can be better than Shakespear, though anybody may now have things to say that Shakespear did not say, and outlooks on life and character which were not open to him.

Nevertheless I am convinced that Shaw is as willing to have his plays compared with Shakespear's as Turner was to have his pictures hung beside Claude's. Yet when he was invited to a dinner in Paris in honor of Rodin, he wrote that he had the honor of being one of Rodin's models, and was sure of a place in the biographical dictionaries a thousand years hence as "Shaw, Bernard: subject of a bust by Rodin: otherwise unknown." He struck the same note when, finding that Rodin, though an infallible connoisseur in sculpture, had no books in his collection except the commonest kind of commercial presentation volumes, he presented him with a Kelmscott Chaucer, and wrote in it

I have seen two masters at work: Morris who made this book:
The other Rodin the Great, who fashioned my head in clay.
I give the book to Rodin, scrawling my name in a nook

Of the shrine their works shall hallow when mine are dust by
the way.

In the same vein is the inscription he proposed for a pedestal to Lady Kennet's[5] statue of him, now in the Bournemouth Municipal Gallery.

WEEP NOT FOR OLD GEORGE BERNARD: HE IS DEAD
AND ALL HIS FRIENDS EXCLAIM "A DAMNED GOOD JOB!"
THOUGH RANKING GEORGE'S CELEBRATED HEAD
HIGH IN THE MORE UNCOMMON SORTS OF NOB

LONG AT ITS IMAGE KATHLEEN'S HAND HAD PLIED
WHEN THE LORD SAID "NOT THUS GREAT WORK BEGAT IS.
COPY NO MORE: YOUR SPIRIT BE YOUR GUIDE:
CARVE HIM SUB SPECIE AETERNITATIS

SO WHEN HIS WORKS SHALL ALL FORGOTTEN BE
YET SHALL HE SHARE YOUR IMMORTALITY"

Later on The Evening News asked him to write his own epitaph. In response he drew a weed-overgrown tombstone and on it the lines

HIC JACET
BERNARD SHAW
Who the devil was he?

Now I confess I am not convinced by this evidence of modesty. I am not sure that it is not rather the final artistic touch to Shaw's swank. For what was the origin of the Rodin bust?[6] Rodin knew nothing about Shaw, and at first refused to undertake the commission. Mrs Shaw thereupon wrote to Rodin pleading that she wished to have a memorial of her husband, and that her husband declared that any man, who, being a contemporary of Rodin, would have his bust made by anyone else, would pillory himself to all posterity as an ignoramus. Rodin, finding that he had to deal with a man who knew his value, weakened in his refusal. Mrs Shaw then ascertained from Rilke, the Austrian poet, then acting as Rodin's secretary, what his usual fee was for a bust. The money (£1,000) was immediately lodged to Rodin's credit on the understanding that he was to be under no obligation whatever in respect of it, and might make the bust or not make it, begin it or leave it off at his pleasure: in short, treat the payment as a contribution to the endowment of his work in general and remain completely master of the situation. The result, of course, was that Rodin sent for Shaw to come to Paris at once; installed him and his wife as daily guests at his Meudon villa; worked steadily at the bust every day for a month until it was finished; and went beyond his bargain in giving the sitter casts of it.

Here we have the diplomatic Shaw, the master of blarney, and the penetrating art critic; and not for a moment do I suggest that there was the slightest insincerity in his proceedings. Had there been, Rodin would not have been taken in. But was there no vanity in it? Would so busy a man as Shaw have left his work and gone to Paris to pose like a professional model for a whole month if he had not thought his bust as important as the busts of Plato which are now treasures of the museums which possess them?

Shaw is an incorrigible and continuous actor, using his skill as deliberately in his social life as in his professional work in the production of his own plays. He does not deny this. "G.B.S.," he says, "is not a real person: he is a legend created by myself: a pose, a reputation. The real Shaw is not a bit like him." Now this is exactly what all his acquaintances say of the Rodin bust, that it is not a bit like him. But Shaw maintains that it is the only portrait that tells the truth about him. When Rodin was beginning the work in his studio, Mrs Shaw complained to him that all the artists and caricaturists, and even the photographers, aimed at producing the sort of suburban Mephistopheles they imagined Shaw to be, without ever taking the trouble to look at him. Rodin replied, "I know nothing about Mr Shaw's reputation; but what is there I will give you." Shaw declares that he was as good as his word. When Paul Troubetskoy saw the bust he declared that there was no life in the eyes; and in three hours frenzied work he produced his first bust of Shaw, now in

America. As a *tour de force* it is magnificent; but it is Mephistopheles, not suburban, but aristocratic. Shaw liked the bust, and liked Troubetskoy; but his wife would have none of it, nor of the curious portrait by Neville Lytton, suggested by Granville-Barker's remark that Velasquez's portrait of Pope Innocent was an excellent portrait of Shaw. Lytton accordingly painted Shaw in the costume and attitude of Innocent; but though the picture shews what Shaw would be like in the papal chair, Pope Bernard will never be identified by an antiquary with the subject of the Rodin bust.

Augustus John's three portraits of Shaw are even less reconcilable with the Rodin. John has projected all Shaw's public strength and assurance at their fullest intensity, indeed at more than lifesize. "There is the great Shaw," says the sitter when he shews his friends the picture. But when he points to the Rodin, he says, "Just as I am, without one plea." De Smet's portrait is that of a quiet delicate elderly gentleman: Shaw likes its resemblance to his father. The statuette by Lady Scott is friendly and literal: the half length statue by Lady Kennet of the Dene (the same lady) is a companion to that of Shakespear in Stratford church. Sigmund Strobl's bust ranks with those by Rodin and Troubetskoy. Troubetskoy finally modelled Shaw at full length, lifesize, in his platform pose as an orator. This fine bronze has come to rest in the National Gallery of Ireland, which possesses also his portrait by John Collier, prosaic, but lifelike enough to have been mistaken by Mrs Shaw for Shaw himself in Collier's studio. Mrs Shaw was fastidious about portraits of her husband. Of Laura Knight's she said to G.B.S., "Laura has given you her own singleminded sincerity; but you are always acting." On seeing a photograph of Epstein's famous bust (the last) she said, "If that thing enters this house I leave it"; and it never did. Shaw admired its workmanship but acknowledged it only as representing some aboriginal ancestor of his. Davidson's bust is a spirited but hasty sketch.

No wonder H. G. Wells complained that he could not move a step without being outfaced by an effigy of Shaw. Modest Shaw may be; but he has sat for memorials of himself by the greatest masters of his time. Can such modesty be justified until he has been dead for at least five hundred years?

Shaw is the greatest pedant alive. Dickens's man who ate crumpets on principle could not hold a candle to him in this respect. Descriptive reporters have said that Shaw wears a flannel shirt. He never wore a flannel shirt in his life. He does not wear a shirt at all, because it is wrong to swaddle one's middle with a double thickness of material: therefore he wears some head-to-foot under-garment unknown to shirt-makers. The flannel fable arose because, at a time when it was socially impossible for a professional man to appear in public in London without a white starched collar, he maintained that no educated eye could endure the color contrast of ironed starch against European flesh tones, and that only a very black and brilliant Negro should wear such a collar. He therefore obtained and wore grey collars. Now that the fashion is changed, he wears collars of various colors; but the dye is always chosen to carry out a theory that the best color effect is that of two shades of the same color. His jacket is of the smartest West End tailoring; but it is unlined, on principle. He formerly addressed his letters high up in the left hand corner of the envelope. A mere affectation of singularity, you say. Not at all: he would talk to you for an hour on the beauty of the system of page margins established by the medieval scribes and adopted by William Morris, and on its leaving space for the postman's thumb. When the postman complained that the postmark obliterated the address Shaw returned to the normal practice.

He justifies his refusal to use apostrophes and inverted commas in printing his books on the ground that they spoil the appearance of the page, declaring that the Bible would never have attained its supreme position in literature if it had been disfigured with such unsightly signs. He is interested in phonetics and systems of shorthand; and it is to his pedantic articulation that he owes his popularity as a public speaker in the largest halls, as every word is heard with exasperating distinctness. He advocates a combination of the metric system with the duodecimal by inserting two new digits into our numeration, thus: eight, nine, dec, elf, ten, and eighteen, nineteen, decteen, elfteen, twenty, and so forth. He likes machines as a child likes toys, and once very nearly bought a cash register without having the slightest use for it. When he was on the verge of sixty he yielded to the fascination of a motor bicycle, and rode it away from the factory for seventy-seven miles, at the end of which, just outside his own door, he took a corner too fast and was left sprawling. He has been accused of being one of the band of devoted lunatics who bathe in the Serpentine throughout the year, rain or shine; but this is an invention, founded on his practice of swimming in the bathing pool of the Royal Automobile Club every morning before breakfast, winter and summer, his alleged reason being that as an Irishman he dislikes washing himself, but cannot do without the stimulus of a plunge into cold water. He is, as all the world knows, a vegetarian, valuing health highly but declaring that men who are any good trade on their stocks of health to the utmost limit, and therefore live on the verge of a breakdown. All really busy men, he holds, should go to bed for eighteen months every forty years to recuperate. I could easily fill another page with his fads; but I forbear.

Shaw's gallantries are for the most part non-existent. He says, with some truth, that no man who has any real work in the world has time or money for a pursuit so long and expensive as the pursuit of women. He may possibly have started the protest against the expensiveness and the exactions of beautiful women which is the main theme of Harley Granville-Barker's Waste and The Madras House. Nobody knows his history in this respect, as he is far too correct a person to kiss and tell. To all appearances he is a model husband; and in the various political movements in which his youth was passed there was no scandal about him. Yet a popular anecdote describes a well known actor manager as saying one day at rehearsal to an actress of distinguished beauty, "Let us give Shaw a beefsteak and put some red blood into him."

"For heaven's sake dont," exclaimed the actress: "he is bad enough as it is; but if you give him meat no woman in London will be safe." [7]

Anyhow, Shaw's teaching is much more interesting than his personal adventures, if he ever had any. That teaching is unquestionably in very strong reaction against what he has called Nineteenth Century Amorism. He is not one of your suburban Love is Enough fanatics. He maintains that chastity is so powerful an instinct that its denial and starvation on the scale on which the opposite impulse has been starved and denied would wreck any civilization. He insists that intellect is a passion, and that the modern notion that passion means only sex is as crude and barbarous as the ploughman's idea that art is simply bawdiness. He points out that art can flourish splendidly when sex is absolutely barred, as it was, for example, in the Victorian literature which produced Dickens. He compares Giulio Romano, a shameless pornographer, pupil of Raphael and brilliant draughtsman, with Raphael himself, who was so sensitive that though he never painted a draped figure without first drawing it in the nude, he always paid the Blessed Virgin the quaint tribute of a *caleçon* in his studies of her, and contrived to decorate the villa of a voluptuary with the story of Cupid and Psyche without either shrinking from the uttermost frankness or losing his dignity and innocence. Shaw contends that when art passed from Raphael to Giulio it fell into an abyss, and became not only disgusting but dull.

The eternal triangle of the Paris stage he rejects as proving adultery to be the dryest of subjects. He wrote Plays for Puritans to shew how independent he was of it. He demands scornfully whether genuine virility can be satisfied with stories and pictures, and declares that the fleshly school in art is the consolation of the impotent.

Yet there are passages in his plays which urge that imaginary love plays an important part in civilized life. A handsome hero says to a man who is jealous of him, "Do not waste your jealousy on me: the imaginary rival is the dangerous one." In Getting Married, the lady[8] who refuses to marry because she cannot endure masculine untidiness and the smell of tobacco, hints that her imagination provides her with a series of adventures which beggar reality. Shaw says that the thousand and three conquests of Don Juan consist of two or three squalid intrigues and a thousand imaginative fictions. He says that every attempt to realise such fictions is a failure; and it may be added that nobody but a man who had tried could have written the third act of Man and Superman. In the final act of that play, too, the scene in which the hero revolts from marriage and struggles against it without any hope of escape, is a poignantly sincere utterance which must have come from personal experience. Shakespear in treating the same theme through the character of Benedick might conceivably have been making fun of somebody else; but Tanner, with all his extravagances, is first hand: Shaw would probably not deny it and would not be believed if he did.

Shaw's anti-Shakespear campaign under my Saturday Review editorship was all the more unexpected because I was one of the few London editors to whom Shakespear was more than a name. I was saturated with Shakespear. That I should be the editor of an attack on Shakespear of unheard-of ferocity was the one thing I should have declared confidently could never possibly occur to me. What made the adventure odder was, first, that Shaw, who delivered the attack, was as full of Shakespear as I: second, that though we were both scandalised by the sacrilege we were committing, neither of us could honestly alter a word in one of the articles. They were outrageous; but there was nothing to withdraw, nothing to soften, nothing that could be modified without bringing down the whole critical edifice.

The explanation is simple enough. Shaw's first shot at Shakespear was fired in 1894. Ibsen's first broadside on England caught the London theatre between wind and water in 1889. Shaw had written his Quintessence of Ibsenism in the meantime, and was judging everything on and off the stage by the standard set up by the terrible Norwegian. Many lesser men fell short of that standard; but Shakespear was the most conspicuous victim. "It is useless to talk of Shakespear's depth now," said Shaw: "there is nothing left but his music. Even the famous delineation of character by Molière-Shakespear-Scott-Dumas-*père* is only a trick of mimicry. Our Bard is knocked out of time: there is not a feature left on his face. Hamlet is a spineless effigy beside Peer Gynt, Imogen a doll beside Nora Helmer, Othello a convention of Italian opera beside Julian." And it was quite true. Only in the Sonnets could we find Shakespear getting to the depth at which Ibsen worked.

Shaw was full not only of Ibsen, but of Wagner, of Beethoven, of Goethe, and, curiously, of John Bunyan. The English way of being great by flashes: Shakespear's way, Ruskin's way, Chesterton's way, without ever following the inspiration up on which William Morris put his finger when he said that Ruskin could say the most splendid things and forget them five minutes after, could not disguise its incoherence from an Irishman. "The Irish," he says, "with all their detestable characteristics, are at least grown up. They think systematically; they dont stop in the middle of a game of golf to admire a grandeur of thought as if it were a sunset, and then turn back to their game as the really serious business of their life." His native pride in being Irish persists in spite of his whole adult career in England and his preference for English and Scottish friends.

It will be noticed that my portrait of Shaw is both more and less intimate than any other I have penned. More, because Shaw tells the whole world all that there is to be told about himself. Less, because I have never sat on a committee with him; and that is the only way to see much of him. Shaw is not really a social man. He never goes anywhere unless he has business there. He pays no calls. Once he was induced by Maurice Baring[9] to go to a bachelor's party of the usual British type, with grown men throwing lumps of bread at one another, telling smutty stories, and conscientiously striving to behave like rowdy undergraduates. "Gentlemen," said Shaw, with deadly contempt for their efforts, "we shall enjoy ourselves very much if only you will not try to be convivial." On their persisting he got up and left. He complains that only in the presence of women will men behave decently.

After lunching at the Savile Club on his arrival in London he resolved that he would never be a literary man nor consort with such. "I might have spent my life sitting watching these fellows taking in each other's washing and learning no more of the world than a tic in a typewriter if I had been fool enough," he says. I tried to cure him of this by inviting him to my Saturday Review lunches at the Café Royal; but it was no use. He came a few times, being sincerely interested in the Café, in the waiters, in the prices, in the cookery: in short, in the economics of the place; but he concluded that Harold Frederic[10] and I ate too many steaks, and that it was a waste of money to pay Café Royal prices for his own plateful of macaroni, which he could obtain elsewhere for tenpence. The fact that I paid for it made no difference: he objected to a waste of my money just as much as of his.

I have sometimes wished that other people were equally considerate; but Shaw's consideration amounts to an interference with one's private affairs that is all the more infuriating because its benevolence and sagacity makes it impossible to resent it. All attempts to draw him into disinterested social intercourse are futile. To see as much of Shaw as I could easily see of any other man of letters in London, I should have had to join his endless committees. Our relations as contributor and editor were useless for social purposes: he came to the office only when we were in some legal difficulty, mostly to demonstrate with admirable lucidity that we had not a leg to stand on. He is accessible to everybody; but the net result is that nobody really knows him.

There is a cutting edge to Shaw that everybody dreads. He has in an extreme degree the mercurial mind that recognizes the inevitable instantly and faces it and adapts itself to it accordingly. Now there is hardly anything in the world so unbearable as a man who will not cry at least a little over spilt milk, nor allow us a few moments murmuring before we admit that it is spilt and done for. Few of us realize how much we soften our losses by veiling them in an atmosphere of sympathies, regrets, condolences, and caressing little pretences that are none the less sweet because they are only anesthetics. Shaw neither gives nor takes such quarter. An Indian prince's favorite wife, when banqueting with him, caught fire and was burnt to ashes before she could be extinguished. The prince took in the situation at once and faced it. "Sweep up your missus," he said to his weeping staff, "and bring in the roast pheasant." That prince was an oriental Shaw.

Once at Westminster Bridge underground station, Shaw slipped at the top of the stairs, and shot down the whole flight on his back, to the concern of the bystanders. But when he rose without the least surprise and walked on as if that were his usual way of descending a flight of steps they burst into an irresistible laugh. Whether it is a missed train, or a death among his nearest and dearest, he shews this inhuman self-possession. No one has accused him of being a bad son: his relations with his mother were apparently as perfect as anything of the kind could be; but when she was cremated, Granville-Barker, whom he had chosen to accompany him as the sole other mourner, could say nothing to him but, "Shaw: you certainly are a merry soul." Shaw fancied that his mother was looking over his shoulder and sharing the fun of watching two men dressed like cooks picking scraps of metal from her ashes. He is fond of saying that what bereaved people need is a little comic relief, and that this is why funerals are so farcical.[11]

In many ways this mercurial gift serves Shaw's turn very well. He knows much sooner and better than most people when he is in danger and when out of it; and this gives him an appearance of courage when he is really running no risk. He has the same advantage in his sense of the value of money, knowing when it is worth spending and when it is worth keeping; and here again he often appears generous when he is driving a very good bargain. When we stand amazed at his boldness and liberality, it is doubtful how far he is capable of facing a real danger or making a real sacrifice. He is genuinely free from envy; but how can he be envious when he can pity every other man for not being George Bernard Shaw? The late Cecil Chesterton has left it on record that when he, as a young nobody, met the already famous Shaw, he was received on terms of the frankest boyish equality. This shews only that Shaw makes no mistakes about men and manners. All that can be predicted of him is unexpectedness.

And so, with all his engaging manners and social adroitness, Shaw often seems one who does not care what he says, nor what others feel. It explains why "he has not an enemy in the world; and none of his friends like him." His Caesar's "He who has never hoped can never despair" is imposing; but who can feel sure that its inspiration is not infernal rather than divine? Compare it with the piously hackneyed "This is the true in life, the being used for a purpose recognized by yourself as a mighty one; the being thoroughly worn out before you are thrown on the scrap heap; the being a force of Nature instead of a feverish little selfish clod of ailments and grievances complaining that the world will not devote itself to making you happy." There is no smell of brimstone about this; but ask any of Shaw's fans which of the two quotations is the more Shavian.

I shall not attempt to carry the portrait any further. Shaw is almost a hopeless subject, because there is nothing interesting to be said about him that he has not already said about himself. All that he has left for me to deal with is something that has escaped not only his biographers but himself. Neither he nor they have ever attempted to explain Wilde's epigram. He is violently resented and hated as well as admired and liked. Pinero signed a friendly private letter to him "with admiration and detestation."

I have tried to depict a consistent character (and Shaw's character is almost mechanically consistent) that can produce such contrary effects. Nobody has yet tried to do this: his defenders have ignored the dislike: his assailants have denied his qualities and invented faults which do not exist. I have made no attempt to sit in judgment nor play the chivalrous friend. I have sketched the man's lines as they appear; and though the resultant figure is free from deformity, yet he can give us all a shudder by saying, "Imagine a world inhabited exclusively by Bernard Shaws!" This is only a trick; for a world of anybody would be unbearable. But there is something in it for all that; and what that something is I leave you to discover, not understanding it myself.

24th May 1919

Notes

Preface

WHO I AM

[1] In October, 1927, the Shaws moved from 10 Adelphi Terrace, where they had lived since their marriage in 1898, and where Charlotte had lived even before that, to a flat in fashionable Whitehall Court. It was their second and last London address.

[2] The incident apparently occurred when Anatole France visited London shortly before the First World War to address the Fabian Society. Shaw as chairman introduced the lecturer, who embarrassed G.B.S. by kissing him on both cheeks.

Chapter 1

PLAYS FOR PURITANS

[1] In April, 1898, a minor foot injury caused by lacing a shoe too tightly developed into a bone infection that required two operations and kept Shaw on crutches for more than a year. It forced him to give up play-reviewing for *The Saturday Review* (which he had tired of anyway) and other activities that had cut into the time he had available for writing.

[2] Terriss soon afterward (December 16, 1897) was stabbed to death outside the stage door to the Adelphi Theatre by a deranged would-be actor who considered the victim to be blocking his rise to fame.

[3] *The Wreck Ashore, or A Bridegroom from the Sea* (1830), by John Baldwin Buckstone (1802–1879) was one of more than one hundred melodramas by the now-forgotten early Victorian actor-manager (Haymarket Theatre) and playwright.

[4] Murray Carson (1865–1917) was a minor actor, producer, and playwright.

[5] Shaw writes about the November 13, 1887, "Bloody Sunday" march on Trafalgar Square to protest restrictions on free speech and assembly on pp. 150–51 of the *Autobiography 1856–1898*.

[6] The story of Shaw's epistolary romance with Ellen Terry is detailed in the *Autobiography 1856–1898* on pp. 233–35. Although Shaw wrote the Lady Cecily role in *Brassbound* for her, it was only in 1906, nearly eight years later, that rehearsals for it at the Court Theatre brought him into closer contact with her than through the mails or across the footlights.

[7] Sir Henry Morton Stanley (1841–1904), journalist and African traveller, is best known for his *How I Found Livingstone* (1872).

[8] Mary Kingsley (1862–1900) was a writer and African traveller of keen scientific observation and labored humor, best known for her *Travels in West Africa* (1897).

[9] Sir Johnston Forbes Robertson (1853–1937) turned from popular Victorian comedies to Shakespearian roles under Sir Henry Irving, after which he became an actor-manager on his own, starring in what is often considered the finest *Hamlet* of his time in 1895, and playing Romeo to the Juliet of Mrs. Patrick Campbell. During his management of the St. James's he achieved memorable performances in *The Passing of the Third-Floor Back* and *The Light That Failed* as well as in Shakespearian revivals.

[10] Pothinus impatiently scolds Caesar, who has offered Cyprus as a consolation prize to Cleopatra's dethroned younger brother Ptolemy, observing, "Cyprus is of no use to anybody."

"No matter," says Caesar: "you shall have it for the sake of peace." Disraeli—by 1878 the Earl of Beaconsfield—"accepted" Cyprus from the Turkish Sultan (after quietly insisting on its being offered) as a base from which to keep the peace—to insure defense of Asiatic Turkey against Russian encroachment. Economically it was then worthless, and, according to Disraeli's biographers (Monypenny and Buckle, *viii*), "it is quite certain that until he arranged for its acquisition, very few people in England indeed ever cherished the slightest wish for it."

[11] For many decades after the Literary Copyright Act of 1842, ambiguous

phrasing led playwrights to believe that if a play were published before it was performed, performing rights were irretrievably beyond protection. Actors were therefore hired to give what amounted to one-time public readings of manuscript plays, without costumes or scenery, during off-hours at a legitimate theatre. The Copyright Act of 1911 made the "old copyrighting farce" unnecessary, and ended Shaw's minuscule acting career, which had consisted almost entirely of appearing in his own and his friends' copyright performances under real and joking names. (Shaw, for example, read the Anthony Anderson part in his own *Devil's Disciple* under the name of Cashel Byron.)

[12] The "Ra" prologue was first used by Forbes Robertson in October, 1912.

Chapter 2

CEREBRAL CAPERS

[1] The Comte de Buffon (1707–1788), a famed theoretical biologist in his time, was best known for his *Natural History,* reprinted often and in many languages for more than a century after its first publication.

[2] Grant Allen (1848–1899) was a famous popularizer of the new science as well as author of such social problem potboilers as *The Woman Who Did* (1895).

[3] Slum-landlordism (*Widowers' Houses*), pseudo-Ibenism (*The Philanderer*), prostitution (*Mrs. Warren's Profession*), militarism (*Arms and the Man*), marriage (*Candida*), history (*The Man of Destiny*), current politics (*John Bull's Other Island*), natural Christianity (*The Devil's Disciple*), national and individual character (*Captain Brassbound's Conversion*), paradoxes of conventional society (*You Never Can Tell*), husband-hunting (*Man and Superman*), questions of conscience (*Major Barbara*), professional delusions and impostures (*The Doctor's Dilemma*). There are possibilities for other classification among Shaw's first dozen plays but the foregoing indicates the thrust of his remark.

[4] Sydney Olivier (later Lord Olivier). For Shaw's recollections of their earlier Fabian days see *Autobiography 1856–1898.*

[5] William Poel (1852–1934) founded the Elizabethan Stage Society in 1894, a group that freed Shakespeare and his contemporaries from cumbersome Victorian staging and production and profoundly influenced Elizabethan revivals thereafter.

Chapter 3

THE COURT EXPERIMENT

[1] Shaw's reference is to the Lord Chamberlain, in his capacity as censor of plays. Chapter 4 concerns his encounters with this official.

[2] Benozzo Gozzoli (1420–1497) was a Florentine painter of frescoes under the patronage of the Medici family.

[3] The gentleman was J. H. Leigh, a businessman.

[4] Shaw's flattery of Lillah McCarthy goes beyond normal bounds here because the passages were written as a foreword to her autobiography (see Sources).

[5] B. C. Stephenson (1839–1906) composed lyrics for popular Victorian light operas, one of them, *Dorothy* (with Alfred Cellier's music), playing nearly two thousand performances in London and the provinces in the eighteen-eighties. He was also an English adapter of Scribe and Sardou. (See also Note 5 to Chapter 11.)

[6] Sir Oliver Lodge (1851–1940), a physicist turned psychical researcher, published *Evolution and Creation* (1926) and *Beyond Physics,* as well as the spiritualistic *Raymond, or Life and Death* (1916).

[7] Dr. Stanton Coit (1857–1904), briefly an English professor at Amherst College, became an Ethical Culture preacher after turning to philosophical studies, and in 1887 replaced Moncure Conway at South Place Chapel in London.

[8] W. T. Stead (1849–1912), editor of the *Pall Mall Gazette,* 1883–88, and social and political activist, was lost in the *Titanic* disaster.

[9] Bacteriologist Sir Almroth Wright (1861–1947) and his laboratory staff at St. Mary's Hospital often worked late, stopping to make tea at midnight. Visitors from Sir Almroth's wide circle of friends would often turn up for tea and talk, Shaw being there on a night when a discussion arose among the physicians about admitting a tuberculosis patient for treatment by a new experimental method. John Freeman, Wright's assistant, objected, "We've got too many cases on our hands already."

Shaw asked, "What would happen if more people applied to you for help than you could properly look after?"

"We should have to consider," legend has Wright answering, "which life was worth saving."

According to André Maurois (biographer of the discoverer of penicillin,

Sir Alexander Fleming), Shaw laid a finger to his nose and announced, "Ha! I smell drama! . . . I get a whiff of a play!"

[10] Shaw remained hostile to vaccination all his life, probably an outgrowth of his being inoculated for smallpox as a youth, yet falling a victim to the London epidemic of 1881 anyway. Later he developed scientific reasons for his stand, upholding them publicly and often.

[11] Elie Metchnikoff (1845–1916) was a Russian-born French bacteriologist and originator of the phagocyte concept.

[12] The particular model Shaw refers to was Edward Aveling (1849–1898), a scientist and unsuccessful playwright who, according to Hesketh Pearson, "would borrow sixpence from the poorest man within his reach on pretence of having forgotten his purse, and three hundred pounds from the richest to free himself from debts that he never paid." When his wife—whom he had deserted—died, freeing him to marry Eleanor Marx, with whom he was living, he married another woman, with whom he had been deceiving Eleanor. On learning the news Eleanor committed suicide, Aveling did not survive her very long. There were complications from a serious operation he had had before her death, and Aveling, realizing his condition was grave, determined to die in his study amid his books, facing Battersea Park. On August 2, 1898, only four months after the death of Eleanor, he put down a book he was perusing and closed his eyes, ending as he had intended.

There were other models from life, notably the artists Rossetti and Beardsley, the former having Louis Dubedat's money morals and unscrupulous amours, the latter having his physique and tubercular condition as well as his wit.

[13] *John Bull's Other Island* was to have played the standard opening six matinees, but Beatrice Webb brought the Prime Minister, A. J. Balfour, to a performance. He was so delighted with it that he returned twice, first with one leader of the Opposition (Campbell-Bannerman) and then with the other (Asquith). It assured the play's popular success. A Command Performance had to be staged when King Edward VII expressed a desire to see it also, for the play by that time had completed a second scheduled run. It put the seal of the Crown upon Shaw's reputation as England's leading playwright, especially when it was learned that the King had laughed so heartily that he had broken his chair. It made it a costly evening for the frugal Vedrenne, for the furniture in the Royal Box had been specially rented for the occasion.

[14] The four Shaw plays produced "expressly" for the Court were *John Bull's*

Other Island (actually written for the Abbey in Dublin), *Major Barbara, The Doctor's Dilemma,* and the one-act farce *How He Lied to Her Husband*. There were eight other plays theoretically at the disposal of the Court Theatre, but one—*Mrs. Warren's Profession*—had been banned by the censor, leaving only the other seven previously written plays for production. They ranged in number of performances given from eight (*Don Juan in Hell* and *The Philanderer*) to 176 (*Man and Superman* without the Hell scene), 149 (*You Never Can Tell*), and 121 (*John Bull*).

[15] The Shakespearian season at the Savoy Theatre (*The Winter's Tale* and *Twelfth Night*) drew rave notices for faithfulness to the texts, freedom from elaborate staging, and the urgency of the acting. Granville-Barker's directorial star was at its zenith after the 1912–13 productions, but they nevertheless lost money.

[16] Shaw's memory is somewhat faulty here. Lord Howard de Walden backed two Barker productions, putting up half the amount (£1000) needed to finance *Fanny's First Play* in 1911, and purchasing a four months' lease of the St. James's Theatre in September, 1913, for the production of *Androcles and the Lion*. Between the two came Shakespeare, financed by £10,000 from Lord Lucas.

[17] Lillah, following her divorce, married the distinguished biologist Frederick William Keeble, in 1920. When he was knighted two years later she became Lady Keeble.

[18] Since Helen Huntington was still alive when Shaw, past ninety, wrote this, he treated her gently; however his bitterness about what she had done to Barker's career, and to Shaw's surrogate-son relationship with Barker, nevertheless shows through. She was, at best, a minor poetess, trivial fictionist, and undistinguished translator from the Spanish, indulging herself in writing on a large inherited income.

[19] After appearing in the audience at a lecture Granville-Barker gave in London in 1925, G.B.S. and Charlotte never saw him again. In September, 1943, G.B.S. wrote a postcard to Barker to tell him that Charlotte had died, at eighty-six. "You will not, I know," he added, "mind my writing this to you." Barker died in Paris three years later, at the age of sixty-eight.

Chapter 4

THE PRACTICAL IMPOSSIBILITIES OF CENSORSHIP

[1] Until September, 1968, for more than three centuries one Royal appointee had despotic power to decide what plays could be publicly performed in

England. As censor, the Lord Chamberlain could order an offending word, line, or scene stricken from a script or ban a play from the stage altogether by refusing to issue a license to it. Stage censorship, first enforced on religious and moral grounds, was actually instituted through the Lord Chamberlain on political grounds in 1737 when Prime Minister Walpole sought a way to suppress the political satire of Henry Fielding. The three Shaw plays interdicted by the censor were *Mrs. Warren's Profession* (1893), *Press Cuttings,* a satire on suppression of suffragette agitation (1909), and *The Shewing-Up of Blanco Posnet* (1909).

[2] *Arms and the Man* (1894).

[3] The production Shaw refers to was that of Arnold Daly's company in New York in 1905. The entire cast was arrested on charges of disorderly conduct, after a complaint filed by Anthony Comstock, Secretary of the Society for the Suppression of Vice. Eventually the defendants—released on bail—were acquitted when the judge ruled that the play, rather than being indecent, was a dramatized social tract.

[4] One of Harcourt's comedies, *A Question of Age,* had been presented by the Vedrenne-Barker management at the Court Theatre in 1906.

[5] Viscount Samuel (1879–1963), first elected to Commons in 1902, held numerous posts in the Cabinet and as a colonial administrator, remaining in public service for six decades.

[6] Lockwood (1847–1928), the first Baron Lambourne, had retired from the Army with the rank of lieutenant-colonel in 1883 and entered Parliament in 1892, where—except for his horticultural passions, symbolized by his lush and ever-present carnations—he was regarded as a typical country squire member.

[7] Reginald Bunthorne in Gilbert and Sullivan's *Patience* (1881), an "aesthetic poet," paid the young Oscar Wilde the compliment of satirizing him; but while the extravagantly garbed Bunthorne walked down Piccadilly "with a poppy or a lily in his medieval hand," Wilde later affected the notorious Green Carnation in his buttonhole, providing Robert Hichens with the title for the damaging *roman à clef* (1894) which hinted at what Wilde's three trials proved the following year.

[8] Shaw published eight letters on censorship in *The Times* during 1909, one on *Blanco Posnet* and two on *Press Cuttings,* and the others (June 4, 7, 26, and 30, and July 31) on the Committee hearings.

[9] The technically private performances under the Stage Society were a legal

evasion of the Lord Chamberlain's interdict. No such problem arose in Ireland, where the Lord Chamberlain's powers did not extend.

Chapter 5

SHAVIAN BUSTS

[1] Alvin Langdon Coburn (1882–1966) was one of the rare photographers who turned camera portraiture into an art. A friend to many of the famous in Edwardian art and literature, they live in his photographs of them, as does early twentieth-century London in his cityscapes.

[2] Coburn wrote of the incident:

> On 21st April [1906] I accompanied Mr. and Mrs. Shaw to the unveiling ceremony of Rodin's sculpture "Le Penseur" outside the Pantheon. The next morning G.B.S. surprised me by suggesting that after his bath I should photograph him nude in the pose of "Le Penseur." I had photographed him in almost every conceivable way, he said, so now I might as well complete the series as "The Thinker"—his true role in life. . . . I think G.B.S. was quite proud of his figure, and well he may have been, as the photograph testifies. When exhibited under the title "Le Penseur" at the London Salon of Photography it aroused considerable comment in the press. Reporters asked me if it were really a photograph of Shaw, and they asked him the same question, but I referred them to him for verification and he referred them to me, so they remained mystified. During his lifetime the photograph was never published, although G.B.S. had no objection to this, saying I could do what I liked with it.
>
> —*Alfred Langdon Coburn, Photographer. An Autobiography,* New York, 1966

[3] Pierre Puvis de Chavannes (1824–1898) was a French academic painter and portraitist at the height of his fame in the 'nineties.

[4] Prince Paul Troubetskoi (1867–1938) was a Russian emigré sculptor for whom Shaw was as much friend as artistic subject.

[5] John Singer Sargent's famous studio, on Tite Street in Chelsea, diagonally across from the house where Oscar Wilde lived, still stands.

[6] See Appendix II for another Shavian version of how Rodin worked on Shaw's bust. Yet another account appears in two letters written by the poet Rainier Maria Rilke, then Rodin's secretary:

. . . hardly ever has a portrait been so much aided in its making by the subject it represents as this bust of Bernard Shaw. Not only that he stands excellently (with an energy in his keeping still and with such an absolute giving of himself to the hands of the sculptor), but he knows too how to collect and concentrate himself to such a degree in the part of his body which, within the bust, will after all have to represent so to speak the whole Shaw, that the nature of the man springs over from it with unbelievably heightened intensity, feature by feature, into the bust.

—to S. Fischer, the Berlin publisher, April 19, 1906

Bernard Shaw comes out daily with his wife, we see each other often, and I was present at the first sittings and saw for the first time how Rodin tackles his work.—First there is a firmly shaped clay dummy, consisting of nothing but a ball set on something that supports it like a shoulder. This dummy is prepared for him and contains *no* armature *at all;* it only holds together by firm kneading.—He begins his work by first placing his model at a very short distance, about half a step from the stand. With a big iron compass he took the measurement from the top of the head to the tip of the beard, and immediately established this proportion on the clay dummy by lumps of clay. Then in the course of the work he took measurements twice more: nose to back of head, and ear to ear from behind. After he had further cut out the eye sockets very quickly, so that something like a nose was formed, and had marked the place for the mouth with an indentation such as children make on a snowman, he began, with his model standing very close, to make first four profiles, then eight, then sixteen, having his model turn after about three minutes. He began with the front and back views and the two full side-profiles, as though he were setting four different drawings vertically against the clay ball, then fitted half-profiles, etc., between these contours. Yesterday, at the third séance, he seated Shaw in a cunning little child's armchair (that ironic and by no means uncongenial scoffer was greatly entertained by all this) and cut off the head of the bust with a wire (Shaw, whom the bust was already remarkably like, in a superior sort of way, watched this decapitation with indescribable joy) and worked on the recumbent head, partially supported by two wedges, seeing it from above, at about the same angle as the model sitting low down a step away. Then the head was set on again and the work is now going along in the same fashion. In the beginning Shaw *stood,* often very close to the stand, so that he was somewhat higher than the bust. Now he sits right next it, exactly as high as the work, parallel with it. At some distance away a dark cloth has been hung up, so that the profiles always stand out clearly. . . .

—to Clara Rilke, postmarked April 19, 1906

[7] Sarah Bernhardt, Shaw wrote in the essay from which this autobiographical piece is extracted, "is very clever with her fingers."

Chapter 6

TREE AND A POTBOILER

[1] Robert Macaire was a character in *L'Auberge des Adrets* (1823) who became the nineteenth-century prototype for the clever and audacious rogue. Lord Dundreary was a minor character in Tom Taylor's dull farce *Our American Cousin* (1858), remembered now primarily for being in performance at Ford's Theatre in Washington on the evening Abraham Lincoln was shot. The character of Dundreary—all that is now remembered of the play itself—was assigned only some forty-odd lines, but Edward Sothern, who played the brief role in the first New York production, was mollified by being told that he could "gag" it as much as he pleased. Dressing in outlandish clothes, lisping and stuttering behind drooping whiskers, hopping about in a gait that was half shuffle, half jig, he created a set of mannerisms which were taken as caricature of the well-bred, obtuse eccentricity of the English lordling. The play became a smash hit on both sides of the ocean and caused a "Dundreary boom" in fashion—and in whiskers.

[2] Joseph Grimaldi (1778–1837) is traditionally the funniest of clowns, all of whom since have owed their "Joey" designation to him. At Covent Garden Theatre he created the role of Clown since associated with the designation. The original clown in the harlequinades was a country bumpkin, afterwards sophisticated into a varicolored Pierrot. Via Grimaldi the Clown became a combination of knave and butt.

[3] Eugène Brieux (1858–1932) was a French naturalistic, social-problem dramatist in the tradition of Zola, best known for Shaw's espousal of him (the Preface to *Three Plays,* in 1909) and for his *Les Avariés* (1902), a study of venereal disease produced in English as *Damaged Goods.* It created a sensation.

[4] Richard Carton (1856–1928) was an actor who turned to writing comedies of a Dickensian flavor, the best known being *Liberty Hall* (1892) and *Lord and Lady Algy* (1889). Shaw's comment, although obvious flattery of a friend, was meant less to indicate that Carton wrote masterworks than that Carton was a deft handler of stage business.

[5] The ambiguity of Shaw's ending, meant to not quite close the door on a reconciliation between Eliza and Higgins (who is nevertheless not of the marrying type), was thus romantically warped by Tree, who left the audience happily anticipating wedding bells. To provide an antidote Shaw wrote a prose epilogue for the published play in which Eliza marries Freddy, the young—and shiftless—upper-class beau whom she had rejected earlier.

[6] In 1917.

[7] When Shaw returned on July 8, 1914 (the play had opened on April 11), he found not only the flagrantly false ending but an episode in the second act in which Mrs. Campbell, as Eliza, pretended to walk through a wall. At the last moment Tree warned, "Don't go in there; that's my bedroom." In the audience there was some faint laughter and a good deal of shocked silence.

[8] Shaw's account is more generous than it might have been had it not been written originally as a contribution to a memorial volume prepared by Tree's half brother, Max Beerbohm.

[9] Henry Sweet (1845–1912) had a Readership in Phonetics specially created for him at Oxford in 1901.

Chapter 7
WAR MADNESS

[1] Rolland, in the fall of 1914, initiated a protest of intellectuals against the German destruction at Louvain and Rheims which his London publisher, Heinemann, circulated among prominent Englishmen. Only a few refused to sign, among them Shaw, who wrote Rolland that the only way to preserve libraries and cathedrals was to prevent war.

[2] Shaw's *Daily Chronicle* articles were "Armaments and Conscription: A Triple Alliance against War" (March 18, 1913) and "The Peace of Europe and How to Attain It" (January 1, 1914).

[3] The Protestant-dominated northern counties comprising Ulster and led by

Sir Edward Carson threatened rebellion and secession if Home Rule legislation for Ireland being considered in Parliament did not exclude them. Eventually their demands were met, and in the meantime they succeeded in delaying Home Rule altogether.

[4] A secret understanding, revealed by Foreign Secretary Lord Grey on August 2, 1914, prior to the German ultimatum to Belgium demanding passage rights into France, committed Britain to defence of the Channel and North Sea coasts of France against Germany.

[5] Shaw was already at Torquay (the "hotel in Devon" he mentions three paragraphs later) when England declared war. He remained there, but for a single brief business trip to London, until he had completed *Common Sense.*

[6] General Friedrich von Bernhardi (1849–1930) had published *Germany and the Next War* in 1911. Three of its chapter titles, "The Right to Make War," "The Duty to Make War," and "World Power or Downfall" indicate its point of view. Heinrich von Treitschke (1834–1896), a German historian, saw the increase of national power as the highest duty of the state. Friedrich Nietzsche (1844–1900) told Germans that Supermen were above ordinary morality.

[7] In early January, 1918, an Air Ministry came into being, with Lord Rothermere—brother of the newspaper proprietor Lord Northcliffe—as first Secretary of State for the Air Force. One of his first acts was to demand that the British Museum be vacated to make room for administrative offices for himself and his staff. Public reaction was overwhelmingly negative. He resigned in April, 1918.

[8] Barrie and Shaw. The air raid occurred on September 4, 1917.

[9] A. E. W. Mason (1865–1948), a prolific writer of historical novels (*The Four Feathers*), had an earlier career as an actor and appeared in a minor role in the first production of *Arms and the Man* in 1894.

[10] Former Senator Albert J. Beveridge of Indiana (1862–1927) had been traveling in Europe to do articles on the war for *Collier's* and *The Saturday Evening Post.* The March, 1915, interview with Shaw by the future biographer of John Marshall and Lincoln created a storm because Shaw again insisted that England would have gone to war on the French side even if Belgium had not provided a pretext.

[11] It appeared in London in *The Nation* on November 7, 1914, and was widely reprinted in America.

[12] Sir Hall Caine (1853–1931) authored a number of popular novels, many of them dealing with the Isle of Man. The Belgian Relief volume he edited for *The Telegraph* was *King Albert's Book*.

[13] One of the founders of *The New Statesman*, G.B.S. owned shares in the company. Although he resigned from its Board in 1916 in protest against the editorial policies of Clifford Sharp, he never threatened to withdraw his funds or use his shares to get his way.

[14] The published verbatim record of Parliamentary proceedings.

[15] Charles Frohman (1860–1915) at the time of his death was probably the most successful theatrical manager in America, and had turned theatrical management into big business.

[16] Charles Klein (1867–1915), once associated with Frohman, was co-author of the farce *Potash and Perlmutter*, a 1915 London hit.

[17] Sir Hugh Lane (1875–1915) was an Irish art collector whose collection of French impressionists was bequeathed to the National Gallery in London. An unwitnessed codicil, judged to be of no legal effect, left the paintings instead to Dublin and created a new source of Anglo-Irish acrimony.

[18] Also known as Aubers Ridge (May 9, 1915). The defeat cost 11,500 British casualties, and *The Times* in a leading article (May 14) protested that "British soldiers died in vain on Aubers Ridge . . . because more shells were needed. The Government, who have so seriously failed to organise adequately our national resources, must bear their share of the grave responsibility." Even more ordnance would have only obtained a local and temporary success, however.

[19] Lord Derby actually did write to Shaw, "It is very good of you to take the trouble to let me know about these sort of things. . . . Don't you think you could be tempted to come to me here in the official position as Stage Manager of Trafalgar Square Recruiting Meetings [?]. . . ."

[20] James Keir Hardie (1856–1915), leader of the Scottish miners, was a founder of the Labour Party and one of its few chieftains opposed to the war. James Ramsay MacDonald (1866–1937), an early Fabian and leader of the Labour Party, consistently spoke out against the war but survived execration to become the first Labour Prime Minister of England in 1924.

[21] Shaw's outspokenness on the niggardly family allowances granted to soldiers even prompted the intervention of George V with Asquith's cabinet; but the increase agreed upon was more token than real.

[22] Shaw's friend Rutland Boughton (1878–1960), who was organizer of the Glastonbury Festival.

[23] Shaw intervened in a number of cases, notably those of Clifford Allen and Stephen Hobhouse (1916–17), and offered advice (which had been asked for) in the case of Bertrand Russell. His major effort, however, was the publicity he brought to the cause via his letters-to-the-editor, most of which appeared in *The Nation*.

[24] See the next chapter for more on Montague.

[25] Cecil Chesterton (1879–1918) died in a hospital in France on December 6, 1918, less than a month after the armistice.

Chapter 8

JOY RIDING AT THE FRONT

[1] *Augustus* was first presented in London on January 21, 1917, at the Royal Court Theatre, and was repeated on January 22. It satirized the well-meaning but obstructive mediocrities who had been left with home-front responsibilities.

[2] Sir William Beach Thomas (1868–1957) was then war correspondent for *The Daily Mail*. He was knighted in 1920.

[3] C. E. Montague (1867–1928), novelist and drama critic, enlisted as a private at the age of forty-seven. After serving in the trenches he was made an officer and given the task of squiring distinguished visitors. After the war he returned to the *Manchester Guardian*, where he wrote cynical articles about his experiences afterwards collected as *Disenchantment* (1922).

[4] H. M. Tomlinson (1873–1958), author of *The Sea and the Jungle* (1912), *Gallions Reach* (1927), and *All Our Yesterdays* (1930), was war correspondent for *The Daily News*.

[5] Sir Philip Gibbs (1877–1962), journalist and novelist, published several postwar volumes about his experiences as a war correspondent, the best of them *Now It Can Be Told* (1920).

[6] Captain Matamore (from the Spanish for "slayer of Moors"); the later dramatic equivalent of the Roman comedy's *Miles Gloriosus*, the boastful, swaggering—and usually cowardly—soldier.

[7] In Chapter 21 of *Don Quixote* another misadventure begins when the Don convinces himself that a village barber riding toward him on an ass, with

his brass basin on his head to protect himself from the rain, is really a knight on a dappled steed wearing the magical gold helmet of Mambrino. The original helmet of Mambrino, satirized by Cervantes, appears in Boiardo's *Orlando Innamorato* (and Ariosto's sequel, *Orlando Furioso*), where Mambrino is a Moorish king whose magical helmet is acquired by Rinaldo.

[8] Shaw, in a burst of belated Irish patriotism, clearly exaggerates. The quelling of the Easter Rising (in the last week of April, 1916) damaged or destroyed buildings in a very small sector of central Dublin.

[9] General Sir Henry Rawlinson was then commanding general of the Fourth Army, on the Somme front.

[10] Ben Tillett (1860–1943) was Secretary of the Dock, Wharf, Riverside and General Workers' Union of Great Britain and Ireland from its inception in 1887 until its amalgamation with the Transport and General Workers' Union in 1922.

[11] Shaw's memory fails him here in his eagerness to get at Lord Northcliffe, who, as proprietor of several powerful newspapers which had complained about munitions shortages and the conduct of the war, had much to do with the eclipse of Earl Kitchener *a year earlier*. Kitchener, the hero of Khartoum, had become Secretary of State for War two days after the war began. By early 1916 he had lost much of his power to dictate strategy to the General Staff; and in June, 1916, set off by sea for Russia to discuss Russian demands for military supplies and credits. His ship, the *Hampshire*, struck a mine off the Orkneys, and Kitchener was one of the many lost. According to Arnold Bennett, Northcliffe's personal animus toward Kitchener had resulted from Northcliffe's loss of several nephews in the war. When questioned about his attitude toward Kitchener he was reported to have said, "But he's murdered my nephews!"

[12] Sir Almroth Wright, the inspiration for Shaw's *The Doctor's Dilemma* (see Chapter 3), was then an Army colonel doing research on wound infections at a hospital in France.

[13] Major Robert Loraine (1876–1935), then commander of 40 Squadron, was a veteran Shavian actor and—like Granville-Barker—a Shavian surrogate son. Seriously wounded twice while flying early in the war, he returned to duty and was severely wounded again in July, 1918, nearly losing his leg. After the war he returned to the stage.

[14] Shaw's *Daily Chronicle* articles appeared on March 5, 7 and 8, 1917.

Chapter 9

CRASH OF AN EPOCH

[1] *Peace Conference Hints,* a 1919 pamphlet, is best summed up by Shaw's own recapitulation of its main points:

1. As far as the planning of the war and the preparations for it are concerned the parties enter the Peace Conference on equal terms morally. . . .
2. The war was decided by the naval blockade, which proved that the British Empire has militant powers of starvation and ruin at present possessed by no other State.
3. . . . The United States must build a fleet capable of coping with any existing naval armament.
4. As a similar resolution on the part of the German Empire was the first step towards the present war, this declaration may be taken as the first step towards the next war unless and until the League of Nations becomes an established fact.
5. The League of Nations must begin as a combination of States with settled responsible governments of the modern democratic type, and will differ from an alliance by having a joint legislature and tribunal for enacting and administering a body of international and supernational law. The present alliance presents so obvious a nucleus for such a League, that it must at once anticipate its attitude and accept most of its moral responsibilities.
6. As republican federations of the North American type will be eligible as constituents of the League of Nations without question, whereas monarchies will have to satisfy the League that their governments are really responsible, the League, without directly imposing any form of government, or denying to any nation its right of self-determination, must, by the mere fact of its existence and the conditions of admission to it, act as a high premium on federal republicanism and responsible government, and as a veto on autocracy.
7. Germany cannot be admitted to the League until she has a settled government of the type desiderated; but the League cannot seriously ensure peace in Europe until Germany is admitted.
8. . . . The campaign of hatred against Germany, which has now served its turn, should be discontinued in England and America.
9. Disarmament (including nominal abolition of conscription) is

possible as regards land forces, but delusive. Naval and aerial armaments must be balanced and morally controlled by the League of Nations. The production of high explosives and artillery on a threatening scale, and the equipment of submarine vessels with torpedo tubes, should be made an offence against supernational law; but the League cannot make war physically impossible and should not try to.

10. There is not, and there never can be, any such thing as neutrality in war or in peace. . . . The extent to which any nation can be permitted to limit the general human right of way or to monopolize any natural product is one of the most difficult and pressing subjects for the supernational legislation which the League of Nations will have to set up.

11. The influence of party politics and Balance of Power diplomacy on the Peace Conference may produce a reactionary combination of the present European war Governments with the American Republican Opposition. . . . It is important that America should wake up to this situation, and not leave her President in the position of a prophet with less honor in his own country than in Europe, on which he has made a tremendous impression.

[2] The last act of *Heartbreak House,* which concludes with an air raid and the explosion of a bomb nearby, is taken from life—the dramatization of a 1916 Zeppelin raid observable from Shaw's country house at Ayot St. Lawrence.

[3] Although Shaw conceived *Heartbreak House* before the war, he apparently did not begin the actual writing of the play until March, 1916.

[4] H. G. Wells's *Anticipations* (1901; reissued 1914) actually bears the longer title *Anticipations of the Reaction of Mechanical and Scientific Progress upon Human Life and Thought.* In it Wells forecast the changes in home and family life, in personal relationships and in the class structure, that seemed inevitable in an age bound to become increasingly technological.

Chapter 10

BURGLARS

[1] "On my first visit," Hesketh Pearson wrote about a trip to Adelphi Terrace in 1916, "I was astonished by the formidable spikes that topped the wicket-

gate leading up to his flat and wondered whether they were a war-time measure. He [G.B.S.] explained their presence as already recorded." (Pearson was referring in his biography to the lines which this annotates.)

[2] Shaw describes this, the "Dod Street" affair, in Chapter 7 of the *Autobiography 1856–1898.*

[3] *The Silver Box,* which concerned the existence, in effect, of one law for the rich and another for the poor; and *Justice,* which repeated the message while scoring the inhumanity of British prison practices, were produced in 1906 and 1910, respectively. *Justice* actually effected a change, for it was seen by Winston Churchill, then Home Secretary, who instituted some overdue reforms.

[4] Shaw's comments on imprisonment were originally written as a preface to the report of the Hobhouse-Brockway committee; but, Shaw wrote, "I did not find it possible to keep a thorough sifting of the subject within the limits of the sixth commandment, on which Mr. Hobhouse took an uncompromising stand. . . ." According to Stephen Hobhouse (*Autobiography,* 1952), when Shaw's preface arrived, "to my horror I found that, though he said many wise and witty things about our present penal system, he advocated in it also a policy of 'euthanasia for incurables,' i.e. of 'extirpating' by consigning to the 'lethal chamber' criminals who were found to be 'utterly unmanageable.' He even suggested the same treatment for hopeless invalids and idiots. And this proposal to extend the existing rights of the community to kill men was actually intended for a volume compiled by writers whose crime had been that they had refused to admit the community's right to kill anyone, even the most hardened aggressor. . . . I at once told the Committee that, if this outrageous Introduction were included, I could not allow my name to appear as Joint Editor. The Sidney Webbs called a meeting of the Committee at their Grosvenor Road home to decide whether to throw G.B.S. or myself over. He appeared, having made a real but, to me, quite inadequate attempt to modify the crudity of his euthanasia proposals, which he read out to us. I stuck to my determination to resign; it was amusing to see how my aunt Beatrice was divided between her estimation of me as a sentimental fool for rejecting G.B.S.'s contribution (which would inevitably have greatly increased the number of readers who would at least open the pages of our rather formidable treatise) and her desire to secure that advantage for her and her husband's *History of English Prisons under Local Government,* which was to appear concurrently with our book (and actually did so with G.B.S.'s Introduction)."

Chapter 11

A MEMBER BY BAPTISM

[1] Ayot St. Lawrence, in Hertfordshire, where "Shaw's Corner" is now a National Trust house.

[2] Lucinda Gurly Shaw died in February, 1913. G.B.S. (accompanied by Granville-Barker) oversaw her cremation at Golders Green, having arrived by tube while the coffin proceeded in a horse-drawn hearse. A parson read the Church of England burial service to the audience of two, and when the coffin disappeared into the nearby furnace G.B.S. went behind the scenes to observe. "And behold!" he wrote to Mrs. Campbell. "The feet burst miraculously into streaming ribbons of garnet coloured lovely flame, smokeless and eager, like pentecostal tongues, and as the whole coffin passed in it sprang into flame all over; and my mother became that beautiful fire."

[3] Rhoda Broughton (1840–1940) had a reputation for audacity among mid-Victorian novelists, but outlived her reputation by not changing with the times. "I began my career as Zola," she said wryly of herself; "I finish it as Miss Yonge."

[4] Lucy actually published two books, both modelled after the *Letters of Lord Chesterfield to His Son. Five Letters of the House of Kildonnel* (1905) was followed three years later by *The Last of the Kildonnel Letters*. They became rare books almost immediately.

[5] Charles Butterfield played opposite Lucy in the light opera *Dorothy*. G.B.S.'s observations about their performance appears in the *Autobiography 1856–1898* in Chapter 10 ("How to Become a Musical Critic").

[6] Lucy Shaw died on March 27, 1920. Her will, dated February 14, 1918, specified, "My body to be cremated if possible and the ashes scattered. No funeral, no flowers, no mourning." G.B.S. attempted to carry out her instructions, but added the impromptu service. In other respects the compliance was complete, for there was no mourning implicit in his note to Mrs. Campbell on March 31, "Lucy is now Cinderella."

[7] Jonathan Wild (1682–1725) was a notorious London thief and organizer of bands of thieves. After his hanging at Tyburn his adventures were narrated by Defoe and satirized by Fielding. Shaw's sarcastic reference is to *Exodus* 12:35–36 (King James Version), where, after the final plague in which firstborn sons are found dead, the Egyptians are desperate to induce the Israelites to leave. "And the children of Israel did according to the word

of Moses; and they borrowed of the Egyptians jewels of silver, and jewels of gold, and raiment:/And the Lord gave the people favour in the sight of the Egyptians, so that they lent unto them such things as they required. . . ."

Chapter 12

BACK TO METHUSELAH

[1] The cycle, five plays in one, was begun during the last year of the war and completed late in 1920. The plays are *In the Beginning, The Gospel of the Brothers Barnabas, The Thing Happens, The Tragedy of an Elderly Gentleman,* and *As Far as Thought Can Reach.*

[2] Ivan Pavlov (1849–1936) was a Russian physiologist whose treatise *Conditioned Reflexes: An Investigation of the Physiological Activity of the Cerebral Cortex* was published in London in 1927.

[3] August Weismann (1834–1914) was a biologist whose theories of heredity precluded the transmission of acquired characteristics from one generation to another.

[4] Sir Barry Jackson (1879–1947) founded the Birmingham Repertory Theatre in 1913 and maintained it personally for twenty-two years, largely in the face of local indifference. In 1935 the Theatre was turned over to a governing Trust, while Sir Barry continued operating the nearby Malvern Festival (founded in 1929, largely to produce Shaw), which—although it failed to survive the Second World War—initiated the English theatre into the festival habit. His *Methuselah* production, originating in Birmingham in October, 1923, was transferred to London in February, 1924. These were not the pioneering productions of the cycle, for it had been premiered by the Theatre Guild in New York in February and March, 1922.

[5] St. Januarius, patron saint of Naples, is believed to have been martyred during the persecutions initiated by Diocletian in 305. A dark mass in a sealed reliquary in the Naples Cathedral, preserved as a sample of the blood of St. Januarius, is believed to liquify eighteen times a year.

[6] Jan de Witt (1625–1672), and his brother Cornelius, leaders of the republican, anti-Orange party in Holland, were seized by a royalist mob in August, 1672, and brutally murdered.

[7] In *The Tragedy of an Elderly Gentleman* the Gentleman is struck down dead when the Oracle gazes steadily into his face. He had been warned by her to return home or die of discouragement.

[8] Joseph Needham (1900–), biochemist and Master of Gonville and Caius College, Cambridge, published *Chemical Embryology* in 1931.

[9] Dr. Alexis Carrel (1873–1944), who achieved fame with *Man the Unknown* (1939) pioneered artificially induced circulation of the blood.

[10] Maurice Ernest (1872–1955) published *The Longer Life; A Critical Survey of the Many Claims to Abnormal Longevity, of Various Theories on Life and Old Age, and of Divers Attempts at Rejuvenation* (1938). He also founded in London (1928) the Centenarian Club, the aim of which was to investigate the means "whereby health and vigour may be retained beyond the century."

[11] St. John Hankin (1860–1909) considered, after Shaw and Granville-Barker, as the major playwright in the Edwardian theatrical revolution, committed suicide by drowning himself in the River Ithon. The best of his sardonic comedies are *The Return of the Prodigal* (1905) and *The Cassilis Engagement* (1907).

Chapter 13

HOW TO WRITE A PLAY

[1] Shaw overstates his case. In a number of his plays he deliberately employs a player who is both actor and character in the same person—the self-conscious character, or actor directly aware of his audience. This was a Shavian anti-illusionary device used as early as the turn of the century. He used other reminders of a theatrical theatre as well, from having a roguish character in *The Doctor's Dilemma* confess to being a disciple of Bernard Shaw to an old-fashioned, pre-naturalistic prologue in *Caesar and Cleopatra* spoken by the Egyptian god Ra, who makes the audience well aware that it *is* an audience, and that the play is a play. And after the lines here annotated were written Shaw concluded the improbable events in the first act of *Too True to Be Good* (1931) with the announcement by one of the cast: "The play is now virtually over; but the characters will discuss it at great length for two acts more. The exit doors are all in order. Goodnight." And the play ends with the impassioned but interminable oration of a young man which goes on while the other characters exit, leaving him to preach in solitude; while at last he is enveloped in fog and darkness. In the opening words of Shaw's last stage direction, "The audience disperses. . . ."

[2] See *Autobiography 1856–1898*, Chapter 8 ("Love Affairs") and its notes.

[3] The climactic scene—Eliza's triumph at passing herself off as a duchess at a fashionable garden party—occurs between Acts 3 and 4. For the film version Shaw wrote in part of the scene; and in the musical version by Alan Jay Lerner (*My Fair Lady*) it is moved to Ascot and expanded into one of the major scenes in the play.

[4] Mrs. Clandon in *You Never Can Tell* (Mrs. Besant); Sergius in *Arms and the Man* (Cunninghame Graham); Professor Adolphus Cusins in *Major Barbara* (Gilbert Murray); Lady Britomart Undershaft, Cusins's future mother-in-law in *Major Barbara* (the Countess of Carlisle, Murray's actual mother-in-law); Bluntschli in *Arms and the Man* (Sidney Webb); Sir Colenso Ridgeon in *The Doctor's Dilemma* (Sir Almroth Wright); the Rev. James Morell in *Candida* (the Rev. Stopford Brooke); the Bishop of Chelsea in *Getting Married* (Mandell Creighton, the Bishop of London); the unseen General Sandstone in *Press Cuttings* (Lord Haldane); the drama critic Trotter in *Fanny's First Play* (A. B. Walkley); Burge and Lubin in *Back to Methuselah* (Lloyd George and Asquith); the Inca in *The Inca of Perusalem* (Kaiser Wilhelm). Some of these personalities modeled for other Shavian characters as well.

[5] See Shaw's description of the incident in the *Autobiography 1856–1898*, Chapter 6 ("The Fabian Experience").

[6] Shaw elaborated on this point, turning *Macbeth* into a Bennett-Galsworthy novel, in an article in *The Nation,* "Mr. Arnold Bennett Thinks Play-Writing Easier Than Novel Writing" (March 11, 1916, reprinted in *Pen Portraits and Reviews*).

[7] H. G. Wells, in a letter (February, 1905) to Shaw about *John Bull's Other Island* in which he curiously saw himself caricatured as Broadbent, diagnosed Shaw's comic style as blemished by "perversity." He added: "You have every element of greatness except a certain independence of your own intellectual exciteability. You can't control your own wit and love of larking. You ought to dull yourself with meat and then you'd be vast." (Lovat Dickson, *H. G. Wells,* 1969).

Chapter 14

SAINT JOAN

[1] Rodin's massive "Burghers of Calais" was completed between 1884 and 1895, having been commissioned as a monument in memory of the heroes of the siege of Calais by Edward III in the 14th century. As Froissart re-

counted they went to Edward "bareheaded, barefooted, nooses round their necks and the keys to the city and to the castle in their hands." Although the idea for the play came to Shaw before 1914, the play was not written until 1934.

[2] Shaw's *The Six of Calais,* subtitled "a mediaeval war story in one act, by Jean Froissart, Auguste Rodin and Bernard Shaw," was first presented at the Open Air Theatre, Regent's Park, London, on July 17, 1934. The Queen Philippa was Phyllis Neilson-Terry.

[3] The *Chronicles of Jean Froissart* (1338–c.1410) remain the most graphic, anecdotal, account of fourteenth-century French history. Shaw's objection to their reliability is that their perspective is that of the Court and Castle.

[4] This may be Shavian sarcasm, for the conservative Pius IX was responsible for the *Syllabus of Errors* (1864), a compilation of eighty liberal theses he denounced, including one that "Everyone is free to adopt and profess that religion which he, guided by the light of reason, holds to be true" (Condemned Proposition 15). Short of conversion, Pius IX could not have supported young Irish Protestant Shaw's bid for a heavenly destination.

[5] Jules Quicherat, *Procès de Condemnation et de Réhabilitation de Jeanne d'Arc, ditte la Pucelle: Publiés pour la première fois d'après les manuscrits de la Bibliothèque royale, suivis de tous les documents historiques qu'on a pu reunir et accompagnés de notes et d'éclaircissements,* 5 vols., Paris, 1841–49.

[6] *The Suffragette Movement. An Intimate Account of Persons and Ideals,* London, 1931.

Chapter 15
FABIAN POLITICS

[1] Shaw discusses his early Vestry experience also in the *Autobiography 1856–1898* on pp. 258–60.

[2] Hermann Alexander, Graf von Keyserling (1880–1946), wrote *The Travel Diary of a Philosopher* (1925), *The World of the Making* (1927), and *Creative Understanding* (1929), an account of his *Schule von Weisheit.*

[3] The affair of the automobile and the baronetcy was only unusual in that MacDonald was leader of a party espousing Socialism. There had been a considerable traffic in honors available through the Prime Minister's office during the last years of Lloyd George's ministry, a knighthood allegedly

going for £5000 and more, and baronetcies beginning at £20,000. Peerages were more expensive. All of this was denounced by MacDonald, but in the summer of 1924 (he had become Prime Minister himself in January) it was revealed that he had accepted a gift of 30,000 shares in the prosperous biscuit company of McVitie and Price from its head, Sir Alexander Grant. *The Daily Mail* then discovered that in the next Honours List the donor had been granted a baronetcy. To make matters worse, *The Daily Mail* then learned that a Daimler automobile had been provided for MacDonald, also from Sir Alexander. In his defense MacDonald lamely pointed out that the Prime Minister was provided with no automobile, and that the income from the shares was for the upkeep of the gift automobile. A better defense might have been that the Prime Minister did not receive a sufficient salary to maintain his office, and that many of his predecessors had been subsidized by the wealthy, Asquith for many years receiving £3500 from the millionaire contractor Lord Cowdray.

[4] G. D. H. Cole (1889–1959), author of dozens of treatises on economics, many supporting syndicalism and Guild Socialism, was Chichele Professor of Social and Economic Theory at Oxford, 1944–57, and Chairman of the Fabian Society, 1939–46 and 1948–50.

[5] St. John Ervine later became hostile to the Fabians, especially the Webbs.

[6] In the 1908 elections to the Fabian Executive, Wells was supported by 78 per cent of the membership. His wife was also re-elected.

[7] His letter of resignation was printed in full in the *Fabian News* in October, 1908. In it he concluded that conversion of the Fabians to his point of view was "not worth making."

[8] Shaw unreasonably downplays the impecuniosity of Wells's childhood and youth, yet he could not have known how difficult life really had been for Wells since reticence about the period extends even to Wells's autobiography. Yet Wells celebrated his twenty-first birthday in poverty and invalided from a teaching job he despised with hemorrhaging lungs and a ruptured kidney. And Wells had come close to starvation while he desperately tried to write something which would sell, once consigning a 35,000 word beginning of a novel to the fire. When he did succeed, however (with the *Pall Mall Gazette* and *Pall Mall Budget,* in 1893, when he was twenty-seven), he was able to sell—quickly—almost anything he wrote.

[9] It was one of Shaw's proud boasts, made often in his last years, that he engineered the interment of the Webbs in the Abbey when Sidney Webb died in 1947. Shaw, ninety-one, made his plea in a letter to *The Times* which

stressed that "great civilisers" and "world-betterers" belonged there as much as "kings and captains, novelists and actors." It was the first time in nine hundred years that a husband and wife were buried together at Westminster in the same ceremony. The address, appropriately, was given by a Fabian, Prime Minister Clement Attlee. It was a fitting gesture to Fabianism for there were ten Fabians in the Cabinet at the time, 229 in Commons.

[10] The Newcastle Programme, a Webb invention, was foisted on the Liberals in 1892.

[11] The tract, number 49, was issued under Shaw's name alone in 1894.

[12] Shaw at the time of writing may not have looked in the 1889 *Fabian Essays* for some years, although it remained—and remains—in print. Marx is actually mentioned twice in one of Shaw's essays, and once (however only in a footnote) in an essay by Sidney Webb.

[13] Sir William Harcourt (1827–1904), when Home Secretary under the Liberals in the 'eighties, was instrumental in reforming the government of London.

Chapter 16

THE APPLE CART

[1] The play was first performed at the Teatr Polski in Warsaw on June 14, 1929. The Malvern Festival Theatre gave it its first performance in English on August 19, 1929.

[2] Gattie's *The Honourable Member* was produced at the Court Theatre on July 14, 1896, and noticed by Shaw in *The Saturday Review* on July 18, 1896, where he called it "a remarkable play; . . . because he [Gattie] seems conversant with ethical, social, and political ideas which have been fermenting for the last fifteen years in England and America. . . ."

[3] Gattie (1856–1925) apparently had invented a system of unloading container cargo that was not only automated but safe for handling fragile and dangerous goods, even explosives. Ambitiously, he then imposed upon that concept a scheme for a Central Clearing House with seven times the interior space of St. Paul's Cathedral, to replace seventy-four London freight stations, many times that number of wharves, and untold thousands of loyal labor unionists. Its roof would have doubled as a landing strip for aircraft, completing a dream of Wellsian proportions. Shaw urged the scheme upon the Chairman of the Board of Trade as an urgent wartime labor-saving

possibility, but was told that the enormous expenditure of men and materials necessary to test the project's practicality on a large scale—even if the foul and abusive Gattie personality were no obstacle—made it impossible under wartime conditions. A victim of the vested interest in inefficiency, Gattie was finally given a formal No in 1919—after the war.

[4] "Here am I, the Powermistress Royal. I have to organize and administer all the motor power in the country for the good of the country. I have to harness the winds and the tides, the oils and the coal seams. . . . I do it, but it costs twice as much as it should. Why? Because every new invention is bought up and suppressed by Breakages, Limited. . . . But for them we should have unbreakable glass, unbreakable steel, imperishable materials of all sorts. . . . I could name you a dozen inventions within my own term of office which would have effected enormous economies in breakages and breakdowns; but these people can afford to pay an inventor more for his machine or his process or whatever it may be than he could hope to make by legitimate use of it; and when they have bought it they smother it. . . . I—I—oh, it is beyond bearing [*she breaks down*]." (*The Apple Cart,* Act I)

Chapter 17

TOURING IN RUSSIA

[1] Shaw left London on July 18, 1931.

[2] Although Shaw implies that he was uninhibited in what he wanted to see and do, this was clearly not so, even if his Soviet guides fostered that impression.

[3] Shaw's reception in the border town of Nigoreloye was quiet, as he had requested in advance, but in Moscow there were thousands at the station to greet him, with welcoming banners, a brass band, and shouts of "Hail Shaw!"

[4] Anatoly Lunacharsky (1875–1933), a Bolshevik leader who had participated in the 1917 coup and was Commissar for Education from 1917 through 1929, had prepared a careful statement about the unpredictable Shaw's visit for *Izvestia,* warning readers, "We realize that Bernard Shaw is our ally. Yet we know quite well that he may sometimes execute some amazing zigzag . . . indulging in witticism at our expense . . . and do so in a manner calculated to evoke a satisfied grunt from the bourgeoisie. . . . The penetrating eye of the 'free man' will surely discern the real truth which, after all, is the only cause that the great Irish writer is always anxious to serve."

[5] Maxim Litvinoff (1876–1951), Soviet Ambassador to London, 1917–18, and to Washington, 1940–41, was Commissar for Foreign Affairs at the time of Shaw's visit.

[6] Philip Kerr (1882–1940) was one of the founders (1910) and editor of the Commonwealth Affairs quarterly, *The Round Table,* private secretary to Prime Minister Lloyd George (1915–21), and Ambassador to Washington (1939–40). It was at his urging that Shaw made the trip to Russia.

[7] Margaret McMillan (1860–1931) was an American-born English social reformer who pioneered nursery school education in England and established the Rachel McMillan College at Deptford for the training of nursery school teachers.

[8] Mariya Aleksandra Spiridonova assassinated the brutal commandant of the district of Boris-Soglebsk, General Luzhenovsky, on January 16, 1906. As he lay dying, a Cossack officer named Avramov, with his men, seized her and beat her with whips and knouts. Somehow she survived imprisonment and further beatings.

[9] Prince Peter Kropotkin (1843–1921), a Russian anarchist philosopher, joined the revolutionary movement in 1872 and spent the next fourteen years in and out of prisons in Russia and France, finally settling in England in 1886, where he became friendly with Shaw and other socialist activists. In 1917 he returned to Russia.

[10] The adjective is adapted from the Forsyte family in the nine-novel *Saga* by John Galsworthy (*The Man of Property,* 1906), the epitome of nineteenth-century English materialistic acquisitiveness. Some lines later Shaw also turns it into a noun.

Chapter 18

BURNING THE CANDLE AT BOTH ENDS

[1] Shaw is referring to the period of reaction to the First World War, approximately 1918–1930, the latter date the point at which this chapter begins.

[2] Two other "dismal" subjects were dealt with by Shaw in full-length comedies during this period, one failing at the box office and the other failing even to find a hospitable theatre. *On the Rocks* (1933) is built around an imaginary English depression-inspired Cabinet crisis. *The Millionairess* (1935) concerns economic inequality, and (in the person of the title character) the mysterious personal force that renders an individual a "born boss." Shaw wrote little

in retrospect about either one, using the opportunity of their prefaces to expound on larger issues than the plays themselves.

[3] What became of Shaw's play was its eventual eclipse by events, for he had written (as in *On the Rocks*) about events so contemporary in *Geneva* (even providing Hitler, Mussolini, and Franco under disguiseless disguises) that the play had to be kept topical by rewriting during 1938 and 1939. When it toured in Canada and the United States in 1939, Hitler ("Battler") had already invaded Poland, causing Shaw to write a new act. Because of its intrinsic defects, exacerbated by the need for topicality, the play is likely to be revived only as a period piece.

[4] *Sweet Nell of Old Drury* (1900) was the first London success of the now-forgotten American playwright Paul Kester (1870–1933).

[5] Sir Godfrey Kneller (1648–1723) was an English portrait painter of German ancestry. He came to England at the invitation of the Duke of Monmouth and met Charles II, soon becoming the King's official portraitist. He remained Court Painter through the many shifts in the political winds, surviving several monarchs after Charles and holding the position into the reign of George I.

[6] Henry Perigal (1801–1898), the courtly English astronomer Shaw refers to, must have been about eighty-seven at the time of the Broadstairs meeting, if he died, as Shaw notes later in the anecdote, ten years later. (The identification of the astronomer as Perigal is made by Dan Laurence in *Platform and Pulpit.*)

[7] Shaw either remembered the incident at Broadstairs, or remembered into the late nineteen-thirties his mention of it in the 1920 Oxford talk from which the anecdote here annotated was drawn; for in *Good King Charles* (1939) he included a scene in which Louise de Kéroualle (the Duchess of Portsmouth) reacts skeptically to Isaac Newton's insistence upon the importance of his work in attempting to ascertain the exact distance of the sun from the earth:

LOUISE: But what a waste of time! What can it possibly matter whether the sun is twenty miles away or twenty-five?

NEWTON: Twenty or twenty-five!! The sun is millions and millions of miles from the earth.

LOUISE: Oh! Oh! Oh!!! You are quite mad, Monsieur Nieuton. At such a distance you could not see it. You could not feel its heat. Well, you cannot see it so plainly here as in France, nor so often; but you can see it quite plainly sometimes. And you can feel its heat. It burns your skin, and freckles you if you are sandy-haired. And then comes a little cloud over it and you shiver with cold. Could that happen if it were a thousand miles away?

NEWTON: It is very, very large, madam. It is one million three hundred thousand times heavier than the earth.

LOUISE: My good Monsieur Nieuton: do not be so fanciful. [*Indicating the window*] Look at it. Look at it. It is much smaller than the earth. If I hold up a sou—what you call a ha-pen-ny—before my eye, it covers the sun and blots it out. . . . You must never let your imagination run away with you. When you think of grandiose things—hundreds of millions and things like that—you must continually come down to earth to keep sane. You must see: you must feel: you must measure.

NEWTON: That is very true, madam. Above all, you must measure. And when you measure you find that many things are bigger than they look. The sun is one of them.

LOUISE [*rising and going to the table to coax him*]: Ah! You are impossible. . . .

[8] Not one of the more frequently revived Shaw plays, in spite of its wit, wisdom, and theatrical qualities, it is difficult to see a production of *Good King Charles;* however it has had several successful post-1939 productions.

Chapter 19

ENDING AS A SAGE

[1] The minor incident Shaw refers to was that of the German cruiser *Graf Spee,* in December, 1939, here merged misleadingly with the far more crucial air battles of August–September, 1940.

[2] Browning's long dramatic monologue, "Mr. Sludge, the Medium," was based upon Dunglas Home, an expatriate American spiritualist who attracted much attention in the circle in which the Brownings moved in Florence.

Appendix I

LAST WILL AND TESTAMENT

[1] The paragraph ending with a reference to "the cloister" almost certainly is a guarded suggestion that Westminster Abbey was not ruled out if his trustees had that option. Since he had initiated the successful campaign to inter the Webbs at Westminster shortly before, the Abbey must have been

very much in his mind. There was no similar campaign for Shaw, however, and his ashes were scattered in the garden at Ayot. In any event, the next paragraph would very likely have ruled out an Abbey ceremony, for paragraph four excluded almost any kind of interment or memorial service likely under Abbey—and Anglican—auspices.

[2] Shaw's copyrights (valid in England until fifty years after the author's decease and in the United States—assuming renewal—for fifty-six years after publication) were so astronomically valued by the Estate Duty Office that the Shaw Estate remained penniless for years, although Shaw left considerable liquid assets and his copyrights brought in substantial and even unexpected, income, especially after the success of the *My Fair Lady* adaptation from *Pygmalion* (1956–). The result was that the Estate could only use its income to pay its tax indebtedness to the Government, and the interest on the deficit. The value of the estate was announced early in 1951 as amounting to £367,233 (then $1,028,252.40), with a net value of £301,585, on which death duties of £180,571 were assessed.

[3] Shaw's correspondence with Mrs. Campbell was published according to the terms of the will in 1952. Authority to reprint Shaw's letters to Mrs. Campbell remains, according to the will, the right of Mrs. Campbell's heirs; thus these letters are the only body of Shaw's correspondence removed by his direction from the control of his own executors.

[4] The National Trust accepted the gift of "Shaw's Corner"—but with great reluctance, as is made clear in an extract from the diary of Sir Harold Nicolson, then an official of the Trust:

> I go down to Hertfordshire with Jim Lees-Milne and Jack Rathbone to see Bernard Shaw's house which he left to the National Trust. We first go into the garden. A sloping lawn and rough grass intersected by a few rose-beds. A bank, with a statue of St. Joan. A hut in which he worked. Everything as he left it. Postcards, envelopes, a calendar marking the day of his death, curiously enough a Bible and prayerbook and Crockford's Directory, a pair of mittens. The grass path and the bed around the statue of St. Joan are still strewn with his ashes and those of Mrs. Shaw. The Trustees and the doctor got both urns and put them on the dining-room table. They then emptied the one into the other and stirred them with a kitchen spoon. They went out into the garden and emptied spoonfuls of the mixture on to the flower beds and paths. All this some fifteen days ago, but the remains are still there. Just like the stuff Vita puts down for slugs.

We see the housekeeper, a nice Scotch body. She would like to stay on, but how can we afford her? Shaw has left us nothing at all. The house is dreadful and not really lettable. It will, moreover, be difficult to show to tourists as it is so small. It will be essential to keep the furniture exactly as it is. All his hats and coats and nailbrushes etc. are here. His long woollen stockings and his thick underclothes. The pictures, apart from one of Samuel Butler and two of Stalin and one of Gandhi, are exclusively of himself. Even the door knocker is an image of himself.

We decide that morally we must accept Shaw's house. I am not happy about it. I do not think that Shaw will be a great literary figure in 2000 A.D. He is an amazingly brilliant contemporary; but not in the Hardy class.

—Harold Nicolson, *Diaries and Letters, III: The Later Years,* ed. Nigel Nicolson (New York & London, 1968), entry for 11 December 1950.

[5] The transliteration of *Androcles and the Lion,* with facing pages in "Dr. Johnson's Alphabet," was eventually published by Penguin Books as Shaw directed; but only after settlement of the alphabet trust clauses in Chancery (see below).

[6] Deciding *In re Shaw's Will Trusts,* Mr. Justice Harman of the Chancery Division of the High Court of Justice in London held in February 20, 1957, that funds accruing to the estate of G.B.S. could not be applied to the testator's project of revamping the English alphabet into a phonetic one of forty characters. The opening of the litigation on January 16 had had a setting and dialogue Shaw himself might have envied.

"And who appears for the poor alphabet?" asked Justice Harman of the assembled solicitors.

"The Attorney-General, my Lord."

The action on the will was brought to the Chancery bench by the residuary legatees of the trusts—The British Museum, The Royal Academy of Dramatic Art, and the National Gallery of Ireland—and the Public Trustee, as Shaw's executor. Arguing for the Public Trustee, the Attorney-General contended that the alphabet trusts were established for a charitable and educational purpose. In his decision Justice Harman held that it was doubtful that the trusts were in fact charitable: that the value of such an alphabet as a public benefit was too much in doubt, and that its operation "would involve a change in the law of the land." Further, he found the trusts invalid since there was no beneficiary to enforce them. In December, 1957, after prolonged discussion among the contending parties, a settlement was reached out of court between the residuary legatees and the Public Trustee by which a sum not exceeding £8,300 was to be allocated from the income of the estate for the alphabet project, the remainder thenceforth accruing to the residuary legatees.

A competition, with prize money derived from the £8,300, was held to develop a new alphabet according to Shavian standards, and the result was the *Androcles and the Lion* edition Shaw wanted. Today a dedicated group of adherents to the new "Shavian" continue to use the alphabet, and some of its features are paralled in a revolutionary program for the teaching of reading in many English schools, students returning to "Dr. Johnson's Alphabet" after they have mastered basic reading and pronunciation. Thus, in some form, Shaw's dream lives.

[7] F. E. Loewenstein not long after Shaw's death put aside his bibliographical efforts and returned to his native Germany. Work on a definitive Shaw bibliography was later taken up by Professor Dan H. Laurence.

[8] Shaw's witnesses were Mr. and Mrs. Harold White, of The Leagrave Press, Ltd., in nearby Luton. It was The Leagrave Press that was then producing *Bernard Shaw's Rhyming Picture Guide to Ayot Saint Lawrence,* Shaw's last completed work. He took all the photographs himself and wrote the rhymes shortly before his fatal accident, which occurred three months after he signed his will. On September 11, 1950, while working in his garden, Shaw fell, fracturing his left femur. Immobility left him prey to other ailments, and he died on November 2, 1950. He was ninety-four.

Appendix II

"HOW FRANK OUGHT TO HAVE DONE IT"

[1] Harris died—broke—on August 26, 1931, more than a decade after Shaw wrote the original version of his facetious self-portrait in the Harris style. At the time, Harris—seventy-five and ill—had been theoretically at work on a biography of Shaw. In the end, most of it was written by Frank Scully, with Shaw's additions and "improvements," in order to fulfill the contract and provide funds for Harris's widow. It was published in 1932.

[2] The Yahoos were a subject race of bestial, depraved subhumans (opposed to their masters, the Houynhnhnms, a race of graceful, educated horses) in the fourth book of Swift's *Gulliver's Travels.*

[3] The American actress was Elinor Robins.

[4] The preface to *Caesar and Cleopatra,* actually part of the collective preface to *Three Plays for Puritans* (1900).

[5] Kathleen, Lady Scott (1878–1947), widow of the polar explorer and a talented sculptress, afterwards married Hilton Young, the first Lord Kennet.

[6] The section on the Rodin bust and other attempts at sculpting Shaw was cribbed by G.B.S. from himself (see Chapter 5).

[7] The actor and actress were Sir Herbert Beerbohm Tree and Mrs. Patrick Campbell, then rehearsing *Pygmalion* (see Chapter 6).

[8] The lady in *Getting Married* (1908) is Lesbia Grantham.

[9] Maurice Baring (1847–1945) was an English diplomat turned journalist, novelist, and poet.

[10] Harold Frederic (1856–1898) was *New York Times* correspondent in London in the 'nineties and author of the novel *The Damnation of Theron Ware* (1896).

[11] For Shaw in the first person on family funerals see Chapter 11 ("A Member by Baptism") and *Autobiography 1856–1898,* pp. 16–17.

Sources

AUTOBIOGRAPHICAL INTENTION (rather than private confession) was the sole criterion for admissibility of material. Thus no private letters or manuscripts clearly intended for a limited audience have been included. Chapter headings are the editor's, but the words themselves —as everywhere else in the *Autobiography*—are Shaw's own, adapted from his nonfiction and nondramatic prose.

Some editorial license has been taken in matters of paragraphing and capitalization, and here and there a date or a name has been corrected where Shaw or his printer was clearly in error; however normal autobiographical inconsistencies have been retained.

Although the material comprising the *Autobiography 1898–1950* was written over a period of fifty-two years, and for a variety of audiences, and has here been utilized in lengths ranging from a single phrase to a thousand or more unaltered words, in no case is the rearrangement for reasons other than fuller narrative continuity. Ellipses indicate editorial cuts, and square brackets enclose the few bridging or clarifying words supplied by the editor. Punctuation and spelling—including the unitalicized titles and apostrophe-less contractions—are Shaw's own: variations in them through the text result from the vagaries of original publication.

Preface

WHO I AM

page 1
The celebrated G.B.S. . . . it never is). "The Chesterbelloc," *The New Age*, 15 February, 1908; reprinted in *Pen Portraits and Reviews* (1931).

pages 1–2
I have been . . . heaven and earth. "The Chesterbelloc."

page 2
It happens that . . . theory or practice. *Everybody's Political What's What?* (1944), p. 326.

pages 2–3
Far from being . . . else on earth. "The Chesterbelloc."

page 3
Authors are not . . . a confirmed crank." *Everybody's Political What's What?*, p. 22.

page 3
The explanation seems . . . from another world. *Everybody's Political What's What?*, p. 21.

pages 3–4
When I was . . . coat of arms. *Everybody's Political What's What?*, pp. 186–87.

page 4
No doubt every . . . it behind him. "The Artstruck Englishman," *The Nation*, 17 February, 1917; reprinted in *Pen Portraits and Reviews*.

pages 4–5
Granted that . . . Perhaps I shall. *Everybody's Political What's What?*, p. 327.

page 5
I am myself . . . Te Deums to them. "The Artstruck Englishman."

Chapter 1

PLAYS FOR PURITANS

pages 6–7

Since I gave . . . books and plays. Preface to *Three Plays for Puritans* (1900).

page 7

When I began . . . has to a sermon. "Playwrights' Texts," *Times Literary Supplement,* London, October 25, 1917.

pages 7–9

They tell me . . . old-fashioned playwright. Preface to *Three Plays for Puritans.*

page 9

One day . . . of a play. *"Vornehmlich über mich selbst,"* in Program No. 88 of the Schiller Theatre, Berlin; reprinted in Archibald Henderson, *Bernard Shaw* (Cincinnati, 1911), p. 354.

page 9

He wasted very . . . collaboration and produced. "On the Living and the Dead," *The Saturday Review,* 25 December, 1897; reprinted in *Our Theatres in the Nineties,* III, 278.

page 9

one of the most . . . The Devil's Disciple. *"Vornehmlich . . . ,"* Henderson, pp. 354–55.

page 9

When it was . . . at anything else. "On the Living . . ."

pages 10–12

Robert Buchanan . . . all was over. Preface to *Three Plays for Puritans.*

pages 12–14

I claim as . . . have been written. Notes [Appendix] to *Captain Brassbound's Conversion* (1900).

page 14

Written in 1899 . . . with the play. Program notes for the Little Theatre (London), October 15, 1912; reprinted in Mander and Mitchenson, *Theatrical Companion to Shaw* (London, 1954), p. 75.

pages 14–15
which I had . . . thing is done." "Bernard Shaw Talks about Actors and Acting," *The New York Times,* January 6, 1929 (from an address to the Royal Academy of Dramatic Art, December 7, 1928); reprinted in *Shaw on Theatre,* ed. E. J. West (New York, 1958), p. 195.

pages 15–16
Even Miss Terry . . . on the stage. Program Notes for the Little Theatre; *Theatrical Companion,* pp. 75–76.

page 16
I wrote Caesar . . . in such conceptions. "The Heroic Actors," *Play Pictorial,* No. 62 (October, 1907); reprinted in *Theatrical Companion,* p. 63.

pages 16–18
Technically, I do . . . spared a disappointment. Preface to *Three Plays for Puritans.*

pages 18–20
As to Caesar . . . any merit whatever. Notes to *Caesar and Cleopatra* appended to *Three Plays for Puritans.*

pages 20–21
The American notices . . . for Forbes Robertson. "The Heroic Actors," *Theatrical Companion,* pp. 63–64.

page 21
Caesar and Cleopatra . . . my own editions. "Playwrights' Texts," (London) *Times Literary Supplement,* October 25, 1917.

page 21
But there is . . . the god Ra. "Bernard Shaw Self-Revealed," *Fortnightly Review,* CXXV (May, 1926), 613.

pages 21–22
But the difficulty . . . about the discrepancies. "Playwrights' Texts."

Chapter 2

CEREBRAL CAPERS

pages 23–25
One day in . . . we are emerging. Preface to *Back to Methuselah* (1921).

page 25
Shelley and Wagner . . . of the Evolutionists. Preface to the 1911 cheap edition of *Man and Superman.*

pages 25–27
Ibsen was Darwinized . . . a few times. Preface to *Back to Methuselah.*

page 27
But I hear . . . way of appendix. Preface to *Man and Superman.*

page 27
I supplied the . . . of aphoristic fireworks. Preface to *Back to Methuselah.*

page 27
It is a . . . in that sense. Preface to *Man and Superman.*

pages 27–28
The effect was . . . taken seriously themselves. Preface to *Back to Methuselah.*

pages 28–29
I should make . . . form still splendid. Preface to *Man and Superman.*

Chapter 3

THE COURT EXPERIMENT

page 30
The first performance . . . her own pocket. "Commentary" by Shaw in the 25th Anniversary Souvenir Program of the Birmingham Repertory Theatre; reprinted in *Theatrical Companion,* p. 305.

page 30
Now what had . . . possible in England. Preface to *Heartbreak House* (1919).

page 30
Yet for ten . . . Germany and America. "Commentary"; *Theatrical Companion,* p. 305.

pages 30–31
In Germany and . . . of its household. Preface to *Heartbreak House.*

page 31

In the year . . . "ham" technique. "Granville-Barker: Some Particulars," *Drama,* New Series No. 3, Winter, 1946.

page 31

When little private . . . of dramatic faculty. "An Aside," a preface to Lillah McCarthy's *Myself and My Friends* (London, 1933).

pages 31–32

In looking about . . . for your heroine. "Granville-Barker . . ."

page 32

This difficulty was . . . heroic or nothing. "An Aside."

page 32

in the course . . . immature Mrs Siddons. "Granville-Barker . . ."

pages 32–33

It is a . . . what I needed. "An Aside."

page 33

We were now . . . June 1907. "Draft Letter to Millionaires," an appeal for funds for a National Theatre, undated, to be distributed as a printed memorandum. Undated. British Museum.

pages 33–34

went through with . . . out his ideas. "Granville-Barker . . ."

page 34

There is no . . . a considerable reputation. "Draft Letter . . ."

page 34

You may say . . . had never heard. "The Court Theatre," Shaw's reply to a toast by the Earl of Lytton at a complimentary dinner for the managers of the Court Theatre, at the Criterion Restaurant, July 7, 1907. Text from the souvenir menu, *Complimentary Dinner to Mr. J. E. Vedrenne and Mr. H. Granville-Barker.*

pages 34–35

But I kept . . . in the theatre. "Granville-Barker . . ."

pages 35–36

As we rehearsed . . . already helped themselves. "The Court Theatre."

pages 36–38

John Bull's Other . . . in a dream. Preface to *John Bull's Other Island* (1904).

page 38

Years ago . . . never taken place. "Literature and Art," a lecture delivered at the City Temple, October 8, 1908, *The Christian Commonwealth,* October 14, 1908; reprinted in *Platform and Pulpit,* ed. Dan H. Laurence (1961).

pages 38–39

We must not . . . dont we?" *Everybody's Political What's What?,* p. 157.

page 39

In Major Barbara . . . hope for everybody. "To Audiences at *Major Barbara,*" a memorandum circulated to the press in advance of the Grace George production in New York in 1915; reprinted in *Shaw on Theatre,* p. 120.

pages 39–40

When Major Barbara . . . and dazzling vice. Preface to *Major Barbara* (1905).

pages 40–41

The Salvation Army . . . our suburban nurseries. Program Note to the Wyndham's Theatre revival, March 5, 1929; reprinted in *Theatrical Companion,* p. 106.

page 41

The play develops . . . methods for me. *Table-Talk of G.B.S.,* ed. Archibald Henderson (1925), p. 75.

page 41

Some time back . . . understand the feeling. "Smoke and Genius," a speech delivered before the Annual Meeting of the Coal Smoke Abatement Society, London, June 13, 1911, and published in the Society's annual transactions, 1910–11; reprinted in *Platform and Pulpit,* p. 84.

pages 41–42

I must not . . . work fairly well. Preface to *Major Barbara.*

page 42

In my play . . . The Doctor's Dilemma. Preface to the 1907 reprint of *The Sanity of Art;* reprinted in *Major Critical Essays* (1932).

pages 42–43

the character of . . . for expensive vices. *Sixteen Self Sketches,* XIV (1949), pp. 103–04.

pages 43–44
I have recognized . . . notions of propriety. Preface to the 1907 reprint of *The Sanity of Art.*

page 44
Dubedat . . . and upheld it. *Sixteen Self Sketches,* XIV, p. 104.

pages 44–45
Even the very . . . a National Theatre. "Draft Letter to Millionaires."

page 44 [footnote]
The Euripidean verses . . . ways than one. Preface to *Major Barbara.*

page 44 [footnote]
The part of . . . translations of Euripides. "To Audiences at *Major Barbara.*"

page 45
Howebeit . . . ancient Athenian drama. Preface to *Heartbreak House.*

page 45
In the end . . . up the shutters. "Granville-Barker . . ."

page 45
The deficit was . . . £6000. "Draft Letter to Millionaires."

pages 45–48
Having ruined Vedrenne . . . than she foresaw. "Granville-Barker . . ."

page 48
We [had] clicked . . . nonagenarian ex-playwright. "[Letter on the death of Granville Barker]," *Times Literary Supplement,* London, September 7, 1946, p. 427.

Chapter 4

THE PRACTICAL IMPOSSIBILITIES OF CENSORSHIP

pages 49–50
As a playwright . . . on public grounds. Preface to *The Shewing-Up of Blanco Posnet* (1909).

page 50
In 1902 . . . and one afternoon. Preface to *Mrs Warren's Profession* (1902).

pages 50–51
In consequence . . . of my career. "Shaw on Censorship," an extract from the minutes of evidence before the Joint Select Committee of the House of Lords and House of Commons on Stage Plays (1909); reprinted as *Shavian Tract No. 3* (London, 1955).

pages 51–60
Few books of . . . the Lord Chamberlain. Preface to *Blanco Posnet.*

page 61
The Lord Chamberlain . . . was impossible. "Censorship as a Police Duty," address delivered before the Special General Conference of the Chief Constables' Association, Harrowgate, June 8, 1928, and published in the Conference *Reports,* 1928; reprinted in *Platform and Pulpit,* pp. 195–96.

page 61
There is . . . reading the dialogue. Preface to *Blanco Posnet.*

pages 61–62
I remember the . . . to the performance. "Censorship as a Police Duty."

page 62
It is immorality . . . the world began. Preface to *Blanco Posnet.*

Chapter 5

SHAVIAN BUSTS

page 63
In Munich once . . . in the theatres. Preface to the French edition of *Common Sense About the War* (1919).

pages 63–67
In the year . . . hold of it. "Rodin," *The Nation,* 9 November, 1912 (reprinted 24 November, 1917); reprinted in *Pen Portraits and Reviews.*

page 67
Busts outlive plays . . . otherwise unknown." *Table-Talk,* pp. 90–91.

Chapter 6
TREE AND A POTBOILER

pages 68–69
Like Shakespear . . . drawingroom ballads. "Postscript after Twentyfive years" to the Preface to *Back to Methuselah* (1944).

page 69
Take Pygmalion for . . . Beerbohm Tree's Higgins. "This Year's Program," *Malvern Festival Book,* 1936; reprinted in *Shaw on Theatre.*

pages 69–77
Tree was the . . . allowance and correction. "Beerbohm Tree," a contribution to the memorial volume (1920) edited by Max Beerbohm; reprinted in *Pen Portraits and Reviews.*

pages 77–80
Pygmalion Higgins is . . . be anything else. Preface to *Pygmalion* (1915).

Chapter 7
WAR MADNESS

pages 81–82
In compiling this . . . foreign policy. *What I Really Wrote About the War* (1931), 1–2.

page 82
What woke me . . . except myself. *What I Really Wrote,* pp. 4–5.

pages 82–83
In desperation . . . not contradict him. *Peace Conference Hints* (1919), reprinted in *What I Really Wrote,* pp. 309–10.

page 83
There was nothing . . . was too late. *What I Really Wrote,* p. 21.

pages 83–84

The dead silence . . . less placid spirits. *Peace Conference Hints,* reprinted in *What I Really Wrote,* pp. 310–11.

page 84

I made such . . . their moral behavior. *Peace Conference Hints,* reprinted in *What I Really Wrote,* p. 352.

page 84

And so my . . . but drift along. *Peace Conference Hints,* reprinted in *What I Really Wrote,* p. 311.

page 84

England did not . . . unmasked at last. *Peace Conference Hints,* reprinted in *What I Really Wrote,* pp. 311, 309, 311.

pages 84–85

Knowing little about . . . 14th November 1914. *What I Really Wrote,* pp. 21–22.

page 85

It is part . . . bit like it. "What I Said in the Great War," typescript apparently completed in the early fall of 1918, and used in part in *What I Really Wrote.* British Museum.

pages 85–86

At the outbreak . . . in every sentence. *What I Really Wrote,* p. 197.

page 86

Only those who . . . heaped on them. Preface to *Heartbreak House.*

pages 86–87

In 1914, this . . . the theatre landlord. "Authors in War-Time," *The Author,* 29 February 1940, p. 58.

page 87

During the War . . . hearers in front. "Commentary," 25th Anniversary Souvenir Program of the Birmingham Repertory Theatre.

pages 87–88

The fortunate lessee . . . of demanding before. "Authors in War-Time."

page 88

Thus the higher . . . and newspaper articles. Preface to *Heartbreak House.*

pages 88–89

Common Sense grew so . . . by the enemy. *What I Really Wrote,* pp. 116–17.

page 89

Through the accident . . . of my pen. "What I Said . . ."

page 90

Early in the . . . that of conciseness. *Peace Conference Hints,* reprinted in *What I Really Wrote,* pp. 355–56.

pages 90–91

I was specially concerned . . . therefore entirely wasted. *What I Really Wrote,* pp. 117–18.

pages 91–92

I must now . . . the British case. *What I Really Wrote,* pp. 126–27.

page 92

The editor to . . . my personal goodwill. *What I Really Wrote,* p. 141.

pages 92–93

The idea that . . . a successful bombardment. "The Limitation of Christ," *The Nation,* 26 November, 1921; reprinted in *What I Really Wrote,* pp. 396–97.

pages 93–95

Most people could . . . or a shipwreck. Preface to *Heartbreak House.*

pages 95–96

My anxiety as . . . of voluntary service. *What I Really Wrote,* pp. 154–55.

page 96

When I said . . . a huge fortune. *What I Really Wrote,* p. 142.

page 96

It was gravely . . . provinces every day. "War Reputations," *To-Day,* 13 May, 1916; reprinted in *What I Really Wrote,* pp. 213–14.

page 97

In private . . . had no brains. "What I Said . . ."

page 97

I could multiply . . . to one another. "War Reputations."

pages 97–100

In 1916 came . . . as they find it. *What I Really Wrote,* pp. 221–26.

page 97 [footnote]

Early in the . . . and the announcement. "In Praise of Guy Fawkes," a lecture delivered under the auspices of the Fabian Society on November 25, 1932, and published in *The New Clarion,* 3 December, 1932; reprinted in *Where Socialism Stands Today* (1933) and *Platform and Pulpit.*

pages 100–102

During the first . . . my vegetarian diet. *What I Really Wrote,* pp. 183–84, 182–83.

Chapter 8

JOY RIDING AT THE FRONT

page 103

Early in 1917 . . . of my profession. *What I Really Wrote,* p. 248.

pages 103–104

Thus I had . . . we took it. Preface to *Augustus Does His Bit* (1919).

page 104

I equipped myself . . . except the enemy. *What I Really Wrote,* pp. 248–49, 253.

pages 104–106

At the chateau . . . never came off. Recollections of Montague, in Oliver Elton, *C. E. Montague: A Memoir* (1929), 162–65.

page 106

The battle seemed . . . energetic citizens did. *What I Really Wrote,* pp. 248–49.

pages 106–107

When I last . . . to do it. "The Technique of War," *Daily Chronicle,* 7 March, 1917; reprinted in *What I Really Wrote,* pp. 264–65.

page 107

The artillery major . . . he said. "Consolations and Responsibilities," *Daily Chronicle,* 8 March, 1917; reprinted in *What I Really Wrote,* p. 274.

page 107

War is frightfully . . . it borrowed it. *The Intelligent Woman's Guide* (1928), p. 289.

pages 107–108
It is sometimes . . . service at all. *The Intelligent Woman's Guide,* p. 115.

pages 108–111
Though still a . . . taste of frostbite. "Bombardment," *Daily Chronicle,* 5 March, 1917; reprinted in *What I Really Wrote,* pp. 257–62.

page 111
The Commander-in-Chief . . . did not matter. "The Technique of War," reprinted in *What I Really Wrote,* pp. 267, 270.

pages 111–113
The Commander-in-Chief had . . . they were drifting. *What I Really Wrote,* pp. 249–51.

page 113
The danger of . . . always come off. "The Technique of War," reprinted in *What I Really Wrote,* pp. 267–68.

pages 113–115
I enjoyed my . . . in perfect peace. *What I Really Wrote,* pp. 251–54.

page 115
At that station . . . is child's play. "The Technique of War," reprinted in *What I Really Wrote,* p. 266.

pages 115–116
My professional instincts . . . appealed to me. *What I Really Wrote,* pp. 254–55.

page 116
What I actually . . . rest was unchallenged. *What I Really Wrote,* p. 255.

pages 116–117
The following may . . . *Military Secretary*). *What I Really Wrote,* pp. 278–79.

Chapter 9

CRASH OF AN EPOCH

pages 118–119
The war dragged. . . . They went home. *What I Really Wrote,* pp. 280–81.

page 119
In 1918 the . . . published in 1919. *What I Really Wrote,* pp. 296–97.

page 119
This utterance of . . . the next war. *What I Really Wrote,* pp. 368, 370.

pages 119–123
As for myself . . . of their elders. Preface to *Heartbreak House.*

page 123
The mess made . . . and sensibly stabilized. *What I Really Wrote,* p. 404.

page 123
I remember Germany . . . made me pay. *Everybody's Political What's What?,* p. 89.

Chapter 10

BURGLARS

page 124
The burglar in . . . experienced family solicitor. "Imprisonment" (Preface to *English Local Government,* by Sidney and Beatrice Webb, 1921).

page 124
I blush when . . . as a juryman. *Everybody's Political What's What?,* p. 299.

pages 124–126
Besides the chances . . . trouble for nothing. "Imprisonment."

pages 126–129
When I was . . . modern model prison. Foreword, 1925, to the separate publication of "Imprisonment."

Chapter 11

A MEMBER BY BAPTISM

page 130
So far I . . . called a religion. Preface to *Farfetched Fables* (1948).

pages 130–131
If I were asked . . . wrong for me. "The Church Versus Religion," an essay originally meant for a Collected Edition volume on religion; published as "On Ritual, Religion, and the Intolerableness of Tolerance," in *Shaw on Religion,* ed. W. S. Smith (1967), pp. 163–64, 161–62.

pages 131–133
Our indifference . . . at Golders Green. *Sixteen Self Sketches,* XIV, pp. 94–95, 96, 95–96.

page 133
and she left . . . my own words. "The Church Versus Religion," p. 162.

page 133
I delivered a . . . doctor told me. *Sixteen Self Sketches,* p. 96.

pages 133–134
This was possible . . . open to me. "The Church Versus Religion," pp. 162–63.

page 134
The chapel may . . . my own business. Letter to the editor, *The Times,* London, November 8, 1913.

pages 134–135
It may seem . . . the Shropshire Anglicans. Preface to *Farfetched Fables.*

pages 135–137
Once, when I . . . creeds, and colors. *Everybody's Political What's What?,* pp. 360–61, 362–63.

Chapter 12

BACK TO METHUSELAH

page 138
If anyone had . . . the world. But. "The Birmingham Repertory Theatre," in Bache Matthews, *A History of the Birmingham Repertory Theatre* (London, 1924), p. 168.

page 138
when the childish . . . in the laboratories. *Everybody's Political What's What?,* p. 189.

pages 138–139
If Darwin had . . . Tom or Dick. Preface to *Back to Methuselah.*

page 139
But they must . . . incalculable and uncivilized. "Sixty Years of Fabianism. A Postscript by George Bernard Shaw" to the 1948 reprint of *Fabian Essays;* reprinted in the sixth edition, 1962, p. 315.

pages 139–141
In writing Back . . . of his audiences. Preface to *Back to Methuselah.*

pages 141–142
When I contributed . . . degree is death. *Everybody's Political What's What?*, pp. 286–87.

pages 142–143
Our villagers . . . into wise senators. "Postscript after Twentyfive Years" to the Preface to *Back to Methuselah.*

pages 143–144
Considering . . . of oracular senatorism. Preface to *Geneva* (1945).

page 144
Physically I am . . . years or so. "Postscript after Twentyfive Years."

page 144
I started as . . . of their incredulity. Interview with Hayden Church, "En Route to Maturity," *Saturday Review of Literature,* July 27, 1946, p. 7.

pages 144–146
We are only . . . it is nothing. "Postscript after Twentyfive Years."

Chapter 13

HOW TO WRITE A PLAY

page 147
It is quite . . . symphonies all noise. "The Play of Ideas," *New Statesman and Nation,* May 6, 1950; *Theatre Arts,* August, 1950; reprinted in *Shaw on Theatre,* p. 290.

page 147
It is never . . . for your money. Preface to *The Apple Cart.*

pages 147–148

Now a playwright's . . . be laughed at. Preface to *The Six of Calais* (1935).

pages 148–150

An artistic presentment . . . they deserve. Preface to *Great Catherine* (1913)

pages 150–151

The art of . . . and did. "My Way with a Play," *The Observer*, London, September 29, 1946; reprinted in *Shaw on Theatre*, p. 269.

pages 151–152

In writing a . . . to write plays. "Bernard Shaw Self-Revealed," *Fortnightly Review*, April, 1926, pp. 438–39, 439–40.

page 152

If you want . . . *chevaux de bataille*. "This Year's Program," *Malvern Festival Book*, 1936.

pages 152–153

Characters have to . . . possibly unrealised selves. "Bernard Shaw Self-Revealed," pp. 440–41, 442.

pages 153–154

Theatre technique begins . . . in no time. "The Play of Ideas," *New Statesman*, May 6, 1950; reprinted in *Shaw on Theatre*, p. 292.

pages 154–155

My first play . . . like Galsworthy. "Bernard Shaw Self-Revealed," *Fortnightly Review*, May, 1926, pp. 615–16.

page 155

Side by side . . . most dreadful way. "Bernard Shaw Talks About Actors and Acting," *New York Times*, January 6, 1929; reprinted in *Shaw on Theatre*, p. 194.

page 155

But the object . . . still aspiring vehicles. *Fortnightly Review*, May, 1926, p. 618.

page 156

All my plays . . . hang of them. "The Simple Truth of the Matter," *Malvern Festival Book*, 1935; reprinted in *Shaw on Theatre*, p. 238.

Chapter 14

SAINT JOAN

pages 157–158
When I was . . . as it is. Preface to *Farfetched Fables.*

page 158
Until I began . . . in the calendar. *Table-Talk,* p. 83.

page 158
I wrote it . . . in Cartesian geometry. "The Ten Birthplaces of 'Saint Joan,' a letter from G.B.S. [letter to the editor of the *Irish Independent,* November 9, 1943]," *The Shaw Review,* VII (January, 1964), p. 24 (part of an article by Ronald Ayling).

pages 158–159
Not long before . . . Burgesses of Calais. "Bombardment," *Daily Chronicle,* March 5, 1917; reprinted in *What I Really Wrote,* pp. 255–57.

pages 159–160
The Six of . . . in my opinion. Preface to *The Six of Calais.*

page 160
He told the . . . Rodin into words. Program note to the first production of *Saint Joan;* reprinted in *Theatrical Companion,* p. 246.

pages 160–161
Joan is a . . . botched the job. *Table-Talk,* pp. 44, 40, 44–45.

page 161
I was impressed . . . religion at all. "*Saint Joan* Banned: Film Censorship in the United States," letter to the editor, *The New York Times,* September 14, 1936; also in *The London Mercury,* October, 1936; reprinted in *Shaw on Theatre,* pp. 249–50.

pages 161–162
St Joan did . . . Church to Nature. Preface to *On the Rocks* (1933).

page 162
The Church may . . . so too often. Preface to *Saint Joan* (1924).

pages 162–163
Galileo is a . . . *se muove.*" Preface to *On the Rocks.*

page 163

Since the report . . . of striking beauty. "Shaw on 'Saint Joan,'" *The New York Times,* April 6, 1924, p. X2 (a dispatch from James Graham, primarily a complete transcript of a Shavian written interview published in the Parisian theatrical magazine *Comoedia*).

page 163

A straightforward attempt . . . as they exist. Interview with Walter Tittle, "Mr. Shaw Talks about St. Joan," *The Outlook,* June 25, 1924, p. 313.

pages 163–164

The Frenchman . . . upon burning her. "Shaw on 'Saint Joan.'"

page 164

Although the burning . . . of St Joan. "Saint Joan," *The Listener,* June 3, 1931 (transcript of a B.B.C. radio talk, May 30, 1931); reprinted in *Platform and Pulpit,* pp. 214–15.

pages 164–166

For the story . . . in my hands. Preface to *Saint Joan.*

page 166

The protagonists of . . . the boulevardiers. "Shaw on 'Saint Joan.'"

pages 166–167

In London the . . . take them home. Preface to *Saint Joan.*

pages 167–168

As a playwright . . . temporal and spiritual. "Sullivan, Shakespear, and Shaw," *The Strand,* CXIV, October, 1947, and *The Atlantic,* CLXXXI, March, 1948; reprinted in *Shaw on Theatre,* p. 278.

Chapter 15

FABIAN POLITICS

page 169

If I, a . . . of my experience. Foreword to the first edition, *The Common Sense of Municipal Trading* (1904).

page 169

the most romantic . . . political party considerations. Preface to the Fabian Edition, *The Common Sense of Municipal Trading* (1908).

pages 169–172
What, then, should . . . in the least. *Everybody's Political What's What?*, pp. 270–74.

pages 173–174
The Fabian vogue . . . instalment of Socialism. "Sixty Years of Fabianism," *Fabian Essays*, sixth edition (1948), pp. 297–98.

page 174
On the platform . . . but by Nature. Letter to the editor, *Time and Tide*, April 21, 1945; reprinted in Allen Chappelow, ed., *Shaw—"the Chucker-Out"* (London, 1969), p. 323.

pages 174–175
In 1911 the . . . a free lance. "Sixty Years of Fabianism," pp. 298–300.

pages 175–176
He literally cost . . . of the poll. "H. G. Wells on the Rest of Us," *The Christian Commonwealth*, May 19, 1909; reprinted in *Pen Portraits and Reviews*, p. 280.

page 176
I forced myself . . . so well beloved. "The Man I Knew," *New Statesman & Nation*, August 17, 1946, p. 115.

page 176
He repaid these . . . parcel of sweeps. "H. G. Wells on the Rest of Us."

pages 176–177
He was the . . . local government areas. "The Man I Knew."

pages 177–178
As for me . . . of our dailies. "Sixty Years of Fabianism," pp. 300–01.

page 178
My speeches were . . . British daily newspapers. Preface to *Farfetched Fables*.

page 178
British freedom of . . . was talking sensibly." "Sixty Years of Fabianism," pp. 300–01.

pages 178–179
During my greatest . . . the giddiest rabbit. "The Telltale Microphone," *Political Quarterly*, VI (1935), 463–64.

page 179
I was specially . . . at the end. "The Play of Ideas," reprinted in *Shaw on Theatre,* p. 293.

page 179
But whether my . . . part in it. "The Telltale Microphone," p. 464.

pages 179–180
This state of . . . call the tune. "Sixty Years of Fabianism," pp. 301–02, 315, 302.

pages 180–181
Fabianism . . . was meant . . . missed the bus. Article in *The Daily Herald,* March 10, 1943, quoted in *The Chucker-Out,* p. 320.

page 181
British Trade Unionism . . . landlords and capitalists. Message to the *Labour Monthly* on its 20th anniversary, July, 1941; quoted in *The Chucker-Out,* p. 227.

page 181
The Fabians, preoccupied . . . soon contradicted it. "Sixty Years of Fabianism," p. 303.

page 181
Though I am . . . fundamental in Socialism. Message to the *Labour Monthly;* in *Chucker-Out,* pp. 227–28.

pages 181–182
I had awakened . . . Guide to Socialism. "Sixty Years of Fabianism," p. 303.

page 182
The book in . . . a paradoxical joke. Preface, unpaged, to the Standard Edition of *The Intelligent Woman's Guide.*

page 182
Nowadays the word . . . Church of England. "Sixty Years of Fabianism," p. 313.

pages 182–183
When Ibsen was . . . world is round. Letter to the editor, *The New Statesman & Nation,* July 3, 1943.

page 183
I could expatiate . . . Mister Bernard Shaw." Draft article, "The Party System and Socialists" (1944), quoted in *Chucker-Out,* p. 335.

Chapter 16

THE APPLE CART

pages 184–186
The first performances . . . the people's will. Preface to *The Apple Cart* (1930).

page 186
A Prime Minister . . . Big Business. Interview with Andrew E. Malone at Malvern, July 24, 1934 (Pattee Library, Pennsylvania State University).

page 186
The Apple Cart . . . the Royal Family. "Bernard Shaw on the Festival Habit," *Malvern Festival Book,* 1937, p. 9; reprinted in *Shaw on Theatre.*

page 186
I never dreamt . . . of King Magnus. "Bernard Shaw's Denial: King Magnus Not Based on Any Living Person," *The Star,* London, September 30, 1929.

pages 186–191
And now a . . . message for us. Preface to *The Apple Cart.*

Chapter 17

TOURING IN RUSSIA

page 192
When Lenin . . . into power. *Intelligent Woman's Guide,* p. 463.

page 192
I was . . . out its mistakes. *Intelligent Woman's Guide,* p. 462.

pages 192–195
September and October . . . to any amount. "Touring in Russia, Part I," *Nash's Magazine,* January, 1932, pp. 6–9.

page 195
Not a band . . . and concert). *Sixteen Self Sketches,* p. 83.

page 195
where they . . . seventy-fifth birthday. "Touring in Russia, Part II," *Nash's Magazine,* February, 1932, p. 16.

page 195
in the Hall . . . seemed natural enough. *Sixteen Self Sketches,* p. 83.

page 195
and the chairman . . . coat and cap. "Touring in Russia, Part II," p. 6.

pages 195–196
Lunacharsky spoke . . . Churchill in Moscow. *Sixteen Self Sketches,* pp. 83–84.

pages 196–197
The other thing . . . one all through. "The Only Hope of the World," *The New Leader,* London, August 7, 1931, from a lecture delivered at the Independent Labour Party Summer School; reprinted in *Platform and Pulpit,* p. 219.

page 197
When we left . . . and thirtyfive minutes. *Sixteen Self Sketches,* p. 84.

pages 197–198
Tourists who are . . . quickly allayed. "Touring . . . , II," pp. 18–19.

pages 198–199
The moment a . . . a smiling countryside. *The Rationalization of Russia,* ed. H. M. Geduld (Bloomington, Ind.: 1964), p. 70.

page 198
where she . . . and brought up. *Intelligent Woman's Guide,* p. 467.

page 199
where good farming . . . of the Kulaks. *Rationalization of Russia,* pp. 70–71.

page 199
It was hard . . . anti-Fabian blunder. *Intelligent Woman's Guide,* p. 467.

page 199
I visited Krupskaya . . . forgive worse things. *Rationalization of Russia,* p. 71.

pages 199–200
The persecution . . . was set up. *Rationalization of Russia,* pp. 80–81.

page 200
I had great . . . they said. "Touring . . . , II," p. 19.

page 200
As far as . . . in social competition. *Rationalization of Russia,* p. 81.

pages 200–201
There is so . . . led for efficiency "The Only Hope . . . ," *Platform and Pulpit,* pp. 219, 219–20.

page 201
I saw nothing . . . after the war. *Rationalization of Russia,* p. 88.

pages 201–203
In the country . . . our prisons produce. *Rationalization of Russia,* pp. 90–92.

pages 203–204
I went one . . . Britain and America. "Touring . . . , II," pp. 17–18.

Chapter 18

BURNING THE CANDLE AT BOTH ENDS

page 205
The central error . . . peace without it?" *What I Really Wrote,* pp. 405–06.

pages 205–206
When wars were . . . at first; but. "Too True to Be Good," *Malvern Festival Book,* 1932; reprinted in *Shaw on Theatre,* pp. 215–16.

pages 206–207
Somehow my play . . . a maddening dissatisfaction. Preface to *Too True to Be Good* (1933).

page 207
The despair of . . . against mere fluency. "The Simple Truth of the Matter," *Malvern Festival Book,* 1935; reprinted in *Shaw on Theatre,* p. 241.

page 207

Long ago I . . . who were not. *Everybody's Political What's What?*, p. 283.

pages 207–208

The increasing bewilderment . . . the same background. Preface to *The Simpleton of the Unexpected Isles* (1935).

pages 208–209

What I miss . . . into the bargain. "The Simple Truth of the Matter," *Shaw on Theatre*, pp. 239–40.

pages 209–210

How many people . . . become of it. Program note printed in the program of the first London production of *Geneva;* reprinted in *Complete Plays with Prefaces* (New York, 1963), V, 649–50.

page 210

In providing a . . . on their periods. Preface to *In Good King Charles's Golden Days* (1939, 1945).

page 210

I became a . . . more to read. *Everybody's Political What's What?*, p. 181.

pages 210–212

A much commoner . . . matters is stupendous. Preface to *Good King Charles.*

page 212

The most gifted . . . the world is. *Everybody's Political What's What?*, p. 49.

pages 212–213

But I refuse . . . all his contradictions. Preface to *Good King Charles.*

pages 213–214

I recall a . . . are all right. "Foundation Oration," delivered before the Union Society of University College, London, March 18, 1920; reprinted from Shaw's corrected copy of the Union Society's pamphlet version in *Platform and Pulpit*, pp. 149–50.

page 214

Please do not infer . . . where we are. *Everybody's Political What's What?*, p. 49.

pages 214–215
As to Charles . . . from cheese biologically. Preface to *Good King Charles.*

Chapter 19

ENDING AS A SAGE

page 216
When I was . . . a long time. "School," *The Listener,* June 23, 1937, from a B.B.C. radio talk; reprinted in *Platform and Pulpit,* p. 276.

page 216
I remember using . . . in the wall. *Everybody's Political What's What?,* p. 20.

pages 216–218
When I had . . . on two Japanese cities. Preface to *Geneva.*

pages 218–219
I am in . . . once start me. "Woman—Man in Petticoats," *New York Times Magazine,* June 19, 1927; reprinted in *Platform and Pulpit,* p. 177.

pages 219–220
I commit this . . . we now are. Preface to *Farfetched Fables.*

page 220
My powers are . . . Christians at iconography. Preface to *Back to Methuselah.*

page 220
Shakespear, with all . . . sentimentalizer, and the like. Preface to *Man and Superman.*

pages 220–221
I am myself . . . in the least. Preface to *Farfetched Fables.*

page 221
And the ordinary . . . beliefs and disbeliefs. Preface to *Man and Superman.*

page 221
I am not . . . and Bernard Shaws. *New Statesman & Nation,* July 3, 1943.

pages 221–222
My experience as . . . a basement hell. Preface to *Geneva.*

page 222
I know now . . . kind yet seen. "Wagner and Vegetables," *The Academy,* 15 October, 1898, p. 79.

pages 222–223
Of these reminiscences . . . Hail and Farewell. "Envoi," *Sixteen Self Sketches,* p. 134.

Appendix 1

pages 224–244
Last Will and Testament. Text, hand engrossed by Edward Giles, in the custody of the Probate Registrar, Somerset House, London. Reproduced as a printed pamphlet by the Apple Tree Press, Flint, Michigan, 1954. Reproduced as part of the text of *Shaw: the Chucker-Out,* London, 1969.

Appendix 2

pages 245–262
"How Frank Ought to Have Done It," *Sixteen Self Sketches,* XVII, pp. 116–134.

INDEX

Y

BIOGRAPHICAL INDEX: G.B.S.

References are to Volume **I**, An Autobiography 1856–1898, *and to* Volume **II**, An Autobiography 1898–1950.

WITHDRAWN